# CITIZEN GREG

# CITIZEN GREG

## The extraordinary story of Greg Dyke and how he captured the BBC

Chris Horrie and Steve Clarke

SIMON & SCHUSTER

A VIACOM COMPANY

First published in Great Britain by
Simon & Schuster UK Ltd, 2000
A Viacom company

1 3 5 7 9 10 8 6 4 2

Simon & Schuster UK Ltd
Africa House
64–78 Kingsway
London WC2B 6AH

Simon & Schuster Australia
Sydney

A CIP catalogue record for this book is available
from the British Library

ISBN 0-684-86671-4

Typeset in Book Antiqua by
SX Composing DTP, Rayleigh, Essex
Printed and bound in Great Britain by
Butler & Tanner Ltd, Frome and London

In memory of Andrew Dignam,
who had the talent but not the luck

# Contents

# Preface and Acknowledgements

This book attempts to tell the story of one of the most extraordinary and charismatic characters in British creative and public life. Greg Dyke's career in television over the last twenty years has tracked every significant development in the industry. At the same time his progress from suburban tabloid newspaper journalist (via incarnations as a down-at-heel, inner-city community relations worker, trade union militant, investigative reporter, fun-loving inventor of contemporary televisual 'infotainment', hyper-competitive breakfast TV editorial wizard, new wave football financier, multimillionaire TV mogul, Harvard Business School alumnus, libertarian scourge of regulators and politicians, international business wheeler-dealer) to take up one of the key positions in the British establishment says much about the way the country has changed in the last few years.

Greg Dyke told us that he did not want to have his story told at this particular time. When we approached him, he was keen to leave the spotlight after being subjected to several months of scrutiny from certain parts of the press that were trying to block his appointment as the BBC's thirteenth Director-General. Dyke believed that the attention he had received was out of all proportion to his news value, as far as most readers were concerned. He was also worried about the effect that taking the job might have on his family, and this was another reason why he was evidently concerned about the book. We assured him that, although some discussion of his personal background would be necessary, we were writing what was essentially a business biography. After all, Greg Dyke's career as a TV executive, we thought, was colourful and dramatic enough. And his personal life is, by all accounts, remarkable mainly for its stability, warmth and guarded privacy.

We were fortunate in being able to speak to many of the people he has worked with most closely in the various stages of his career. This was made easier by the fact that Dyke has largely worked with the same group of journalists and TV executives since his early days in the media. The majority of these people expressed huge admiration for Dyke, helped, possibly, by the fact that he had been responsible for boosting some of them into the millionaire bracket. As journalists, writing about a rich and powerful person, we therefore found ourselves in the odd situation of having – in the interests of balance – to go out of our way to find criticism. Normally when dealing with somebody in Dyke's position it is more a matter of tracking down somebody who can put, as it were, the case for the defence. This had certainly been the case when we wrote a book a few years ago featuring John Birt, Dyke's immediate predecessor as Director-General.

We would therefore like to thank all the people who helped us, listed here in alphabetical order: Roy Ackerman, Roy Addison, Simon Albury, Keith Aldeman, Charlotte Atkins MP, Emily Bell, Paul Bonner, Alan Boyd, Warren Breach, Simon Channon, Judith Chegwidden, James Conway, Peter Coppock, Barry Cox, David Cox, Paul Donovan, Colin and Rod Fry, Nick Evans, James Gatward, David Glencross, Tom Gutteridge, Peter Hain MP, Jane Hewland, Mark Hill, Peter Hitchens, David Housham, John Howard, Lucian Hudson, Martin Jackson, Clive Jones, Mark Mildred, Peter Montieth, Helen Oldfield, Sally Osman, Quentin Peel, Mike Phillips, William Phillips, Marcus Plantin, Angus Shaw, Laura

# Preface and Acknowledgements

Smith, Ray Snoddy, Brian Tesler, Daniel Wiles, Nick Wright and Will Wyatt. We also spoke to numerous other people who, for one reason or another, have asked that we do not mention their names.

Thanks are also due to the staff of the Department of Communications at the University of Westminster, the staff of *Broadcast* magazine, press officers at LWT, Pearson and the BBC and, especially, to the staff in charge of the LWT internal archives (maintained, since the 1994 takeover, by Granada), to Dr David Griffiths and his staff at York University library and to the staff of the Independent Television Commission and its library, the Press Association research library and the newspaper section of the British Library at Colindale. We also wish to thank Martin Fletcher, our editor, and his team at Simon & Schuster, and Robert Kirby, our agent at Peters, Fraser & Dunlop, as well as our partners, Clare and Kim, for their advice, encouragement and, on occasion, patience and tolerance. All these people gave a great deal of help, but if we have erred in any way then the fault is entirely ours.

Most of the people we spoke to repeatedly emphasized Greg Dyke's abilities as a leader. He was frequently described to us as being an 'inspirational' person to work with – and even for. Much of this appears to be connected with Dyke's personal philosophy, which is based on a few, simple, bedrock points. One is the cheerful contempt he shows for pomposity and the class system. This trait is so marked that sometimes people have bizarrely mistaken him for an Australian or American. Dyke, in common with the vast majority of the popular audience, is a great fan of most things American – from pop music, breakfast TV, jeans, Disney, sunshine, cable TV, digital gadgetry and surfing, to libertarian politics, the cult of consumer choice and guilt-free enjoyment of vast salaries. Much of the sneering about Dyke's supposed role in 'dumbing down', it seems to us, misses the point. Greg Dyke has so far been riding a wave of 'globalization' which, as far as TV is concerned, means the American-ization of the English-speaking world. If he is to succeed in reviving the fortunes of the BBC at this critical time in its history, restoring the institution's self-confidence and sense of collective purpose, he will have to demonstrate that he can do more than run with a commercial imperative and build on the BBC's emphatically British strengths.

Dyke's manifest popularity – there was spontaneous cheering in parts of the BBC when he was appointed – may also owe something to the astonishing amount of good luck to which Dyke himself has often attributed his own success. Looked at overall, one interesting aspect of Dyke's career is the way he has managed to 'quit while he was ahead', claiming the full measure of credit for successes and sometimes walking away from companies which were later to hit the rocks. It was forcefully put to us by people who, otherwise, were great fans, that if the result of the greatest defeat of Dyke's business career – the hostile takeover of LWT by Granada – had been reversed, his reputation and legacy might have been very different. It is certainly true that most of Dyke's accomplishments so far have involved joining a company, shaking it up and then moving on.

It is often said that a leader only really succeeds when he hands over a thriving and still-growing organization to his own chosen successor. If that is true then Greg Dyke has so far largely failed. Broadcasting organizations tend to thrive when Greg Dyke is associated with them, and then go downhill when he leaves.

# Preface and Acknowledgements

This book ends with Greg Dyke's appointment as Director-General. It is far too early to say how the BBC will fare under his leadership. One problem will involve playing down the vast expectations inside the Corporation which surrounded his arrival. At the time of writing, Greg Dyke has already moved to stamp his style on the BBC, concentrating much more power – or responsibility – in the hands of himself and a group of trusted lieutenants and thus making himself potentially the most powerful Director-General in the BBC's history. In so doing he has, not for the first time, decided to walk a high wire. He may well repeat his earlier successes. But if he fails, the damage will be of historic rather than merely commercial proportions – and he will have no opportunity to pass the buck, as others might be tempted to do.

Greg Dyke is not likely to spend too much time worrying, however. He frequently and approvingly tells a story of how a friend had once summed-up his personality by saying: 'The trouble with you, Greg, is that you always think things are going to work OK, because you just haven't got enough imagination to see what it would be like if you failed.'

'And y'know,' Dyke customarily adds with a roar of delight, 'that's dead right! . . . It's absolutely bloody true!'

CHRIS HORRIE AND STEVE CLARKE
London and Bristol
May 2000

# 1.
# Little Greg

Greg Dyke is sitting on the sofa in the modest suburban living room of the Dyke family's modest suburban semi in west London next to his brother Howard, one year older. It is 1955 and Greg Dyke is eight years old. Unusually, the boys are quiet and relatively still as, goggle-eyed, they watch a family drama unfold, centred on their older brother Ian. Bill Dodgin, the manager of Brentford FC, is making a scouting call, arriving at a small, neat, pebble-dashed house in Cerne Close, Hayes, in the catchment area of his club. He is negotiating with Dyke's parents, Joseph and Denise. He wants to sign Greg's 14-year old brother as an apprentice. He talks of potential and possibilities. Greg soaks up the promises and blandishments of the unfamiliar grown-up visitor, the excitement and wheedling of his teenage brother, the anxious questioning and worries of his parents. Dodgin hands over his card and departs, asking Joseph to think about it.

Greg is enthralled. But Ian is to be disappointed. Joseph thinks that the life of a professional footballer is too risky. Ian – all the boys – must stay on at school and prepare themselves for life in a secure trade – maybe skilled manual work. Or, perhaps, white collar or clerical work of some sort.

The excitement soon passed. Ian stayed on at school and later played senior amateur football while working for a while as a bricklayer and then, like his dad, getting a job selling insurance. But what Greg Dyke had witnessed would stay in his mind for the rest of his life – an early, exciting, formative glimpse into the strange world beyond the happy and secure, but decidedly limited, horizons and respectable aspirations of suburban life in the 1950s. Bill Dodgin's visit had provided a glimpse into a strange and implausible world where grown-ups did not become housewives or disappear each morning with a briefcase to a temporary non-existence which they never talked about. There was a world where they did what they wanted – where they were allowed to play all the time and somehow got paid for it. Could it be true?

As Dyke grew into his teens in the 1960s he began to realize that there was a big new world opening up, a chance to leave behind the Thirties' haunted grey austerity of his parents' generation and embrace a new world full of possibilities and aspirations beyond Joseph and Denise's wildest dreams. By the time Greg Dyke was forced to think seriously about what he might do with his life, he was convinced that the new world of excitement and opportunity existed.

He knew it was there because he had seen it on television.

Greg Dyke was born in May 1947, the youngest of the three sons born to Joseph and Denise Dyke of Middlesex. Joseph was quietly spoken, reserved and conservative, with a cultivated, middle-class accent. Denise, in contrast, was a bundle of energy, a working-class Tory from Hackney, with an East End accent and a sharp wit. She stayed at home to look after the boys, having a big influence on them all. In later life, friends visiting Dyke's parents would be amazed by the similarity between Greg and Denise's boisterous personality and mannerisms. Later Dyke would tell friends how, when he had been naughty at home as a child, his mother's dire 'wait until your father gets home' warnings never worried him. Joseph would arrive home to reluctantly administer a gentle clip round the ear, winking all the time to show that he did not mean it, but was just going through the motions to please mum. What Joseph and Denise had in common was a loathing of pomposity and a rough and ready sense of egalitarianism. According to legend, Joseph would spend an hour talking to a road sweeper. He brought up the boys to believe that nobody was better than them. But at the same time they weren't better than anybody else.

The family had settled in Hayes, an area of west London nicely balanced between the blue-collar world of soon-to-be-booming light engineering, domestic appliance and electronics factories strung out along the Western Avenue and the solid suburban respectability of the gin-and-chintz belt beyond. The house was respectable enough – pebble-dashed with gardens front and back – wedged between the Grand Union Canal and the dilapidated terraced streets and industrial estates of Southall which, in the Sixties and Seventies, was to become home to a thriving Asian community. Dyke himself later described his background as 'elevated working-class'. Others said it was 'lower middle-class'.

The Dyke boys enjoyed an idyllic childhood, doted upon by their parents. Joseph had sacrificed much to provide an environment of utter security for the family. Demobbed from the army, he had turned his back on his father's pub and taken a grinding job in the insurance business. He was unhappy in his work. But at least it carried a decent pension. That was the thing. He could support the family so that they never need worry.

With such a tight focus on family life, radio and then television played an important role in the Dyke family and some of Greg's earliest memories involved the family gathering round the set – or listening to music on one of the two transistor radios proudly purchased by the Dykes. Joseph preferred radio to TV. He was convinced it was a more respectable medium than the telly. In common with many British households in the Fifties, Dyke senior would insist on the family listening to the cloying but wholesome melodies of *Sing Something Simple* on the BBC's Light Programme. This Sunday evening ritual invariably ended in Joseph falling asleep to the soporific music, providing the chance for Greg and his brothers to go and find something less boring to do. *Sing Something Simple* was too dull for words for kids growing up to the distant pulse of rock 'n' roll. As a schoolboy, Dyke was a big fan of BBC radio comedy shows like *Round The Horne* and *Beyond Our Ken*, and the Sunday night drama, *Journey Into Space*, listened to on his brother's portable in a bedroom. Much of Dyke's early exposure to pop music came via the erratic signal of Radio Luxembourg, often listened to under the bedclothes.

Joseph believed that watching too much television was harmful. For years the family got by on a set that could only receive the staid BBC service. This was a cause of much irritation to Dyke and his brothers, who had to go round to their cousin's house to catch up on the latest adventures of *The Invisible Man* or *William Tell*. Dyke loved the wave of imported American series like *Rawhide* and *Wagon Train* which ITV brought to the screen. Later, when Joseph agreed to have a set which could get ITV, the family would gather around the TV just as the characters in *Wagon Train* met up around the campfire at the start and end of each episode with reassuring regularity.

Dyke meanwhile struggled at school and found the 11-plus test at the end of his primary school years traumatic. He was encouraged by the family to excel and win at everything, but only managed to pass the test by the skin of his teeth, coming – he later claimed – bottom of a list of 126 children selected to go to the local grammar school. Dyke was devastated to find that many of his primary school friends had been written off as failures before their lives had really begun. The experience was to scar Dyke deeply, as it did many others, and gave him a lifelong sense of social injustice.

He was not an academic success at the local Hayes Grammar School. He was remembered as noisy and competitive – always on the go, keen to harmlessly put one over on somebody, chirping away ten to the dozen in what some thought was a carefully cultivated 'rough diamond' Cockney accent. He was known as 'Little Greg' because he was short and stocky, and to differentiate him from his brother, who was in the year above. In the playground and on the sports field he was an organizer. Eventually he made it into the Rugby first XV, where he played inside-centre or fly-half and was admired for his swerve in running round the opposition. He liked to play practical jokes. One Saturday lunchtime after a rugby match Dyke, by then in the sixth form, invited the younger members of the team to the local pub, the Queen's Head, to introduce them to their first pints of beer. He set them up with drinks and then rushed off, leaving them to face a ferocious bollocking from the Rugby teacher, Dai Griffiths, who promptly walked in from the bar next door.

Dyke left Hayes Grammar in 1965 after getting just one A-level, a grade E in maths. His life seemed to be following the pattern of his older brother, Ian – except that he was never good enough at football to have a trial with Brentford. He had no career plans and, it seemed, few prospects. All he knew was that he wanted to avoid the sort of job his dad had – the dull grind of respectability and boredom. His mum and dad fretted and told him that in the world of work you couldn't do just what you felt like, you had to knuckle down. And so he reluctantly accepted a management traineeship with Marks & Spencer, arranged by an uncle. He hated it and decided to drop out the moment his bosses – mostly failed public schoolboys, as Dyke thought of them – started asking, with genuine surprise, why his grammar school had not insisted on elocution lessons. He left after four months, later claiming that his main achievement was, one day, breaking all the biscuits on the tea trolley. He had learned that progress up the ladder in an established business like M&S was mainly a matter of family connections, time-serving and class prejudice, and that – whatever else happened to him – this was a game he could not play, even if he wanted to.

After Dyke left M&S his father offered him a choice of working as a solicitor's clerk or an insurance salesman. Dyke turned him down, saying that he wanted to look around for something more interesting. This, after all, was the 1960s. London – especially west London – was booming. Every day the local papers carried dozen of adverts for well-paid jobs in the surrounding factories. It was a safety net. He wanted to look for something more exciting. If things did not work out, he could always be re-united with his old mates on the production line at the Hoover factory near the family home, or the nearby London Underground repair shop. Dyke later said: 'My dad worked for the same company for forty years and hated every day. He spent the last fifteen years of his working life worrying that if he left he wouldn't get his pension. I was determined when I left school that working life for me was going to be more exciting.'

But Joseph was horrified and Dyke was given an

ultimatum. Either he got himself sorted out in three months flat or he would have to take one of the jobs Joseph had arranged for him. The deadline that, as Dyke saw it, spelled the end of his freedom, was approaching when he heard that a local newspaper, the *Middlesex Advertiser*, was looking for a school-leaver. He knew nothing about journalism and newspapers but, as he later put it, 'it sounded sexy'. Anyway, he was desperate. Slightly to his own surprise, Dyke landed a job as an apprentice, or 'indentured' reporter, not on the well-established if somewhat dowdy broadsheet *Middlesex Advertiser* but on the *Hillingdon Mirror* – a weekly sister paper about to be launched by the same publisher, King and Hutchins. The paper was designed to cater for the swelling ranks of 'baby-boomers' – the 'TV generation' who, like Dyke, were now leaving school and, for the first time, had money of their own to spend.

The *Hillingdon Mirror* began publication in January 1966. Amazingly, for the times, instead of news it had a full-page colour 'feature' picture on page one. This made it look, in many ways, more like a weekly magazine than a newspaper. Early editions went in for cute front-page pictures – a ballet dancer comes to town, amateur theatricals, local beauty queens, a parachute display, crocuses in front of the town hall and kiddies-in-a-paddling-pool to celebrate the arrival of spring – in other words, a genre known in the trade as 'kitten in a wineglass' pictures. A few weeks after launch the front page featured a picture of the Gardeners' Arms, the pub used by the hacks on both the *Advertiser* and the *Mirror*, on the not very newsworthy grounds that the publican had decided to re-paint the front and cheer things up with some flower tubs.

The news was run on the inside pages as a series of short paragraphs written in a passable imitation of the national *Daily Mirror*. There were sensational shock-horror 'news exclusives' and 'investigations', such as HILLINGDON GRIPPED BY DRUGS CRAZE – 'Just one ounce of hashish can provide addict with thirty cigarettes'. But the news soon gave way to more full- and double-page picture spreads with captions. There was heavy emphasis on fashion and huge sections on setting up home, buying cars and going on holidays to the 'exotic' Costa Del Sol. The young feel was bolstered by endless 'bonnie baby' competitions, designed to appeal to the target market of young newlyweds. There was a full-page colour cartoon strip called 'Prince Valient', which relied on an exceptionally weird storyline about King Arthur and Ancient Britons transported back to modern day Uxbridge. From day one there was a big pull-out section called *Mirror Pop Parade*. This acted as a 'newspaper within a newspaper', and was a reasonable imitation of a pop-music weekly like *Melody Maker*, right down to the crudely hand-drawn, psychedelic typefaces, self-consciously hip writing style and cheesy publicity pictures of the likes of Donovan and Manfred Mann.

As an 'indentured' apprentice reporter, Dyke was expected to work for very little, keep his mouth shut and learn from his elders and betters. But on the *Hillingdon Mirror* things were different. The paper was put together by a young, rowdy and inexperienced team of about a dozen people, held in check by the editor Brian Cummings, a more establishment figure who was in his thirties, and Peter Hurst, the chief sub-editor. There were few seniors on the paper to learn from and so Dyke turned to his opposite number on the *Advertiser*, an old Glaswegian pro called Alan Price. Price's attitude to life had been toughened-up by the fact that he had a humped back and a withered arm – thought to have been the result of polio. He was remembered by some of the younger hacks on both papers as 'a torrent of enthusiasm and anger'.

Dyke and Price worked across the corridor from each other (both papers had the same publisher, and the news-rooms, although separate, were in the same building) and went out on stories together. Price took a shine to Dyke and coached him. Dyke was keen and quick to learn. Within eighteen months he had risen above the other rookies to become, in all but name, the *Mirror's* chief reporter. Most weeks it was, in effect, Dyke and Hurst, the headline writer and the production and picture specialist who put the paper together. Cummings stayed in the background keeping his hand on the tiller, which was fine – except for one point. Dyke and others began to object that the *Mirror* was staffed almost entirely by indentured juniors who were doing the work of fully-qualified seniors for a fraction of the wages. There had been grumbling in the Gardeners' Arms about this state of affairs for months. Some of the reporters on the *Advertiser* were in the same position. Then one day Dyke burst into the pub, announcing that he had the publishers 'over a barrel'. He had discovered that the publisher had failed to sign the reporters' indenture forms, which meant that they could ask for more money before signing up, even though they were not yet formally qualified. Dyke led a delegation to see the publisher, King and Hutchins, where the managing director was Frank Barlow (who, many years later, would again be Dyke's boss as head of Pearson, the multi-billion media conglomerate). Dyke was told: 'There's no point in giving you juniors more money. I know what you are like – you'll only go and waste it buying fancy transistor radios.' And so Dyke led the juniors out on strike, setting up picket lines, that turned away lorries trying to deliver paper. The dispute came to a sorry end when the National Union of Journalists told them not to be so silly, to sign their indenture forms and go back to work.

The strike had ended in fiasco, but Dyke was admired for having a go and it made him all the more popular in the office. He became leader of the local branch of the NUJ, a position known as 'Father of the Chapel', and encouraged journalists even younger than himself who were joining the paper in a steady stream, to get involved and air their grievances. He had been promoted to news editor and seemed to others to be older and more mature than his years. Partly because of his influence, the paper had evolved to become less of a weekly pop and picture magazine than a proper newspaper with stories and headlines on page one and by-lines for reporters.

Dyke would ask the juniors what they were planning to write about and screw up his face when they trotted out the familiar round of flower shows and Rotarian meetings: 'OK then – if you must. But when you go to these things talk to everyone who's there. Don't just do the obvious thing.' And then he would use one of his key phrases: 'Dare to be different'. If he saw reporters hanging around the office he could be sharp with them: 'What are you doing in the office? . . . Get out and knock on some doors . . . ' His worst put-down was the accusation that a reporter was not pulling his weight and, if he was really angry, he would deny them a by-line. 'Your by-line is the only thing you've got in this business,' he would warn them. 'And you've got to earn it.' But he was never really a serious disciplinarian and fitted easily into the social scene at the Gardeners' Arms where, on Fridays after work, the reporters would play poker with their wage packets. Dyke would play a few hands, have a couple of pints and quit while he was ahead. Others – against his advice – would stay all night and be taken to the cleaners.

On top of all this Dyke was a hero in the office because he ran a 'lineage pool', a pot of money earned from moonlighting for national papers and shared out between the reporters. The *Hillingdon Mirror*'s circulation area was brilliant for this because it included Heathrow, which was a constant source of national stories. There was great jubilation in the office when, under Dyke's direction, one junior landed the story of an American film star being busted for dope at Heathrow after the reporter had done a routine check of local police charge sheets. That one was sold to the nationals for a huge sum. Another time a reporter covering a routine meeting of the British Legion in West Drayton found out (using Dyke's 'talk to people and look for something different' method) that there was an arsenal of ancient but potentially dangerous ammunition stored in the basement. With a bit of additional spin that one became another direct hit on the nationals.

Dyke worked closely with a Fleet Street news agency, a rough, tough operation specialising in feeding the best stories from local reporters to the tabloids – by far the best payers. He was becoming well known at the agency and on tabloid news-desks, putting down a marker in the time-honoured way for a move onto a national newspaper. Dyke ended up running two news gathering operations – the local police and council derived parish pump stuff for the *Hillingdon Mirror*, with the more valuable Heathrow material reserved for sale to the nationals. In addition, Dyke covered the Uxbridge beat for London's *Evening Standard*.

Most of the reporters on the *Mirror* assumed that they would move up to Fleet Street one day, but Dyke was ambivalent, and worried about following the conventional career route. He and other young journalists would look at older pros like Alan Price and 'Scoop' Ewing, now in their forties and fifties and starting their descent through the ranks of the regional local press after a run at the top. The sight of Scoop, a massive man blowing fumes of chain-smoked cigarettes through his nose like a dragon, shambling about the office of the *Advertiser*, often drunk during the day, was a particularly fearful one. He was a physical and mental wreck, shell-backed from years of slumping over a typewriter; florid-faced and pot-bellied after years of drinking with contacts in the pub. 'Christ!' Dyke and others would say to each other when Scoop bowled into the Gardeners' Arms, 'if that's what Fleet Street does to you, I'm not so sure . . .'

By 1968, Dyke's last year on the *Hillingdon Mirror*, there was a contingent of unabashed hippies on the paper. Dyke himself was never really a hippy, though he dressed in jeans and an open-necked shirt, sported a Beatles-length hairstyle and by now had already grown his famous beard. He took an interest in the 'underground' hippie press, reading magazines like *Oz* that were brought into the office, and even indulging a request from a reporter to cover the Isle of Wight pop festival, Britain's answer to Woodstock. A seminal event was Enoch Powell's 'Rivers of Blood' speech in Birmingham, in the wake of race riots in America. Powell, courting the ever-present strand of racism in white working-class voters, warned that there would be similar trouble in Britain unless immigration was curbed. The speech had a big impact in the *Hillingdon Mirror*'s circulation area, which included the Asian community of Southall and the Heathrow immigration control centre at Harmondsworth – a constant source of race-sensitive stories. There were agonised debates in the Gardeners' Arms about what would today be called 'institutionalised racism' in the press, and discussions of the ethics and merits of 'alternative' press. This was mixed with a growing interest in left-wing politics and the underground scene. Dyke himself drew the line at some reporters' habit of sneaking round the back of the building to smoke joints during office hours: 'What are you doing that for! Don't you know that stuff makes you stupid!' Stoned or clearheaded, many sensed that a generational change was taking place and, casting another glance across the room at Scoop Ewing, few were entirely sure they wanted a conventional career in the newspaper business.

That year Dyke was given promotion in the form of a job on the Slough *Evening Mail*, a new daily paper being launched by King and Hutchins. The idea was that he would set up the Egham and Staines office of the new paper in a two-person team with Ray Snoddy – a reporter on the *Mirror*'s more establishment-minded sister paper, the *Advertiser*. Snoddy, later to become the country's leading media journalist, was a graduate trainee down from Oxford. Dyke, hamming up his pseudo-Cockney persona, teased Snoddy endlessly, winding him up over his intellectual approach. Instead of coming to the pub and joining in the poker school with the *Hillingdon Mirror* boys, the hacks complained that Snoddy spent his lunchtime grooming his long orange beard and playing chess. The plan involved Dyke and Snoddy sharing a flat together. But this cosy arrangement came unstuck when Snoddy accepted an offer to join the Oxford *Evening Mail*.

Many years later, when Dyke became Director General of the BBC, Snoddy, by then media editor of *The Times*, quipped: 'Back then Greg Dyke was the racy tabloid man and I worked on the properly established broadsheet. Nothing's changed.'

# 2.
# Jack the Lad

Greg Dyke, sprawled in his customary position, feet up on the news-desk, tipping his chair well back, is pretending to be deeply absorbed reading the paper. He risks the occasional glance across the desk, managing to keep a faraway look on his face as he watches the Slough *Evening Mail*'s crime reporter, Jim Latham, reading a letter, his jaw almost on the floor.

The letter is written in the characteristic and spookily minute hand of a local exhibitionist transvestite crank, well known in the newsroom for his hobby of bombarding the paper with letters. But instead of the usual communiqué on world affairs, this is a personally addressed love letter asking for a date and promising undying and eternal love. Latham turns white with fear and Dyke and the others crack up with laughter. The letter was a careful forgery.

After a short spell in the Egham office of the new paper, Dyke had again been promoted to work on the broadsheet *Evening Mail*'s Slough newsroom where he again shone, quickly mastering the greater demands of a daily paper and branching out to write longer by-lined feature interviews and longer, more thoughtful political articles. He was in his element. He was a naturally gifted reporter, where his inherited loathing of pomposity and innate self-confidence helped him shine. Above all Dyke loved having a laugh. His beat was local politics. Latham, the victim of the practical joke, worked alongside him covering the courts – difficult for Dyke because it required top-notch shorthand, a skill which was boring to learn and which, therefore, he had never really mastered.

Latham was part of a contingent of journalists who had been moved south from Leeds and Newcastle by the paper's part owners, Thomson Regional Newspapers, to staff the new paper. Dyke was one of a few locally recruited reporters on the paper and the northern contingent would wind Dyke up by imitating and exaggerating his Cockney accent and cocky Southern Bastard, 'Jack the Lad' swagger. Which was why he was so keen to get his own back.

Dyke and Latham ran the paper's NUJ branch and soon after Dyke arrived he was heavily involved in a dispute with the management. By now Dyke was earning around £1200 a year, reasonable white-collar wages, but still not enough to secure a mortgage on a house in boring, but booming, Slough. The issue this time was extra payments for the longer interviews and feature articles the reporters were encouraged to write to fill up the endless columns of the *Evening Mail*'s news pages. Dyke thought that they should get extra money. When more timid souls said they didn't mind helping out, Dyke as Father of the Chapel would loudly announce that the circulation was going up, more money was coming in and if they didn't grab the cash it would only go to the shareholders – 'and what do they do to earn it?' Under threat of strike action Dyke extracted the promise of a review of reporters' earnings. Those providing the most copy would receive extra money according to their contribution. Dyke was suspicious, and when each reporter got a letter saying how much extra they were going to get he called a meeting. The reporters all opened their envelopes at the same time to discover that only Dyke and Latham – the troublemakers – had been offered anything at all. Dyke was highly delighted to have thwarted this devious management attempt at divide and rule. Shortly afterwards they all won an across-the-board pay rise and Dyke was, even more than before, the great hero in the office.

Dyke supplemented his income by working weekends for Cassidy and Lee, the tabloid reporting operation based in Guildford, Surrey. Dyke was building on the success of his lineage pool exploits at the *Hillingdon Mirror*, earning useful extra cash (when Cassidy and Lee couldn't wriggle out of paying him, that is) by selling material to the nationals, learning the black arts of tabloid journalism and winning the attention of Fleet Street news editors. In newspaper circles Cassidy and Lee were legendary operators. While never stooping to actual dishonesty, their methods involved vast amounts of so-called 'needlework' – embroidering and stitching together stories that tabloid news-desks would find irresistible. Often the idea was to think of the story first and then find somebody to 'stand it up' by coming up with the right information, usually a highly embellished quote. A never-ending source of tabloid fodder was a convent in Godalming in Surrey, where the nuns were happy to put their names to almost anything the hacks could dream up. Dyke was involved in an endless stream of funny-old-world Trampolining Nun-type stories. He once supplied a picture-story headlined OFFICIATING AT THE MORNING SERVICE. This featured a nun who swore that she doubled up as a motor mechanic. She was pictured sprawling under a car, spanner in hand, to prove it. Dyke had formed a close working partnership with Jeff Wright, a photographer on the *Evening Mail*'s sister paper, the *Weekly Post*. The two men became lifelong friends.

Meanwhile Dyke was beginning to take his main job on the *Evening Mail* more seriously and becoming increasingly political. His politics beat brought him into contact with people in the Labour Party – the natural focus for the sense of social injustice he had felt since the trauma of the 11-plus and a focus for his rudimentary trade union socialism and gut-reaction loathing of right-wing racism. In the winter of 1968–70 Slough had the rare experience of hitting the national headlines when it became the centre of a sudden influx of Asian immigrants expelled from East Africa by the Ugandan government. Dyke followed the local political fall-out under headlines such as IMMI-GRANT FLOW INTO SLOUGH IS PAST ITS PEAK, run in February 1970. He had developed a friendship with Joan Lestor, the left-wing and fervently anti-racialist Labour MP for Slough. Lestor was preparing to defend her highly marginal seat in the forthcoming General Election, set for later that year. She spent a lot of time cultivating the *Evening Mail*, and was often seen in the office talking to Dyke, the political reporter, and invited all the reporters to the House of Commons for a guided tour.

Dyke covered the 1970 General Election for the *Evening Mail*. The incumbent Labour government of Harold Wilson started well ahead in the national polls, facing a challenge from Tory leader Ted Heath, an enthusiastic amateur yachtsman and musician. Dyke limbered up with a few soft but classily-written background articles on local politics (thus earning his extra lineage payments) such as THREE KNIGHTS CALL IT A DAY – a pun-ridden joint profile of three retiring local backbench Tory MPs who obligingly reminisced about the old days.

At first the election campaign was dominated by concern over inflation, but as polling day approached the race issue erupted once more after Enoch Powell upped the ante by warning that 'coloured immigration' threatened 'the destruction of the British nation'. Powell was immediately denounced by Labour left-winger Tony Benn as a modern-day Hitler. The Labour Party demanded that Heath distance himself from Powell. Dyke covered the story for the *Evening Mail* under the headline: UNITED IN DETESTATION OF RACIALISM – 'The Prime Minister today backed last night's attack on Enoch Powell by Anthony Wedgwood Benn'.

The next day Dyke wrote: 'Now with just two days left, all logical reasoning would point to a second victory in Slough for Labour'. He added: 'Perhaps the one factor which could decide the election is public reaction to the race relations and immigration issue which has blown up in the last two weeks.' The article noted that Joan Lestor was strongly opposed to racialism, and backed Benn's attack on Enoch Powell. Meanwhile Lestor's Tory opponent, Nigel Lawson, Dyke said, was taking 'Ted Heath's line on the issue, against Enoch Powell.' On the eve of polling Dyke dominated the front page under the headline: VOTE TORY PLEA TO PAKISTANIS. Nigel Lawson, Dyke reported, had warned local Asians that they must ignore 'instructions to vote Labour as a block' issued by an organization called the Pakistani Overseas Association.

On the following day Dyke reported a story that was to become familiar in British political life – the 'surprise' news that the Tory party had romped home in a General Election, confounding the predictions of the opinion pollsters. TED HEAVES TO AT NUMBER 10 – HOUSEWIVES HOIST TORY FLAG – JOAN HANGS ON, ran the headline, under which Dyke wrote: 'Ted Heath was today heading for No 10 Downing Street and it was the silent majority – the housewives – who put him on the road.' Despite Labour's national defeat, Joan Lestor was re-elected with a majority reduced by only 2,000 to 2,677 – 'a good result for local Labour as the swing was under 3 per cent'.

Dyke stayed for only another year on the Slough *Evening Mail*, finding himself increasingly bored and disillusioned. The natural next step would have been a reporter's job on a national newspaper. But although, at the time, Dyke thought of himself as a 'pop' – or tabloid – journalist, he was beginning to have second thoughts about the pop end of Fleet Street, telling friends he had come to the conclusion that the tabloids were glib. He had done his bit with Cassidy and Lee, and that had been great fun. But it was teenage stuff.

Dyke was 24 now and wanted to do something more substantial with his life. He attempted a sideways move into the BBC, highly regarded for its news, as a reporter with Radio Teesside. The appointments panel heard his accent and asked him if he thought that people in the north-east would be able to understand anything he said. 'Well, the taxi driver didn't seem to 'ave a problem,' Dyke replied. He did not get the job. Instead, after being encouraged by Joan Lestor and others in the Labour Party, Dyke decided to apply to university. He simply wondered if the people who went to university were any better or cleverer than himself, and wanted to find out. Dyke applied to several colleges and was accepted by both Lancaster and York universities. His choice of subject, naturally enough, was politics, the only thing, apart from football, he knew much about. He chose to go to York simply because he liked the look of the place – especially its artificial lake – the biggest in Europe. Dyke had driven up for his interview in the company of his photographer friend Jeff Wright on a lovely sunny spring day, and both of them had been bowled over by the place.

York University had been set up as part of the Robbins Committee expansion of higher education in the sixties, aimed at making more places in higher education available to the working classes. It promoted itself as 'The University in the Park' and consisted of a series of modernist buildings assembled around an artificial lake with a fountain in the middle. A great many ostentatiously designed walkways, bridges and paths wound through the carefully landscaped grassy knolls, connecting clusters of student flats separated by pleasant streams and leafy groves, to the library and teaching blocks, surrounded by woods. Abstract sculpture was dotted about. As a 'campus' university it had little or no connection with the nearby city of York and was thus a self-contained and somewhat other-worldly community. On a sunny day, with the light shimmering on the fountain and the lake, exotic waterfowl wandering across the lawns, groups of young people – many of them exceptionally attractive young women away from home for the first time – sitting around or wandering leisurely to and fro, the place looked like a sort of paradise. Especially if you came from Slough.

And so in September 1971 Greg Dyke said goodbye to the suburbs – pubs, lineage pools, trampolining nuns and all – never to return.

# 3.
# The Graduate

It is February 1972 and Greg Dyke is in his first year at the University of York, addressing a students' union general meeting in his capacity as Vice-President (external affairs). He is dressed, following the style of the times, in cheesecloth shirt and bell-bottom jeans of heroic flappiness. He has long hair, already thinning at the front, a beard and a moustache, and the overall effect is to make him look remarkably like Tony McPhee, the lead guitarist of The Groundhogs – a blues group popular at the time.

'Over the next five years we are being asked to pay off the £26,000 deficit built up by the university catering committee over the past two years, as well as break even over the same five years . . .'

'Bor-Ring! . . . Siddown Dyke! . . . Bloody bureaucrat!'

Dyke is being heckled by a group of extreme left-wing 'Trots,' mostly belonging to an organization called the International Socialists. Prominent amongst the hecklers is Peter Hitchens, later to make his name as a right-wing, pro-hanging Tory commentator on the *Daily Express*. (Hitchens became famous at York for apologizing after arriving late for a seminar with the immortal words: 'Excuse me, I'm sorry I'm late but I've just been trying to start the revolution.')

Dyke soldiers on. '. . . As I was saying . . . we are being asked break even over the five years. This is only acceptable if the grant increase is large enough, but in fact to do this for the next five years would mean the erosion of the students' purchasing power . . .'

The Trots are not impressed.

'BORING!'

# Citizen Greg

Dyke's interest in politics had flowered after his arrival at York. He had arrived thinking of himself as being pretty far out on the left of politics which, of course, he was when measured by the standards of the population as a whole. But not by the standards of 1970s student politics in general, and politics at York University in particular. Dyke's membership of the boring, mainstream Labour Party, his visceral dislike of the Tory Party, his interest in the roots of the Cuban revolution, about which he wrote essays, and the internal politics of the Soviet Communist Party in the 1920s, his specialist subject, placed him firmly on the right of the political spectrum of the (tiny minority) of student political activists.

Dyke was different from the other students in many ways. Apart from being a few years older and, to general amazement, working fairly steadily at his course, he lived not on the campus – the 'middle-class holiday camp' as some thought of it – but in the city of York. He was almost unique, as a student, in buying his own house in the city, making full use of the generous renovation grants then available to 'do up' a terraced house. Friends coming up to visit from London were mightily impressed at Dyke's initiative and later reckoned that he had used the house to pay his way through college. All this, together with a rare ability to drink his peers under the table, made Dyke seem like an awesome figure to some. He was a London sophisticate who could cook genuine spaghetti bolognaise (still something of a rarity in the early seventies), a journalist with work published in national newspapers (albeit tabloids), who had worked in the real world, knew MPs and powerful people yet was still great fun. His energy and sophistication made him an attractive figure to many, not least women. He soon met and fell in love with Christine Taylor, a younger sociology student who, by common consent, was one of the most good-looking girls at the college.

Naturally enough, Dyke had gravitated towards the university's student newspaper, which was called *Nouse* (a pun on the River Ouse, which flowed through the nearby city) and where he took the post of news editor within a few weeks of arriving. At the time the paper was a passable imitation, in form at least, of a normal local newspaper of the sort Dyke was used to working on. His first front page 'splash' story was about plans by Conservative education secretary Margaret Thatcher to prevent student unions spending their money on political causes. It was run under the headline:

BEWARE – MRS THATCHER IS AFTER YOU.

In 1972, towards the end of Dyke's first year at York, *Nouse* dropped its traditional local newspaper format and became a psychedelic 'underground'-type magazine. The first edition of the new-style paper had a poster front cover based on *A Clockwork Orange*. The paper had abolished all hierarchies and was now being produced by a collective, including Dyke. The paper's content revolved around dope-smoking and the unfathomable minutiae of ultra-left politics – with Black Power, Third World Revolution and Troops Out of Ireland being favoured topics. The paper carried a regular advert for a 'head shop' in York, offering 'loons . . . Indian gear . . . far out jackets . . . tank tops . . . Afghan coats . . . South Sea Bubble gear . . . the lot!' Dyke appeared in these pages under the by-line 'GRYKE' and was a sort of anchor to (relative) reality, penning reports about student politics. In December 1972 it appears that he attended the NUS national conference in Margate – 'four days of smoke, drink, debate and decay' – and wrote: 'there was a rare unification of the various left-wing groups over the grants issue. With the exception of a nutty motion from the International Marxist Group calling for a £20 a week grant all the year round – which of course the popular press had great delight in playing up. Apart from this there was complete unity.'

Dyke frequently lambasted the students at York for their apathy. Less than 3 per cent ever turned up to union meetings and only about 10 per cent voted in student union elections. When the apathetic wrote to the paper complaining that they didn't bother with union affairs because meetings were dominated by left-wingers discussing things like Northern Ireland and Vietnam, Dyke said: 'It's only when the left and the right are screaming at each other that it gets interesting.'

Students were less apathetic when it came to money. Dyke and the York students' union organized a rent strike as part of a national NUS campaign to put financial pressure on universities to support its campaign for higher grants. Dyke reported in *Nouse* that 552 students out of about 3000 had refused to pay their rent, contributing instead over £20,000 into a special bank account run by the students' union. Dyke ran a big article in the paper, surveying the progress of rent strikes across the country and proudly asserting that York's strike was the best supported in the country.

By this time Dyke was in his third year at York and, as his final exams approached, he dropped out of student politics to concentrate full-time on his studies. Dyke's faculty, the politics department, had been convulsed by the early revelations of US President Richard Nixon's role in the Watergate Affair. The department dropped its entire American politics course so that students and academics alike could concentrate on studying the ramifications of the scandal full-time. Dyke took his exams against this extraordinary background and was awarded a 2:1 honours degree.

After graduation Dyke stayed on in York for a few months, uncertain what to do next. He and Christine were now married and she, at least, had a definite career plan. Christine wanted to become a social worker or probation officer and, with this in mind, had been accepted for a postgraduate course at Newcastle University. Dyke was happy enough to follow her to the north-east, where he was able to persuade John Rees, his editor at the Slough *Evening Mail*, to give him a reporting job. By happy coincidence, Rees had been transferred to the *Newcastle Journal*, a big regional broadsheet, the year before. Later Dyke was to look back on the summer and autumn of 1974 as a strange time that somehow signalled the end of an era. In his own mind it meant the Watergate Affair, his departure from the artificial paradise of 'The University in the Park', his return to work as a reporter – something which he thought he had left behind – and the death of his dog, which ran out under a car and was flattened. Even student politics had turned sour. Just as Dyke was leaving, six members of the student union committee were suspended by the university while the fraud squad was called in to investigate the embezzlement of part of the £24,000 rent strike fund. To Dyke, who had been so proud of York's strike, the news of the corruption came as a shock.

Dyke was able to get a job on the *Newcastle Journal* due to a reshuffle caused by the departure of the paper's industrial correspondent, John Kay, who had landed a job on the *Sun* in Fleet Street.

Kay's job had been taken by a reporter called Peter McHugh, causing a reshuffle and an opening for Dyke as a political reporter – the same job he had done for Rees on the Slough *Evening Mail*. The main difference this time was that Dyke had to work in tandem with another reporter, Quentin Peel, later a foreign correspondent on the *Financial Times* but at the time a trainee. Peel, having got to the paper before Dyke, had the better of the two jobs – covering Newcastle City Council which, in the wake of the great north-eastern corruption scandals of the sixties, was a good deal more interesting than Dyke's beat, which was rural Northumberland and its County Council, dominated by tweedy Conservative farmers and landowners.

But beggars could not be choosers and Dyke needed a job to finance the home he was setting up with Christine. His job on the *Journal* paid about £2000 a year. Taking inflation into account, this was what he had been earning before he went to university. Helped by the profits from selling the terraced house in York, the couple were able to set themselves up in a nicely done-up terraced cottage in Wylan, a village up the Tyne from Newcastle. Other reporters on the paper, which included a group of grad-uate trainees who had joined the paper at about the same as Dyke, were jealous of the house, as it was much nicer than the grotty bed-sits off the Westgate Road which they were forced to inhabit. But mostly they were jealous of Christine. They would eagerly accept invitations to visit just so they could gaze upon her beauty. Given the fact that Dyke was no oil painting himself, many wondered how he had managed to pull such a fantastic-looking 'bird'. Behind their backs the couple were given the joint nickname 'Beauty and the Beast'.

Dyke was friendly with the younger reporters on the journal, but he struck them as quite domesticated, settled and shockingly uninterested in making the next career move. This would have meant following John Kay down to London and a job on a national paper. His best friend in Newcastle was a reporter called Nick Evans, who covered the Northumberland politics beat for the rival *Newcastle Chronicle*. Unlike Dyke, Evans was a nicely spoken Oxford-educated public schoolboy. Dyke had first been drawn towards Evans because he was much better at shorthand, and Dyke could recycle his notes. Dyke himself was less than brilliant at taking an accurate record of a lengthy council debate, especially if it was boring. Evans, for his part, was somewhat awed by this amazingly loud and hairy character roaring around the genteel world of the County Set, effing and blinding in his Cockney accent, impersonating the crustier Tories, including their leader Lord Ridley, a local Tory moneybags, and spreading scurrilous gossip about them. Evans and his girlfriend Penny would often form a social foursome with Dyke and Christine, thinking the stripped-pine Wylan house the height of provincial chic.

But Dyke was not happy. He had gone to university, he kept telling himself, to unlearn popular journalism, but here he was again, working for Rees and facing what he thought of as the second-rate standards of regional journalism. Kids like Nick Evans who had gone straight from school to university and then on to the news desk might have liked it. He had loved the life himself when he had left school some ten years earlier. But not any more. 'This is no good,' he kept telling himself. 'It's time to move on.'

# 4.
# Vote Greg Dyke

It is a warm spring evening, May 1977. The telephone in the Putney Labour Party office rings. It is Greg Dyke, candidate for the GLC constituency of Putney, calling from a phone box deep in a Roehampton council estate.

'Judith . . . I'm lost . . . I can see a sign that says "High-cliffe Gardens" or something . . . but I can't see it on the map . . . how do I get back to the office?'

Judith Chegwidden gives directions. Not for the first time. Dyke's main problem, as a canvasser, was that he had no sense of direction and seemed completely incapable of reading a map. In the end, party officials had to arrange for somebody to go with him. It was feared that he might just set off in a westerly direction and keep going day and night until he had canvassed every house all the way back to Slough. Then, if you did go with him, there was another problem. Dyke seemed to want to personally convert every single voter to his own version of the Labour cause. He delighted in finding committed Tories and loudly arguing the toss. Others in his team would move on quickly, complete an entire council block and wince as they heard Dyke's voice echoing up and down a stairwell involved in something just short of a bar-room slanging-match.

Chegwidden and others sometimes thought he was a less than ideal candidate, but there had not been many potential candidates to choose from. Still, they all fell for Dyke's charm. Chegwidden had a particularly soft spot for him. She saw him as being a bit like Tigger from the *Winnie the Pooh* stories, 'a furry, hairy ball of energy' who would go bouncing around the streets with his big party rosette and clutch of leaflets with enthusiasm which far outstripped any tangible results.

Dyke had returned to London with Christine two years earlier. He had seen an advert placed in the journalists' trade paper, the *UK Press Gazette*, by Wandsworth Community Relations Council, a group set up to promote racial harmony, who wanted an 'information and campaigns officer'. Dyke had applied as a way of abandoning journalism and returning to London where, in addition, there were better prospects for Christine. She had completed her course at Newcastle University and was now a qualified probation officer. The other hacks on the paper thought he was mad.

Dyke was interviewed for the job and, according to one person on the interview panel, was by far the strongest candidate. But following an argument about whether the organization should employ mainly or only black people, Dyke was rejected in favour of a black woman activist. It was only when she turned down the offer that Dyke got the job.

At first Dyke and Christine moved not into Putney but to Balham, where the Community Relations Council was based. They bought a flat in a converted Victorian house in Granard Road, just off Wandsworth Common. The flat was on the edge of an area known to residents as the Nightingale Triangle, the local gentrification beachhead in an otherwise run-down and desperately poor area. Within a decade houses in streets like Granard Road would be lovingly restored by their young, middle-class, professional owners and be worth a fortune. But in the mid-seventies they were regarded as the absolute pits – full of damp, with leaky roofs and flaky plaster – and often left empty, semi-derelict or, as in Dyke and Christine's case, chopped up into multiple tiny flats with no sound insulation. This was a particular problem, as the flat above theirs was occupied by a Mexican bongo player who insisted on practising all night.

Granard Road was in the Battersea North parliamentary constituency which, at the time, was held by Douglas Jay, the veteran left-wing anti-European Labour MP, and father of Peter Jay, the journalist. Both Dyke and Christine plunged into the Shaftesbury ward organisation of the Battersea Party, working during the day at their jobs as caring professionals and, in the evenings, attending the endless round of political meetings centred on the Party's Lavender Hill headquarters, with the politicking continuing afterwards over the obligatory trip to The Cornet of Horse pub.

Dyke was keen to get onto the Battersea party's General Management Committee as Shaftesbury ward representative, but found it difficult because there was so much competition. Other ward members included Hugh Stephenson, who in 1982 became editor of the *New Statesman*, Brian Sedgemore, later an MP and, later still, Clare Short. The good thing about South London was that there was a clutch of ancient Labour MPs (such as Jay himself in Battersea) sitting on huge majorities who were all due to retire soon. Their departure would open up possibilities for the ambitious. Like many in the Shaftesbury ward, Dyke put himself forward for inclusion on the 'B-list' of party members approved by Labour's national HQ for consideration as potential parliamentary candidates. He failed to get on the list because of lack of experience in local government.

Things were not going well for Dyke in his job at the Wandsworth Community Relations Council either. From almost day one he realized that he had made a mistake in taking it. By all accounts Dyke's boss, Charles Boxer, had done impressive work in building up the organization, one of the first of its type in the country. Early successes had included a survey of Wandsworth Council's housing department, revealing that blacks and Asians had been concentrated in the worst housing stock, creating 'ghetto' council estates. The evidence had caused a complete re-think of housing policy and was later taken up by other housing authorities around the country. The group also did useful, straightforward work translating council advisory leaflets and other bumf into minority languages. They also produced educational pamphlets for black and Asian youths, and filtered specific minority complaints about education and other services to the council. In addition, the CRC ran Saturday night reggae 'sound system' dances in the town hall which regularly attracted 500 youths, at a time when there was virtually nothing else for young blacks to do.

But by the time Dyke arrived, the organization had evidently lost direction. It had grown to employ thirty people. There were accusations that Boxer had done what were described as 'murky' deals with leaders of Asian community groups in which jobs at the CRC were dished out in return for block votes in local elections. At the same time it was said that the CRC was used as a way of providing wages for full-time Labour Party activists and organizers. Boxer eventually came under pressure to employ only blacks and Asians. Dyke, as a male, middle-class, university-educated white, was resented by many of the other staff. He had already been caught up in a row when his department had produced a cartoon comic advising young blacks on contraception, but had failed to find an illustrator who could draw black people. It was felt on the CRC's management board that Dyke wasn't performing well. Dyke himself would complain that the place was 'ludicrously superficial' and 'riddled with racial politics'.

Then, in the spring of 1976, the GLC seat in neighbouring Putney fell vacant when the sitting member Marie Jenkins, wife of Putney MP Hugh Jenkins, retired. Winning the seat offered Dyke the opportunity of getting more involved in politics and a well-paid job. He put his name forward to the selection committee. The most fancied candidate was Tony Banks, already the GLC councillor for Hammersmith. Banks' and Dyke's paths, as it happened, had crossed three years earlier when Dyke had covered Banks' unsuccessful campaign to win the Newcastle North seat in the October 1974 election. But Banks now pulled out, choosing instead to stand for the neighbouring GLC seat of Tooting. The Putney party now had to choose between Dyke and just two other candidates, both far less experienced than Dyke. And so in a ballot of twenty-three people Dyke was selected as the candidate largely by default.

Dyke resigned from his hated job at the Community Relations Council, went on the dole and threw himself into the GLC campaign, able to work full-time dishing out election addresses, organizing meetings and chatting up local journalists. He and Christine moved from the Balham flat to Sefton Street, a street of Victorian terraces running down to the Thames riverside in north Putney. They had got away from the bongo player but now had to deal instead with the noise of building work all around them. Putney was changing and Sefton Street was being rapidly colonized and renovated by Young Urban Professionals like Dyke and Christine.

British politics in 1976 was full of drama. The Labour government elected as a result of the miners' strike in 1974 was attempting to survive without a parliamentary majority, watering down its left-wing policies to secure the support of Liberal MPs in parliament. Chancellor Denis Healey had accepted an IMF plan for huge cutbacks in public spending which were to lead within two years to a wave of public sector strikes – The Winter of Discontent – and the election of Margaret Thatcher in 1979.

The standard view among local party activists like Dyke was that the party's parliamentary leadership was a huge 'sell-out', wilfully ignoring party policy. Inside the party there was a vigorous campaign, centred on London, for 'Party Democracy', meaning a series of rule changes making MPs answerable to local activists. In July 1976, soon after Dyke's selection, the Putney Labour Party passed a resolution in favour of 'compulsory re-selection' of all Labour MPs throughout the country – giving activists the right to throw out MPs who had supported the 'right-wing' IMF-backed measures of the Labour government, rather than the socialist policies agreed at its annual conferences.

Dyke kicked off his campaign with a speech given to a local South London Labour Party rally, calling for an 'Alternative Economic Policy' to the one being pursued by the government. He was particularly keen on creating 'workers' co-operatives' as an alternative to factory closures and unemployment where private sector firms could no longer make a profit. 'There is a real need to rethink the role of the GLC and to re-examine its powers,' he said. 'It needs to press the government to devolve more powers to the GLC. It needs to be able to invest in industry through an industrial development corporation and it must look at ways of encouraging workers' co-operatives.' Dyke announced that the two main issues of the election were housing and transport. 'The housing problem can only be solved with land in the outer London boroughs – the GLC's major housing role is not in management or maintenance, which would be better carried out by the borough, but in strategic planning and building.' If the leafy Tory-controlled outer boroughs refused to co-operate, Dyke said, then the GLC should be 'given powers' to make them comply. When challenged by one of the local newspapers, Dyke summed up his position with characteristic bluntness: 'The Tory outer London boroughs should be made to build more council houses to help solve inner London's housing problems.'

Unfortunately for Dyke, the final weeks of his campaign were dominated by a local strike by dustbin men, then employed directly by Wandsworth's Labour Council. No matter how much Dyke tried to persuade the voters to focus on his plans for workers' industrial co-ops, and forcing the Tory suburbs to build a ring of Utopian council house settlements in the green belt, attention kept returning to the fact that parts of Putney were swarming with what were described in the local paper as 'poison-proof giant super-rats' because, at the end of the day, the Labour party could not get its act together and arrange for the bins to be emptied. ('Off-licence manager George Hunt' told the *Wandsworth and Putney Borough News* that 'giant rats had gnawed their way through my wooden beer crates. I found 38 of them in one crate, and one or two were as big as cats.')

Dyke's manifesto was based on a standard leaflet used by all GLC candidates. It was topped with the headline LABOUR LONDON'S LOOKING GOOD. The choice of this slogan was bad luck for Dyke, since he was acutely aware that he was not the world's best looking bloke, and so the juxtaposition of the headline and Dyke's startled and bearded mug-shot was unintentionally hilarious (at one crowded Labour Party meeting, just after the then

unknown Dyke had arrived from Newcastle, the chairman had referred to him as 'the bald-headed, bearded
man at the back'. Dyke shouted back: 'You mean "the
short, ugly, bald-headed, bearded man" don't you?').

In the part of the manifesto he was allowed to write
himself, Dyke took a populist line – promising to 'get rid
of a lot of the pomp and ceremony found in local
government'. His only specific personal policy
commitment was to promote 'a policy of cheap bus fares
and more bus lanes like the one on Putney Hill and
regular services'.

On the day of the poll Dyke issued a crudely produced
leaflet which simply said:

> Remember you are voting for your landlord.
> The Tories will STOP building council houses.
> They will SELL OFF the best ones and PUT UP
> the rents on all the rest.
> Don't let this happen
> Vote for GREG DYKE

He also issued a last-minute statement to the papers,
saying that the Conservatives had a secret plan to abolish
bus passes for OAPS if they gained control of the GLC.
The claim was rubbished by the local papers and Dyke's
Tory opponent – a strange-looking man called Lionel
'Len' Harris who had a conical quiff – as a 'desperate eve
of poll smear'.

Dyke lost the seat. The Conservatives' man, Harris, got
17,837 votes compared with Dyke's 10,681. The Tories had
done well right across London, but Dyke's result was one
of the worst in the whole capital – turning a safe-ish
Labour seat into a thumping 7000 Tory majority. David
Mellor, the Tory candidate for the Putney parliamentary
seat, said that he would repeat the trick and unseat
Putney's sitting Labour MP, Hugh Jenkins, in the general

election. With the minority Labour government sinking into ever deeper trouble, this was expected at any time. 'Is it merely coincidence,' Mellor gloated, 'that the most spectacular Tory wins came here in Wandsworth and in Hillingdon, both of which are blessed with the most arrogant, extreme spendthrift Marxist Labour councils in the whole of the country?'

Under the headline TORIES WALTZ IT IN PUTNEY, the *Putney Herald* reported how 'Tory golden boy Len Harris wiped the floor with his Labour adversary in Thursday's poll. Conservative champagne corks popped while the socialists and their candidate Greg Dyke went dejectedly home to bed – wondering what had gone wrong with his election campaign.'

For Greg Dyke it was a personal as well as a political disaster. He had not really been happy since leaving York University. He had spent an uncomfortable year in Newcastle, bored and disenchanted with newspaper journalism. Then he had spent another miserable year at the Community Relations Council, which had done much to dent his faith in radical community politics. And it had had been topped off with his humiliating rejection at the polls.

The day after his election defeat Dyke went for a long walk on Wandsworth Common and found himself sitting on a log, head in hands, asking the question, 'Whatever happened to me?' His hopes of a political career lay in ruins. He had burned his boats at the *Newcastle Journal* and had not worked as a reporter in London for seven years. His chances of getting back into newspaper reporting, even if he wanted to, were slim. Reporting was a young man's game and his age now started to count heavily against him. It seemed too late to train for anything else. He had a mortgage on the house in Putney.

He had been with Christine for six years and she was approaching her thirties as well. Soon it would be time to start a family. He later told a newspaper: 'I didn't know what to do with my life. I was worried and depressed.'

Greg Dyke had just turned 30 and he had the terrible feeling that he was all washed up.

# 5.
# Jammy Bugger

Then Greg Dyke got lucky.

Nick Evans, his old mate from the *Newcastle Chronicle*, told him that *Weekend World*, the LWT current affairs show that he had joined after finishing his training on the *Chronicle*, was about to hire a researcher. Evans encouraged Dyke to apply, even though it was a bit of a long shot. *Weekend World* was an odd sort of TV programme, in essence a weekly illustrated lecture and quite unlike any sort of journalism Dyke had done before.

He almost fell at the first hurdle. At the interview Dyke made the fatal error of mixing up John Birt, the head of LWT current affairs and the man, Evans had said, that he had to impress, with the statutory trade union rep. Dyke concentrated on impressing the rep with a series of jokes and off-the-cuff answers. He largely ignored the greying stony-faced and academic figure of Birt, thinking him an 'awkward bastard' who asked detailed questions about economic policy and international diplomacy. But he had made enough of an impression to be offered an interview for a similar job on *The London Programme* – LWT's regional current affairs show.

Dyke did much better at his second interview, where he impressed the panel with his ability to think on his feet and his ace reporter's knack of answering questions crisply and cleanly in a few well-chosen phrases. One member of the panel, Jane Hewland, the head of LWT's Minorities Unit which made programmes for and about lesbians, gays, blacks and the disabled, was dead against hiring him. 'Oh God!' she wrote in her report on the interview, 'I know everyone thought this guy was terrific.

But I didn't think he was intellectually high-powered myself and he was so glib, so fast-talking and so sure of himself I fear we would never be able to break his spirit and bring him to see the light as we see it. I think he would just turn out to be a pain in the arse.' She was over-ruled and Dyke started work on *The London Programme* soon afterwards.

He made an immediate impact on the programme, playing the role of the properly trench-coated old newspaper hack to the hilt, even if he did turn up to work in his customary jeans and open-necked lumberjack shirt. Reasonably enough, Dyke returned to his old contacts for some of his stories. One of the first looked at the state of Labour Party politics in London, focusing on his former stomping ground in Wandsworth. He then produced an edition of *The London Programme* under the unpromising title of 'Slough Sludge'. The programme traced the death of birds and wildlife to the use of Cinagro, a type of fertilizer made from human sewage and containing dangerous levels of cadmium, made in a factory in Slough. Dyke's former mentor Joan Lestor, the Slough MP, featured heavily in the programme, complaining about the fact that 25 million tonnes of the stuff was being spread on fields within an eight-mile radius of Slough. Another early triumph was a programme highlighting the dangers of hormonal pregnancy testing, revealing early research which, in the wake of the famous *Sunday Times* exposé of Thalidomide, established a link between a pregnancy testing pill and foetal deformity. The programme did much to put the issue on the agenda. The pills were banned and, years later, many victims were able to sue for compensation.

Beyond this, Dyke specialized in local government and police stories. He was involved in an exposé of the influence of Freemasonry in the police and in local government. He worked together with Chris Mullin, the investigative journalist and *Tribune* editor, on an exposé of the internal politics of Newham Labour Party, where a right-wing pressure group was secretly funding legal action against left-wing activists who were trying to 'deselect' MP Reg Prentice. Dyke had useful contacts in the world of racial politics, a subject which, in the late seventies, was climbing up the London political agenda. An early journalistic success was a story about the way in which private landlords were persecuting blacks and Asians throughout London, trying to 'winkle' them out of flats in converted Victorian properties so that they could be sold on at a huge profit for development. He had brought the story with him from his job at Wandsworth Community Relations Council.

One of Dyke's main political contacts at the time was Peter Hain, the anti-apartheid campaigner who had join-ed the Putney Labour Party after the GLC election at about the same time Dyke started work at LWT. Although Hain had been in the Liberal party, the two men found that they were on almost exactly the same political wave-length. Some of the old guard were sceptical about Hain's commitment to Labour, but Dyke was enthusiastic about the new convert and did what he could to make him feel welcome. Both regarded themselves as left-wing by the standards of the national Labour Party of the time, but they were more concerned with essentially American political ideas derived from the sixties anti-Vietnam war 'counter-culture' and Martin Luther King's civil rights movement, rather than Marxism or other more traditional forms of socialism. Hain, for his part, found Dyke to be remarkably un-English, and such a living contradiction of class-based politics – the thing that had put him off joining the Labour party in the first place – that he wondered if Dyke might be a fellow South African or an Australian who had somehow quickly developed a thick Cockney accent. Dyke would meet Hain regularly and go for a curry in Clapham, to discuss Labour business and, at the same time, pump Hain, who had a research job with a big trade union, for story ideas for *The London Programme.*

Both Hain and Dyke were on the General Management Committee of Putney Labour Party and would join in the routine work of distributing Party leaflets and attending meetings, followed by trips to the Jolly Gardeners pub where Dyke would boast entertainingly about his job at LWT. He would amaze his mates by telling them how much he was earning – at least three times what he had earned at the Community Relations Council. 'It's a different world,' he would tell them and – to even greater amazement – offer to get the beer in 'now that I'm earning'. Then he would hold forth about the fiddles that the electricians and cameramen used in order to boost their wages or avoid tax, and how, generally, he was having a ball and raking it in at the same time. 'You jammy bastard!' his audience would reply, leaving Dyke, glowing with pride, in a position to deliver the sucker punch. 'I know,' he would say with a wink. 'Thank God the Tories won Putney!'

As Dyke got into his stride he branched out from political stories, carving out a bigger role for himself on the programme by sheer force of personality, and starting to get himself noticed as a cut above the average *London Programme* researcher. Dyke's greatest hit, and the programme that was later most remembered from his time on *The London Programme*, was a special edition analysing what would happen to London if the River Thames broke its banks and flooded the capital, entitled, simply enough,

# Citizen Greg

'The Drowned City'. At the time, the Thames Barrier had not yet been built and a flood was a real possibility. In January 1978 an exceptionally high surge tide was forecast that would take the river to within two feet of the top of the Embankment in central London, and to within a foot of the river defences at their lowest point which, as it happened, was at Putney near Dyke's newly acquired Victorian des-res. High winds, forecasters said, could easily push the river higher and over the Embankment.

Dyke's programme started off by showing archive footage of what had happened all along the Thames estuary and the coast of East Anglia during the last floods in 1928 and 1953, claiming that London was now facing 'potentially its worst calamity since the Blitz'. It was based on the premise that sea levels were rising because of melting ice-caps – which made the programme a good ten years ahead of its time. Talk of 'global warming' did not become commonplace until the late 1980s. The main problem was the London Underground which, the programme said, would completely fill with water in central London if the Embankment were breached. The fear was that the warning system did not really work and thousands, perhaps millions, of commuters would be trapped and drowned. The horror was captured with stunt 'reconstruction' filming, showing great surges of water cascading down darkened concrete staircases with people struggling to make their way out. As it happened, the weather was calm and so the Thames remained a good fifteen inches below the flood mark, even in Putney. But the programme made such an impact that Agriculture Minister John Silkin asked London Weekend to show it again, so that people would be aware of the dangers and, presumably, stay away from tube trains on flood alert days. All of this was brilliant for LWT – public service broadcasting in its purest form – a TV programme which, it could plausibly be claimed, could actually save lives.

After doing his stint on *The London Programme* Dyke transferred to *Weekend World*, the LWT current affairs flagship. His last contribution to *The London Programme* was a special edition on the future of the capital's economy, also later regarded as well ahead of its time in the way it dramatized the demise of manufacturing industry in the capital, predicted the rise of the service industries and, even, the emergence of a new servant class of nannies, gardeners, household cleaners and jobbing builders.

The move to *Weekend World* meant that Dyke was reunited with Nick Evans, and they made a couple of programmes together, including a documentary about community policing in Devon and Cornwall. Dyke's main solo effort on *Weekend World* was to be an explanation of the Common Agricultural Policy – which he attempted to brighten up by using footage of a cow which would moo with either approval or disagreement in time with what was being said. In later years, if anyone suggested that he could not handle heavyweight programming he would loudly point out that he was 'the only man ever mad enough to try and explain the Common Agricultural Policy on television' .

But Dyke did not get on with his boss on *Weekend World*, a scholarly figure called David Cox, who was determined to defend the analytical purity of his programme at all costs. He was worried about Dyke from the beginning, seeing him as a 'story-based journalist' who was much more suited to *The London Programme*. Cox thought that Dyke had 'a low ceiling', meaning that he was not especially interested in agonizing over the subtleties of whatever Gordian knot *Weekend World* was attempting to slice through. In fact, when pushed, Cox would admit that he thought that Dyke was by his own standards 'a bit dim'. What Cox liked about Dyke was the fact he had 'nous'. As Cox saw it, at *Weekend World* he was surrounded by 'tortured souls' and 'bright young things', but Dyke was more like a taxi driver who knew how to get from A to B.

It was part of Cox's style to demand endless discussion and rewriting of scripts for *Weekend World* in the name of intellectual 'rigour'. In contrast to Dyke's forte of thinking of a simple, preferably funny or emotive, story which would illustrate a political point, the business of getting an edition of *Weekend World* on air was more like doing a PhD thesis. Cox was a difficult man to please and would niggle away at any weak points in a programme, demanding more and more alterations. It was a macho working atmosphere where people were well paid, but were expected to work round the clock, rewriting the script a dozen times before a marathon session in the cutting room. There were long holidays in between programme series – in keeping with Cox's donnish style, a bit like university summer vacations – but once the programme was on air, home life was non-existent, weekends and days off virtually unknown. As a result, Dyke had less and less time to devote to Putney politics. And, more dramatically, Dyke's childless marriage began to break up, partly under the strain of his workaholic lifestyle.

The head of current affairs Barry Cox (no relation to David) and his boss John Birt had watched Dyke's progress with interest, impressed by the way the new recruit had quickly mastered the art of making current affairs television. In some ways the decision to move him to *Weekend World* had been a test. If there were any major flaws in his personality as a journalist or a team player, David Cox was bound to find them. They were aware that

*Weekend World* was hardly an ideal environment for Dyke, but he had shown that he was still able to churn it out. They were aware of the tensions, but even if David Cox never really warmed to Dyke, he never said that Dyke could not deliver the goods. Barry Cox decided that if LWT was going to get the most out of Dyke they had to put him in charge of something. In the spring of 1979 it was decided that Dyke should be 'fast tracked' as potential executive material.

# 6.
# The Summer Of Discontent

In May 1979 a Conservative government was elected, wedded to the then relatively unknown creed of 'Thatcherism', which was to transform the country and, not least, the broadcasting industry. Dyke was too busy working at *Weekend World* to play much of a role in the campaign but he watched in horror how the Tories forged ahead in the campaign. One key event in the election campaign was a violent riot near Dyke's home patch of Hayes in West London. The trouble started when demonstrators attacked police protecting a National Front rally taking place in Southall town hall, about half a mile from Dyke's parents' house in Cerne Close. One demonstrator was killed and dozens were seriously injured in a pitched battle along the high street. The incident was given extensive coverage in the press and added a strong racialist aspect to the election, which included a warning by Tory leader Margaret Thatcher, echoing Enoch Powell, that black and Asian communities like those in Southall represented an 'alien wedge' in the country's big cities. *The London Programme* ran a special edition on the Southall riot.

The drama of the General Election was followed by the start of a major strike at all the ITV companies – including LWT – which was to be one of the last successful large-scale industrial disputes before the new government's anti-trade union laws began to bite. Soon after the General Election the TV union ACTT had asked for a 25 per cent pay increase, needed, it said, to keep pace with inflation. The ITV Association, a federation of all the ITV companies including LWT, was offering only 15 per cent, and so the union ordered a work to rule while members at each ITV company were balloted to see whether they were prepared to accept the offer or go on strike.

The union was particularly strong at LWT, where the peculiarities of broadcasting only at weekends had led to all kinds of overtime arrangements. Technicians were routinely on double or triple time and then had to be bribed with on-the-spot payments to finish the job. There was a great deal of foot-dragging to trigger cumulative overtime payments. One LWT videotape editor had earned £100,000 in a single year at 1979 prices. The standard joke in the industry was, 'What's the difference between an Arab oil sheik and an LWT videotape editor? An Arab oil sheik doesn't get London weighting.'

Dyke, as a producer, was on wages of about £17,000 a year. The press reported that the 25 per cent increase being demanded would take them comfortably through the '£20,000 barrier' (roughly £70,000 at year 2000 prices). Dyke, a union militant since he led apprentice reporters in threatening a strike at the *Hillingdon Mirror* more than ten years earlier, was the organizer for the researchers and producers' section of the ACTT at LWT and, along with LWT journalist Andy Forrester, was one of the most out-spoken advocates of staff rights on the editorial side. He had already made himself the bane of LWT personnel director Roy Van Gelder, taking up all sorts of staff grievances. According to legend, Dyke had once threatened a walk-out if researchers were not given overtime payments to reflect the fact that, in effect, they started work over the breakfast table by reading the newspapers, and not just when they turned up at work.

The union called a meeting of LWT staff and urged them to reject the ITV Association's offer and go on strike if need be. Such was Dyke's eloquence at this meeting, helped by the fact that the vast majority of LWT's journalists were strong Labour supporters and saw the strike as a way of causing trouble for the new Tory government, that the vote in favour of strike action was unanimous, even though it would mean going without pay for the duration.

The LWT management, like that of any individual ITV company, was in a weak position. The union's power lay in the tactic of 'secondary action', later to be made illegal, and meaning the ability to call out workers at one station in support of members in dispute at another. The Independent Broadcasting Authority (later the Independent Television Commission, or ITC) would not allow ITV companies to run extra advertising slots at the end of a strike, so as to honour contracts with advertisers, so any time spent off air because of union action was a dead loss in financial terms. And the IBA's main concern was to keep the network on air, in the interests of the viewers it officially represented, regardless of the finances of the ITV companies. So if any individual ITV company wanted to take on the unions it would first have to persuade all the others. It would then have not only the unions, but the advertisers, the IBA, the public and, usually, the government on its back, urging a settlement.

On 3 August 1979 the ACTT told the ITV employers that they had backing for a national strike if the 15 per cent offer was not increased. The employers took a hard line. At 6.30pm the ITV Association said they would withdraw the offer of even 15 per cent if the ACTT did not call off the work-to-rule and order its members to resume working normally. Dyke led the *Weekend World* journalists out on to the street, where they formed a picket line. Within half an hour ITV stopped broadcasting, displaying the message:

# The Summer of Discontent

NORMAL SERVICE WILL BE RESUMED AS SOON
AS POSSIBLE.
WE APOLOGISE FOR INCONVENIENCE.

Dyke helped organize a round-the-clock picket – journalists and researchers standing shoulder to shoulder with the foot-dragging lighting technicians and tape editors who usually made their life a nightmare. But within a few days it was realized that the LWT management was making no effort to break the strike by running a skeleton service. One wag on the picket line noted, in a reference to the Winter of Discontent, when the bins were not emptied, 'The public will support this strike because we are keeping rubbish *off* the screens.'

Dyke's old sparring partner, Roy Van Gelder, was very civilized about it all. In contrast to the barbed wire and riot police deployed against strikers by media companies a few years later, Van Gelder would turn up to chat. Once, when it was raining, he even invited the pickets to stand inside the reception, rather than outside on the street, so that they would not get wet. The strike was rock solid anyway, with many taking the chance to spend some of their already huge wages on an extended summer holiday. The boredom of picket duty was alleviated by a football match against journalists from the *Sunday Times*, who were also on strike that summer. Lewis Chester, a *Sunday Times* feature writer, reckoned that the LWT team won the match because the *Sunday Times* side were on strike pay, sitting around in restaurants all week, while the LWT players were lean, hungry and kept themselves fit by driving taxis and painting houses.

Eventually Dyke got fed up with picketing an empty building. By now he had separated from Christine and was living alone in the large house in Sefton Street, looked after by Judith Chegwidden, his former GLC election agent. Chegwidden had taken Dyke's advice that houses in rapidly gentrifying south Putney were a brilliant financial bet and had moved into the street and got busy with a skip. The strike was rock solid and it was high summer, so Dyke set off with Nick Evans and learned how to windsurf. Dyke took to the new sport in his customary hyper-competitive way, but soon found it all a bit too tame. Eventually they ended up staying with an old mate of Dyke's who had moved out of London to live on the mid-Welsh coast near the mouth of the River Dovey. Dyke loved to windsurf there because the cross-winds and the Estuary rip-tide made it officially one of the most dangerous (but exciting) places to windsurf in the whole of the UK.

After eleven weeks the unions called off the strike, declaring total victory. ITV's increased pay offer was complicated, and phased in over the coming year, but amounted to 55 per cent – more than double what the union had asked for in the first place. The deal was infla-tion indexed, and with prices rising at about 25 per cent a year, the increase could be worth as much as 75 per cent in a single year, taking Dyke's own salary to a little under £30,000 (close to £100,000 in year 2000 prices) – which was not a bad result for a summer spent windsurfing.

Dyke returned to work not only with extra cash, but with promotion to deputy editor of *The London Prog-ramme*, working with his old friend Nick Evans as editor. Their boss, Barry Cox, had put them together as a team, seeing Dyke as the 'man from the streets' and Evans as the intellectual 'slightly poncified public school boy' as he thought of it (David Cox, the *Weekend World* chief, had teased Evans, who had been to a minor public school, about his background: 'If we have to have a fucking public schoolboy, we should at least have a proper one').

# The Summer of Discontent

The first edition of *The London Programme* produced by Evans and Dyke was about pornography in Soho. It did not go smoothly. The premise – or excuse – for the show was that organized crime had moved in to control the business. But they were unable to prove it and the programme ended up as a collection of unconnected interviews and bits of wallpaper filming. Dyke spent hours in the cutting room trying to put it all together in a way that made sense. He watched the final version of the show, just hours before it was due to go out, with a horrified look on his face before, halfway through, slamming his fist down on the mixing desk and shouting, 'I can't understand a fucking word of this . . . it makes no fucking sense at all!' Urgent repairs were made and the show was transmitted. It got good ratings even though Dyke and Evans were far from proud of the programme.

Evans and Dyke pushed the programme towards a 'populist' agenda, only to be warned by Birt and Cox to make sure they covered the routine and sometimes inevitably dull aspects of London political life, in line with requirements placed upon LWT by the regulators. At one management meeting Evans and Dyke were instructed to make a programme about local government finance – years before the subject became remotely sexy with the introduction of the poll tax. At meetings like these Dyke would fidget continuously, or sit there tearing a sheet of paper into little strips. 'How can anyone make a subject like that remotely interestin'?' Dyke would complain. In the end they commissioned a 30 minute animated cartoon explaining the whole thing which – amazingly – came in both on time and under budget and, less surprisingly, scored next to nothing in the ratings.

Dyke and Evans drew closer together the longer they worked on the programme. Evans had inherited a cottage in Devon and, during breaks in the series, would go down there for three or four days of bass fishing and water-skiing. Not that Dyke relaxed much. On one of these trips he didn't catch a fish for two days and, at the end, was almost bursting with frustration. Another time, Dyke managed to snare a water-skiier with his fishing line. After establishing that the victim was all right, he rushed off to a telephone box and, just like the old days on the *Hillingdon Mirror*, sold the story as lineage to the *News of the World*.

Dyke became a member of what amounted to a weekend walking club, whose other members included fellow left-wingers like Barry Cox. They were known as 'The Radical Ramblers' and membership extended beyond LWT to include people like Harriet Harman, a future Labour cabinet minister. Dyke joined in with characteristic gusto, once famously stripping off all his clothes and jumping stark naked into the River Way, near Guildford, to win a bet during a Sunday stroll around rural Surrey.

In the summer of 1980 the separation from Christine became permanent and Dyke was grateful that he could spend a lot of time with Evans and his wife, Penny, instead of going home to an empty flat. He sold the house in Sefton Street, Putney, and moved to a flat in Grafton Square, Clapham Old Town, a few doors away from Evans. He was about to start a new relationship with one of Christine's friends, Sue Howes, an intellectual Mancunian LSE sociology graduate. Dyke and Sue were getting on fine, but he was still pretty lonely and cut up about losing Christine. The final separation was sad but amicable. Dyke blamed himself entirely, putting it down partly to neglect as a result of preoccupation with his own life and career which clashed with her own ambitions, that in many ways were simpler and less ambitious. The couple had married young by modern standards, when Dyke had been an overwhelming and impressive figure and, like many others, they had simply drifted apart. Dyke and Christine were divorced in due course.

To help Dyke get over this setback, he took a long holiday with Evans and Penny, touring California and Oregon in a camper van. Dyke loved America and the Great Outdoors. The trip gave him time to reflect. He had joined the TV industry at a late age and with no experience in the medium. Yet he had found he could do very well at it, without too much difficulty. He was later to say that he had an advantage over many in the TV industry because, unlike the Oxbridge types who in the main dominated the business, his natural instincts were more in tune with the mass of the audience. Many of the public schoolboys in the business, he later said, were 'a bit of a pushover' anyway. It was the same sort of experience he had had at York University. Before becoming a student Dyke had been a bit in awe of people with university degrees. It was only by going to university himself that he found out how ordinary they were in reality.

By now Dyke had done a stint on *The London Programme* and was starting to get bored. His age still counted against him, not that he ever discussed it or seemed on the surface to be bothered about the problem in any way. But the fact was that he had to go up all the rungs of the TV current affairs ladder in double-quick time in order to catch up with those, like Evans, who had started in the business when they were ten years younger than him.

As chance would have it, LWT was developing a new programme to fill an extra hour between six and seven o'clock on Friday evenings that it had been given by the IBA. LWT had long complained that Thames, the weekday ITV company, had no interest in handing over a big audience to LWT for the start of the weekend on Friday night. The LWT management had won the slot from Thames but were, at first, at a loss as to what to do with it.

Greg Dyke was soon to come up with the answer.

# 7.
# 'Will My Mum Like It?'

'Thank you . . . thank you very much . . . good evening and welcome to *The Six O'Clock Show* . . . a new programme that comes to you live – and that's the most terrifying word for anyone who works in television . . .' The camera zooms in on the slightly dishevelled figure of TV smoothie Michael Aspel, wearing a grey safari suit and tinted glasses and wandering around a vast studio surrounded by an adoring studio audience. He emphasizes the difficulties of live TV work, with a raised eyebrow. ' . . . Yes, we are live from our studios on the South Bank of the Thames . . .'

Aspel invites the audience to give themselves a round of applause and then silences them with the instruction to 'save it for the show . . . we may need it.' For some reason the audience finds this absolutely hilarious.

'Well, what is this new show all about?' Aspel continues, in a way that suggests that he is not really very sure. 'Well, the aim is to bring you some of the offbeat news items you might have missed this week and one or two stories that nobody knows about yet.' Without missing a beat, he then delivers possibly the corniest joke in the history of the world: 'For example, I've just been reliably informed that last week a girl ran across Twickenham rugby ground without her blouse . . . I don't think she'll be doing it again unless she's practising for the Oh Calcutta Cup . . .'

Huge mirth from the studio audience.

'We'll be back in a quarter of an hour,' Aspel continues. 'But first, over to Andrew Gardiner at *Thames News* for the more serious side of today's regional news . . . Are you there, Andrew?' Andrew Gardiner, gravel-voiced and dome-headed, appears on a monitor and confirms that he is there. Aspel seems relieved.

For years Thames TV had run a lengthy news and sports preview programme starting in the London ITV region at 6pm. The show had little appeal for at least half the audience – women. By the time Thames handed over at 7pm, the BBC had established a crushing lead in the ratings which they were able to keep all evening. The IBA took the point and, as part of the station's renewed franchise starting in January 1982, ordered Thames to hand over to LWT at 6pm. The idea was that LWT would get the weekend off to a flying start with a popular programme that would get the ratings up and, ideally, hook in an audience for a whole evening's viewing.

It fell to Barry Cox, the head of current affairs, to devise a programme to fill the new slot. Michael Grade, LWT's head of programmes, encouraged Cox to get help and advice from the light entertainment department run by David Bell. Bell said that Cox's current affairs department had no experience in making popular programmes – a fair argument, seeing that *Weekend World* almost took pride in its famously low but elite audience. But Cox had an ace to play. Under the franchise agreement, the new show had to include the day's regional news done absolutely straight by proper journalists. Cox saw that if anyone in LWT was going to do it, it had to be Dyke – only he combined an obsessive interest in politics and current affairs with the light touch that was needed.

Cox had already drafted the outline of a programme that would be a mixture of a studio chat show with a celebrity presenter and short, funny reports filmed using new lightweight cameras. From the start it was agreed that the show had to appeal to housewives. They formed by far the biggest group in the daytime audience and were the most likely to be watching with their kids as they ate their supper and waited for dad to come home from work. Grade liked the idea of the show, seeing it as the ideal vehicle for Terry Wogan, the housewives' favourite.

With the backing of Grade and Cox, Dyke was appointed as editor (designate) of the programme in May 1981, eight months before it was due to go on air. At first Dyke held joint planning meetings with senior people from both current affairs and light entertainment. At one early joint meeting David Bell rubbished Dyke's plans for the show, telling him bluntly that it would not work. A member of Dyke's team, drawn from the current affairs side, listened carefully and ventured the opinion that if, as Bell feared, things didn't work out, they could always change the format. After the meeting, in the privacy of an empty corridor, Dyke delivered a bollocking, telling him that he should always 'stick to his guns'. There was a 'strategic battle' going on inside the company, Dyke said, and they could not afford to 'give an inch' to Bell. Dyke's grasp of corporate politics meant that he manoeuvered Bell and the entertainment people out of the way so effectively that by the time the show went on air they were not consulted at all.

Apart from office politics, the first job on *The Six O'Clock Show* was casting. There was a setback when Grade and Wogan could not agree terms. Cox thought about using Russell Harty, who had just finished fronting a late night chat show called *Saturday Night People*. But he was thought to be lacking in sufficient housewife appeal and so, instead, they turned to Michael Aspel who, eventually, was lined up with Janet Street-Porter. The format was agreed. There would be a studio audience. Aspel would introduce the show and then a series of filmed 'reports' – many of them, according to plan, stunts of one sort or another – would be shown and then talked about in the studio by Aspel, Street-Porter and other invited chat show-type guests. By now the IBA requirement to have 'proper news' wrapped into the show had been dealt with by sub-contracting it to Thames. This involved a complicated handover to the Thames studios five minutes into the programme and then a return to Aspel after they were done.

Dyke then set out his editorial plans in an interview with *Broadcast* magazine. Content, he said, would mainly be decided by the question, 'Will my mum like it?' He said that she watched the telly every day between six and seven, 'unlike me and most of my colleagues'. Denise, his mum, he said, was 'closest to the typical viewer we are aiming at', pointing to market research showing that early evening TV was most watched by people over 55 and that most of these oldies were women. He said the show would, at all costs, be funny, and claimed that he had been given the editor's job because he was the only one who made jokes at editorial meetings.

The show was important to LWT and the station invested heavily in it. The production budget was over £25,000 for each hour-long show and there were three live 'pilot' editions, where everything was done as though the programme was on air, but nothing was broadcast. The pilots turned out to be catastrophic. The production team had little or no experience of working live and, importantly, were very uncertain about which stories fitted Dyke's formula and which did not. It was all very well, and great PR, for Dyke to talk about his mum, but useless as a practical guide to what they should actually be featuring in the show. All he could do was to point to particular stories that he (or his mum) found funny – a man who had been let out of Brixton prison to get married and then escaped . . . idiots in posh north London who had phoned the police saying they had seen a werewolf . . . a pet snake set loose in the drainage system of a council estate causing everyone to block up their toilets . . . that sort of thing.

In the end, items were plucked out of the week's serious news and the video teams set off to get supposedly hilarious public reaction to them. But often as not the general public didn't know what the reporters were talking about, or gave devastatingly dull or obvious answers. The action would switch back to the studio, where Aspel and Street-Porter would try to be witty. But most of the hoped-for amusing put-downs exchanged between smoothie, middle-class Aspel and Cockney knockabout Janet came over bristling with antagonism. Street-Porter was peeved and, during the pilots especially, came close to letting it show. She wanted to be the sophisticated one and was annoyed that she was being paid far less than Aspel while being forced to endure public humiliation as the butt of his naff jokes. The studio-based material was, if anything, worse. An item featuring Nicholas Coleridge, the *Evening Standard*'s camp, café society columnist, demonstrating a spray which supposedly made men irresistible to women – which looked like a good idea on paper – degenerated into farce. All Coleridge could do was struggle through the studio audience, amid deafening silence, asking women to sniff him, to no great or apparent effect.

The horrific thing was that each pilot seemed to be worse than the one before. An appearance by Derek Jameson – 'Sid Yobbo' of *Private Eye* fame and lately the launch editor of the *Daily Star* – did not work out, and a desperate move in the direction of animal stories went badly wrong when a monkey escaped into the lighting rig. The audience, who played a key role in the show and were always on screen, spent the whole time ignoring Aspel and Street-Porter, craning their necks to watch the monkey and missing all the cues to laugh or clap. Eventually the monkey was captured, only for it to bite and scratch a newborn baby unwisely brought into the studio by its father, Tony Cohen – a workaholic member of the production team. The incident was serious and the baby was rushed off to hospital. Later that evening, while Dyke and Barry Cox were engaged in a fraught post-mortem in an office above the studio, Dyke took a phone call from the doctors, who said they urgently needed to see the monkey. Unfortunately, both the monkey and its owner, who was keeping the animal illegally, had disappeared. Dyke explained the problem to Cox, whose only response was to ask: 'Did this take place on London Weekend property?'

After doing what he could to sort out the monkey medical crisis, Dyke promptly went off to get drunk, asking himself how he could have not only produced something as bad as this, but also nearly killed somebody's baby in the process. Over the Christmas break, days before the show was due to go on air, Dyke phoned one of the show's directors, gravely worried. There was a huge danger that the programme was not going to work and they would all end up with egg on their faces. Dyke said he didn't know what to do. He wondered if his career was about to come to a sudden end. He was not used to being associated with outright failure.

The first broadcast edition of *The Six O'Clock Show* went on air on 2 January 1982.

London was caught in a blizzard and almost all forms of transport had been cancelled. The 'proper' news insert was full of reports of snow-related disasters and disruption, which sat uneasily with the cheery *Six O'Clock Show* graphics showing bored and grey commuters on a tube train bursting into colour, throwing away their coats and umbrellas and jumping up the escalators full of the joys of spring. The *TV Times* had announced the programme with a big cheesy picture of a besweatered Aspel on the front cover. Inside the magazine, Dyke hyped the show as 'a Friday tonic for those of the capital's viewers to whom a glance through the newspapers is an invitation to instant depression'. And he gave an example: 'Take the Brixton riots. At the height of the trouble, a police dog got loose and took a bite out of the officer conducting the negotiations. I don't suppose the poor copper found it funny, but it was a touch of comic relief in a very serious story and – let's be honest – there are enough gloomy headlines these days.' Street-Porter was simply quoted as saying: 'I'm the resident weirdo.'

The first show went smoothly enough, even though the tension in the studio was palpable. Once it had finished, Dyke let out a huge sigh of relief and congratulated the production team – reminding them, as is customary on these occasions, that they had to do it all again next week. Then he went off to get plastered.

The first edition of *The Six O'Clock Show* got a 33 per cent share of the London audience, which was an extremely good rating for the time of day. Another good sign was the huge number of complaints about the programme recorded in the LWT duty log – proof that the show was getting a reaction. Many of the complaints were about Janet Street-Porter and her accent, variously described as 'disgusting', 'hateful', 'vulgar' and 'horrible'.

By edition three the show was trouncing the BBC, which was showing *Nationwide* in the same schedule slot. LWT had 31 per cent of the total London audience, compared to the BBC's 19 per cent. Even better, there were signs that LWT was managing to hang on to the audience that the show was winning for the station – earning millions in extra annual advertising revenue. After this early success, all the nervous energy Dyke had put into worrying about a potential flop was translated into pushing the populist formula even further.

Dyke himself produced an item, firmly in the old Cassidy and Lee Trampolining Nun tradition, about a man who had constructed a scale model of the *Titanic*, apparently ten years in the making. Dyke arranged for the model *Titanic*'s launch on Wimbledon pond to be filmed. Pleasingly, but suspiciously, the model boat promptly sank. The disaster was explained by Street-Porter interviewing the model-maker, who claimed that he often spent ten years making model boats in order to sink them, strange though this might seem. But it did enable Dyke to bill the item as '*The Six O'Clock Show* Raises The *Titanic*' by hiring frogmen to rescue the model from the murky shallows. This meant that Aspel, back in the studio, could make quips about Lew Grade's vastly expensive film flop *Raise the Titanic*, which had been released the same week.

Dyke was so pleased with this piece of entertaining flim-flam – marked as it was by extraordinary serendipity – that he roared into the office of LWT's chief spin doctor, Peter Coppock, announcing that he had 'a fantastic exclusive story'. Coppock noted the details and, after Dyke had dashed off again, gave the story to one of his best contacts on the *Daily Express*. Dyke came back a few hours later to ask Coppock how he was getting on, and exploded when he said that he'd given it to the *Express* – 'You what! Can't you do better than the fucking *Express*!' A couple of days later, on the morning of the Friday when the item was due to be transmitted, Coppock showed Dyke a double-page spread with a huge picture of Street-Porter standing in the middle of the pond, wearing waders and holding the *Titanic*. It was, in effect, a huge free advert for the show. 'There you are,' Coppock said, 'a couple of million of your potential viewers will have read this on their way to work this morning . . . ' Dyke stroked his beard – 'Hmmmm . . . yeah . . . *quite* good, I suppose . . .'

Other items on early editions of the show included Janet Street-Porter asking men she met in the street about their underpants, a day out with an obsessive autograph hunter, and another day out with a fun-loving Singing Bus Conductor. Under Dyke's influence there was a lot of humour at the expense of the class system, with items about an upmarket baker's shop trying and failing to make a living on a council estate; a supposed trend for cocktails on the Old Kent Road, and so on. 'I discovered that the working class and the upper class were very, very funny, but the middle classes were a pain in arse,' Dyke later explained. 'You couldn't get a line out of them.'

The technical disasters – the 'degree of anarchy' Dyke had promised in the run-up to the launch of the show – continued to haunt the programme, especially when animals were involved. An Emperor penguin was almost killed when a security guard burst into a dressing room after hearing the creature honking in distress. The penguin's keeper, with about half an hour to spare before going on air, had locked the penguin in the room while he went for a drink in the bar. The guard forced the door open and, in the process, knocked the penguin unconscious. Ice was brought from the bar and the creature made its appearance on the show looking extremely groggy.

Apart from technical cock-ups, one early potential problem for *The Six O'Clock Show* was the Falklands war, which started in the spring of 1982. Contingency plans were made to hand over the whole of 6–7pm to *Thames News* if something seriously unfunny happened – like huge numbers of body bags arriving back from the South Atlantic. Otherwise *The Six O'Clock Show* covered the conflict from its normal oblique angle, reporting a supposed overload on broadcasting facilities for Argie foreign correspondents, illustrated by a number of ridiculously moustachioed Latin journalists gabbling into microphones with no real indication of whether these people really were journalists or actors hired to illustrate the item.

By the end of the first series of *The Six O'Clock Show* in June 1982, it was judged to have been a fantastic success and was on target to become one of LWT's most highly rated programmes ever – a tremendous achievement for a regional magazine show, a type of programme previously thought of as ratings death. Two major new stars had been launched – Danny Baker, recruited to the programme by Janet Street-Porter, and Gloria Hunniford, spotted by Dyke on Ulster TV and identified as a 'TV natural'. The whole place was really buzzing and many on the production team were becoming fiercely loyal to Dyke who, for a TV executive, managed the neat trick of being tremendously popular with the senior managers who ran the place and with the staff (often it was a matter of one or the other). Dyke had such a straightforward and self-deprecating style that he could make the most devastating criticism of people's work or journalistic judgement and turn it into a joke, so that no offence was caused. At the same time, his put-downs were so withering and accurate that he got his way by inspiring a desire to please him. Dyke was naturally popular anyway as a union man responsible, in part, for the success of the 1979 strike, which had doubled everyone's wages, and as a trusted union rep and barrack room lawyer who would take their complaints to senior management and, more often than not, get a result. He did not allow the success of *The Six O'Clock Show* to go to his head, keeping his approachable man-of-the-people persona and joining in the ritual staff football matches (difficult for a while, because they took place on Friday afternoons when he was busy with the show, but compensated for by the scheduling of mid-week matches against a team of London Labour politicos, led by Peter Hain).

Dyke's main headache, in terms of staff relations, was the never-ending efforts of Janet Street-Porter to improve her billing, especially after the programme began to be seen as a success. She had a habit of marching into Dyke's office with about half an hour to go, effing and blinding, demanding to have her name put above Aspel's as the main presenter, claiming that the whole thing was 'her show', that Aspel and others were claiming the credit and getting more money and that she was being discriminated against purely because she was a woman. Dyke would simply say: 'Fuck off, Janet.' Street-Porter would then sometimes stomp off to Dyke's boss, Barry Cox, and in floods of tears complain behind Dyke's back that he was being horrible to her. With ten minutes to go before the show went live, it fell to Cox to calm her down and coax her back on to the set.

Towards the end of the first series of *The Six O'Clock Show*, Dyke received a personal 'hero-gram' from John Birt, who had taken over from Michael Grade as LWT's director of programmes at the start of the year and inherited the show as the starting point of his schedule.

At first Birt had entertained severe doubts about Dyke being able to pull off such an important job for the station. These worries had now evaporated. 'The Board of LWT has asked me to pass its appreciation to the *Six O'Clock Show* team,' Birt wrote, 'for the speedy and remarkable success the programme has earned. May I add myself that the creation of a programme of such wide appeal, with such a delightful and distinctive character of its own, is a tremendous achievement for both you and the team.'

By Birt's austere standards, this counted as gushing praise. But within a few months Greg Dyke would want something much more than a slap on the back for his role in getting *The Six O'Clock Show* off the ground.

# 8.
# Flavour Of The Month

One morning in February 1983, Greg and his new partner Sue were getting ready for the day, Dyke already contemplating the rush-hour train journey to his job on *The Six O'Clock Show* while keeping one eye on the latest offering from the TV industry – the breakfast television station TV-am. Newscaster Anna Ford finished reading the headlines, smiled, shuffled her papers and said: 'After the break. . . Yehudi Menuhin – live in the studio'.

Dyke was nonplussed. 'Who the hell do they think is going to watch that at this time in the morning?' Dyke had nothing against classical violin music – though his own musical preference was mainly for Sixties Golden Oldies. He tried to visualize the process of editorial decision-making that had led to somebody at TV-am thinking that even the greatest Yehudi Menuhin fan in the world would want to sit down and concentrate on a classical recital while they were getting the kids ready for school or rushing off to work. He knew more about the daily family breakfast nightmare now that he was with Sue, who had two young children from a previous relationship. Dyke had finalized his divorce from Christine Taylor in 1982 and was now living with Sue Howes and her two young children, Christine and Matthew, in a family house in Barnes, an upmarket west London Thames-side inner-suburb fast becoming fashionable with media folk. Although Dyke and Christine lived as man and wife, they were described as partners. Dyke's dad was always urging him to remarry, but it was never to be. After all, not many women would have wanted voluntarily to take on the title 'Mrs Dyke' after the term, by the 1980s, had become widely used to mean 'lesbian'.

Dyke, whose populist instincts had proved such a success on *The Six O'Clock Show*, liked the idea of broadcasting to people at this time of day, when most of them needed cheering up. He had seen it work in the States and believed it could work here provided the right techniques were used. But the BBC had got off to a bad start with *Breakfast Time*. Fronted by the avuncular Frank Bough and Selina Scott, a devastating cool blonde who might have stepped out of a Hitchcock movie, the show was an uncomfortable mix of starchy good humour and contrived casualness. The most successful elements, as Dyke realized, were camp astrologer Russell Grant, maverick weatherman Francis Wilson and a striking fitness instructor, Diana Moran, known as the Green Goddess because she wore a lurid green body-stocking.

Two weeks after the launch of *Breakfast Time*, TV-am's *Good Morning Britain*, the commercial version, entered the race for the breakfast TV audience. The station was masterminded by Peter Jay, once a presenter on *Weekend World*. He had finally been given the opportunity to put his 'mission to explain' approach to TV journalism to the big test, having won the keenly contested licence with a celebrity bid fronted by David Frost, Michael Parkinson, Robert Kee, Angela Rippon and Anna Ford – the so-called Famous Five. Jay had concocted this highbrow approach to small-screen journalism in tandem with his intellectual sparring partner John Birt, taking the form of a series of articles in *The Times*. But despite his respect for Birt, Dyke was beginning to think that the last thing breakfast viewers needed was Jay and his 'mission to explain'.

The adverts ended and there he was – Yehudi Menuhin playing the violin beautifully – at completely the wrong time of day and on the wrong medium. With a final sneer, Dyke set off for work, ready to regale *The Six O'Clock Show* team with the latest example of Jay's elitist folly.

The launch of TV-am had, as Dyke had guessed, turned out to be a disaster and within weeks it was well known in the business that the majority shareholders, Jonathan and Timothy Aitken, and their managing director, Michael Deakin, were on the lookout for an editor who could turn things around. For some reason Birt and his LWT colleague Barry Cox had convinced themselves that Deakin had already, in secret, lined up Dyke to take the job. This was not true. But Birt complained to Deakin, asking why he was trying to poach his most successful editor. In fact Deakin had never heard of Dyke, but with such a glowing, if back-handed, testimonial, he phoned him up and offered him the job of joint editor, working in some capacity with Peter Jay. Dyke did not fancy that at all. He was still having fun at *The Six O'Clock Show*, boosting his currency all the time as the ratings continued to climb.

But a year later Dyke decided that he had taken the show as far as it could go. Others might have stayed on, waiting for internal promotion at the company. The tradition in TV at that time was that people joined and stayed with the same company for their entire careers, moving around between departments if necessary, on the model of the civil service-type career structure found at the BBC. But Dyke was different. The success of *The Six O'Clock Show* had made him flavour of the month. The best thing, really, would be to quit while he was ahead, claiming as much of the credit as possible.

At the end of the first series Dyke marched into David Cox's office and told him he deserved a car in recognition of the job he had done. Cox was not sure. The 'issue' of cars for editors was a grey area. Cox himself had reached car status only after several years editing *Weekend World*. Dyke had been an editor for less than a year. Cox said he would look into it and went to see Birt, who, as bad luck would have it, was under pressure at that moment to reduce the number of cars used by his programme-making department and give them to the advertising sales department. Cox broke the bad news to Dyke, who was extraordinarily put out, saying with real bitterness that he must have been the most successful programme-maker in LWT at the time, that his work had earned the company a fortune – and they wouldn't even recognize that by giving him a car. Cox was surprised by the fuss Dyke was making and told him again that if he waited he would probably get one later on. It was clear to Cox that Dyke wanted the car as an official badge of his success – so that he could evermore claim that *The Six O'Clock Show* was down to him personally.

The car dispute rumbled on inconclusively for months, during which time Dyke was again contacted by TV-am, where the Aitkens had taken charge. A phone call led to a meeting at Jonathan Aitken's palatial residence in Lord North Street, where Dyke was aghast to find himself dining off silver plate and being waited upon by an astonishingly camp butler. Aitken, who had been turned down flat by several other more senior figures in the industry, wanted to know if Dyke was interested in taking over. The job was described, in the standard euphemism, as 'a challenge'. TV-am's viewing figures were around 200,000, compared with BBC *Breakfast Time*'s 1.3 million – which was low enough. The station needed a million viewers to start making a profit. At the same time the station's outgoings were vast. According to a plan drawn up by Jay, TV-am's original chairman, there were supposed to be 175 employees led by himself and the Famous Five. By the time the station went on air, the payroll had grown to more than 500. The American breakfast TV show *Good Morning America* managed the same job with seventy-five people. As a result TV-am was losing £600,000 a month. Within six weeks of the station going on air, Jay had been forced out, to be replaced as temporary chairman by Jonathan Aitken, a 38-year-old Tory MP whose company, Aitken Hume, was the largest single shareholder in TV-am with a 16.7 per cent stake.

Dyke was intrigued, but uncertain. He talked to the people he trusted most on *The Six O'Clock Show*, telling them he had the chance to move and that he didn't know what to do. Eventually he mentioned the offer to David Cox, who told him it was a big risk moving from a successful show at a company like LWT, watched by 20 per cent of the population, to a tiny operation seen at the time by virtually no one and which might go bust at any time. Much depended, Dyke thought, on who he would be working with at the breakfast station. Above all, he wanted Sue to be involved in the decision. Women in general, Dyke had decided, were much better judges of character since they were less likely to fall for flattery. He was coming to rely on her judgement and advice more and more.

Dyke and Sue went for dinner with Aitken at his house in Lord North Street. The new management team at TV-am was now being publicly criticized as the bloodletting at the beleagured breakfast station was gleefully reported in all its gory detail in the papers on an almost daily basis. Anna Ford had famously thrown a glass of wine at Jonathan Aitken in full view of the press during a reception held by Lady Melchett. Parkinson had also made clear his feelings concerning the Aitkens. 'I would rather be a chauffeur than work for them. You meet a better class of people,' he said. But Dyke found that Jonathan Aitken – who, according to some, was able to turn on the charm 'like a sun lamp' – was not the great monster he was made out to be. They both agreed that the Famous Five had made a pig's ear of it. Dyke, taking a more detailed interest now, had read Jay's application for the commercial breakfast TV franchise and described it, in public, as 'the biggest load of pompous, pretentious crap I have ever read in my life'. The fact that the IBA had given TV-am the licence in the first place showed little grasp of the realities and preferences of the audience. It was a 'scathing indictment' of British TV regulation, Dyke said subsequently.

After dinner, Aitken and Sue were left to their coffee while Dyke and Clive Jones, recruited to work at TV-am prior to its launch, settled down to talk privately about the problems at the station. Aitken had identified Jones as the best person to keep the show on the road as interim programme boss until a new editor-in-chief could be found. Jones started off brightly enough, filling-in Dyke on Aitken's background. The MP had been the first news-reader at Jones's old company, Yorkshire Television. The launch of Yorkshire had been chaotic as well. So much attention had been given to the technical aspects of get-ting a signal on air that Yorkshire had failed to build even a simple newsreader's set in time for the launch. Aitken had ended up borrowing a lectern from a local Methodist chapel so he could deliver the news with some semblance of authority when the station went on air.

But TV-am was in a far worse state than Yorkshire had been. Jones began pouring out a tale of woe. The place was a complete editorial as well as financial shambles. There was no real schedule to speak of. Producers would just make more or less what they fancied and offer it for transmission. At last the mystery of how Yehudi Menuhin made it on to the screen was solved. The financial position, Jones revealed, was far worse than people realized. The only advertising confirmed was for Wall's sausages and Nivea face cream. After that the books were empty. Before long they would be giving the airtime away. Jones said that he was holding the whole thing together day by day. He was not sure that he would want to go on for much longer.

To Jones' surprise Dyke seemed to take all this in his stride. 'I like a lot of problems, don't you?' he said. After a start like that, things could only get better. Dyke had obviously thought about it all. He told Jones that the basic idea of a commercial breakfast show was a 'great opportunity' for British TV. It was just that the original team, and especially Jay, had got it all wrong: 'What do you expect?' If they could pull it all down and start again from scratch, and analyse where the ineffective BBC opposition was going wrong, and what 'real people' might want to watch in the morning, they were in with a chance. He had the backing of Aitken and the board to start with a clean sheet, and he would be given a reasonable time to make a difference. Jones was struck by Dyke's repeated use of the term 'popular quality'. It was clear that Dyke did not accept the division of TV into 'popular' on the one hand and 'quality' on the other, the terms used to describe tabloid and broadsheet newspapers. This kind of thinking, Dyke said, simply didn't apply to television. Jones was cheered up by this sort of talk and by Dyke's ebullience and repeated promises that they would have a lot of fun 'sorting out all the problems, untying all the knots'. Slightly to his own surprise, he realized that the more he tried to warn Dyke off joining the nightmare that was TV-am, the more interest Dyke showed in wading in.

Walking away from Lord North Street, Sue turned to Dyke and said: 'Whatever you decide to do, you know you must never trust these people'. He decided to take the job anyway, negotiating a salary of £40,000 with a bonus of £20,000 if he got the ratings up to over a million. It meant that Dyke would exactly double his salary if he did the job required of him. If things did not work out, and TV-am went bust before he had a chance to make a difference, he would be paid his annual salary with a further £20,000 compensation on top.

Dyke handed in his notice at LWT. All that remained was to organize his leaving party. This was a riotous affair, enlivened by a commemorative video fronted by Danny Baker and featuring footage of Dyke being mauled by a blonde strippergram girl. 'I've got a special present for you,' the girl purred, producing a Mars Bar. Informative as ever, Dyke yelped: 'Do you know the story about Mick Jagger . . . ?' and started to look uncomfortable as the girl planted dozens of red lipstick kisses on his bald head. Then the video recreated one of Dyke's greatest *Six O'Clock Show* moments. A member of the team, made-up to look like Dyke with a bald wig and rolled-up trousers, stood in a pond on Wimbledon Common taking a long suck on a toy buzzer before breathing deeply, wobbling slightly, looking around dreamily, utterly lost, and saying in a passable imitation of Dyke's Cockney drawl, 'What the fuck is all this about?' as a model ship sailed surreally past in the corner of the shot. There were endless references to the legend of Dyke sitting on his log on Wandsworth Common and deciding to get into television. Bernie Winters, the comedian, was interviewed about 'Gwen Dyke' . . . 'Yeah, I remember him now. He was the bloke on Wandsworth Common . . . he was a flasher, wasn't he?

Yeah, Gwen Dyke . . . the Wandsworth Flasher . . . But he couldn't do it. He could only describe it.' Selina Scott, the BBC breakfast presenter who Dyke was keen to sign for TV-am, was filmed saying: 'I know you are after me. All I want is a million pounds in cash, a chauffeur-driven Rolls-Royce, a fur coat and . . . oh yes . . . a 3am alarm call every day from you personally.' The video ended with Danny Baker sitting in a cubicle in a public lavatory, trousers down, smoking a fag, reading the *Sun* and reciting a limerick: 'There was an old man called Gwen Dyke, who thought he could do what he liked, he went to TV-am and was never seen again . . . serves him fucking well right.' Baker wiped his nose on his sleeve and went back to reading his paper, muttering, 'You c***'.

Naturally, this went down stormingly well. And there was more hilarity when Dyke spotted Roy Van Gelder, the LWT personnel chief, who had slipped into the back of the room to see what all the fuss was about: 'Oi! – there's Roy,' Dyke shouted, getting everyone's attention. 'There's just one thing I need to clear up before I go. You remember when we came in asking for 20 per cent? We were actually expecting to get 10 per cent. And you gave us 30!' A leaving card was circulated, signed by everyone who Dyke had worked with, including David Cox, who wrote, as a joke: 'Fuck off, Dyke, and don't come back'.

The next day Dyke sent everyone a memo saying that his time on *The Six O'Clock Show* had been 'very special and no matter what happens in the future I'm not sure work will ever be such fun again.'

# 9.
# Getting Away With It

'Bad news, Clive. We've had to stop filming . . . '

Clive Jones, the editor at TV-am and Greg Dyke's right-hand man, was on the phone in his office at TV-am talking to a manager of a camera crew halfway up a mountain in Switzerland. It is December 1983. The crew had been sent, at vast cost, to film *Roland Rat's Winter Wonderland* – a televisual skiing extravaganza featuring the glove puppet Roland Rat – the product of puppeteer David Claridge and his febrile imagination.

'Claridge has had an accident. Fell on the ice and banged his head. He's got concussion, apparently. We've had the doctor round. He sent him upstairs to bed.'

Jones was alarmed. Budgets were tight, filming abroad cost a fortune and there was no way they could afford to lose even half a day. 'What are the crew doing?' he demanded. 'Oh, they're having a great time getting pissed outside. They hate the bastard.'

Claridge was seen by all as a great but *difficult* creative talent. His creation, Roland Rat, and the massive following the puppet show attracted were, after all, credited with saving TV-am. But, like many creative people he was, well, *a bit strange*. Jones had had his own spats with Claridge, the latest being over the plane tickets for Switzerland. Claridge had marched into Jones' office saying: 'I've just got my plane tickets, but there's only one . . . can't anybody in this place get anything right?'

Jones, genuinely puzzled, asked Claridge why he thought he needed more than one ticket. 'For Roland, of course!' Claridge was horrified by the idea that Roland might have to go in the luggage hold. Then, once the TV-am team had arrived in Switzerland, Claridge had annoyed the production team by refusing to take Roland out of his plastic bag on the grounds that it was too cold, and made them hunt down or fix up miniature thermal underwear for Roland to wear. Later still, when the crew had run off to safety after seeing the first signs of an avalanche, Claridge had thrown the mother of all tantrums, demanding that they go back into the danger zone – 'RIGHT NOW!' – and rescue Roland. If Claridge was going to be laid low for a bit, it suited them just fine.

'Look,' Jones barked down the phone, 'I know he's difficult, but just show a bit of responsibility, will you? Just go upstairs and make sure he's OK. Phone me back immediately. If it's serious I'll have to do something about it.'

A couple of minutes later the unit manager rang back. 'Clive, sit down – you are not going to believe this . . . Claridge – right – is sitting up in bed with a bandage round his head, and he's got Roland tucked in next to him with an identical bandage round his head as well . . .'

Jones sorted out the problem and paused to reflect on his career to date and, especially, the direction it had taken since he had teamed up with Greg Dyke. He had worked for years on news desks of regional newspapers, ending up as deputy editor of a major provincial morning paper. He'd subsequently had three very successful years at Yorkshire TV, rising from news desk to programme editor in record time. Jones had joined TV-am when the Famous Five were still attempting to put Peter Jay's 'mission to explain' into practice, with a reputation as a serious, level-headed – even dour – journalist who had spent all his life in news, politics, sport and documentaries. Now he had ended up producing *Roland Rat Live*.

# Citizen Greg

Roland was a loud-mouthed Cockney egomaniac rodent fashioned from grey nylon fur who lived with his extended family in the sewers beneath King's Cross Station. He had made his first appearance on TV-am in the early months of 1983, a few weeks before Greg Dyke's arrival. The character had been the brainchild of Claridge and was steered on to the screen by Anne Wood, at the time one of the country's up and coming children's TV producers and, later, creator of the Tellytubbies. Roland had originally featured in a slot called the *Amazing Shedvision Show*. This was shown at around 8am to enable kids getting ready for school to tune in. Dyke thought the character was OK and, crucially, his mum liked it.

Then, one day, as the school summer holidays approached, Dyke was seen clutching ratings figures, squinting at them and twisting his beard with an air of the mad professor about him. 'There's something here with this Roland Rat thing,' he began to mutter. Dyke claimed that, by looking through the ratings for several weeks, minute by minute, comparing it, minute by minute, to what was on the other channel, Roland Rat was producing a higher rating than he should have done. Jones looked over the numbers as well. He couldn't see anything special about Roland Rat. Dyke persisted: 'What we're gonna do is put Roland Rat on in the last half hour. We can fill 9.00–9.30 with it.' Jones was dead against the idea. The last half hour was the only time TV-am got any sort of audience at all. Running a glove puppet ran the risk of killing the only audience they had 'on the basis of . . . what?' But Dyke was adamant: 'Nah, nah . . . trust me, this will work.' And it did. Ratings took off almost immediately, with Dyke 'building back' Roland Rat's dedicated audience, encouraging them to turn on earlier and earlier.

But the Roland Rat revelation came only after Dyke had been at the station for a couple of months and was by no means his first innovation. Programme-makers on the shop floor had noticed a change of atmosphere from day one. The word was that Dyke was a good bloke, a former Labour councillor, a lefty, but a populist who wanted to do more lightweight, fun material. There was an immediate change. Instead of making more or less what they felt like and then offering it to Jones to fit into a schedule as best he could, a more structured approach had begun to evolve. From day one, approval was required before anyone could take out a camera crew. After a couple of weeks, when Dyke had settled in a bit, the system changed again. Instead of producers suggesting items and then getting approval, Dyke would himself, or through intermediaries, tell the film-makers what he wanted, explaining, as best he could, how what he was asking for fitted into the schedule. Large numbers of film-makers and others were laid off. But with the people who remained, Dyke was popular because he immediately imposed some sort of order on the chaos. People finally knew where they stood. They could still put up ideas – Dyke would listen to anybody – but mostly the direction was the other way. Dyke wanted them to focus on what the audience was doing or thinking at any moment when they were on air, and organize their programme-making around that. It was a simple, clear, 'no-bullshit' formula stamped by Dyke on the whole organization very quickly and to a remarkable extent. After the weeks of free-floating anarchy, people were grateful to have some sort of direction. One of his first moves was to bring over Danny Baker from *The Six O'Clock Show*. This was a popular move with people – they could see the sense in bringing in someone more like a radio DJ, since the more perceptive had noted that their main competition in the mornings was not really upmarket BBC *Breakfast Time* but Radio One and commercial chart radio.

Behind the scenes, Dyke's first few weeks in control had been far from smooth. He and Jones spent endless hours sitting on a barge moored alongside TV-am's trendy designer-led headquarters and studios, known as Egg Cup Towers, on the banks of the Grand Union Canal at Camden Lock in north London. They would go through the programmes, revamping running orders, thinking about presenters.

Dyke was taking advice from John Birt who, in many ways, was acting as his mentor. Birt's advice was to create a tight structure of management control and come up first of all with an editorial structure that would work, and then comb through the existing staff to find the people who could implement it. Dyke went on the record about Birt's input, telling *Broadcast* magazine that he had discussed Peter Jay's original 'mission to explain' plan for TV-am with the LWT chief: 'If you ask John Birt, he will tell you that to provide in-depth analysis on a day-to-day basis is difficult.' This was especially true at breakfast time because 'the degree of concentration available from the spectator is limited. Morning is a time for brushing your teeth and having your breakfast'. He then criticized Jay and the Famous Five: 'Peter Jay said he wanted to do "*Daily Mirror* journalism" on TV-am. So do I. The difference is, I don't think Peter Jay ever read the *Daily Mirror*. The five people who won the franchise were all famous personalities – some of whom made the mistake of actually believing their own publicity. The presenters had more power than the producers, which is ridiculous. The result was chaos. It was worse than the average regional magazine programme, with the difference that it had famous presenters.'

By now Anna Ford and Angela Rippon had left the station. The decision to fire them had been taken, Dyke said, before he arrived. Still, he added, they 'would not have fitted with my plans'. At the same time, though, he thought the sudden and public manner of their sacking had been 'shabby' and could have been avoided. Of the other original TV-am big names, Michael Parkinson was still on board, but had been shifted to anchor the Saturday morning edition alongside his wife, Mary. David Frost did the Sunday interview show, which in time added some much-needed gravitas to proceedings. Robert Kee, the veteran television reporter and expert on Irish politics, remained on board to handle the more substantial material on weekdays. But the main weekday-morning presenting team now consisted of Anne Diamond, headhunted by Dyke from BBC Birmingham, and Nick Owen, originally a sports presenter at the station. Dyke liked Anne and Nick for their 'ordinariness'. But the station was still short on glamour and so Jones was ordered to find 'a blonde girl with big tits' who could give the opposition BBC's Selina Scott and Green Goddess exercise instructor, Diana Moran, a run for their money. After a brief search Wincey Willis was hired from Tyne Tees.

Dyke then turned his attention to the set. He thought the original design was awful. The Famous Five had hired a top interior designer to create what was described as a 'brown and beige Conran catalogue set'. A fortune had been spent creating an on-screen newsroom, a sports-room, a lounge, study, multipurpose kitchen, garden, children's play area and separate sets for the reading of horoscopes and weather. Dyke denounced it all as too 'upmarket', bitty and impractical. 'They said it was meant to be classless,' he later told the press. 'That was a joke. It looked like a north London home owned by a middle-class family who shop at Habitat.' Dyke made sure it was demolished. Instead he threw everyone on to a cheap single set 'so that it's easier to set up a shot and so they can all see each other and communicate.' But Dyke was still not happy. 'There are lots of little things that are still not right, such as the sofa. It looks – and is – uncomfortable.' He then moaned that money was so tight at TV-am that they didn't even have enough cash to buy a new one. Instead he put up net curtains to make the modernist windows in the background look less designerish and more homely, and had the tasteful shades of beige and grey repainted in bright 'sunshine' colours. Dyke's final touch was to clutter the set with vases full of tacky, unnaturally bright plastic flowers and robust rubber plants. The set designer resigned on the spot.

Next on the agenda was finding a 'proper' newsreader to do the regular news headlines alongside the sofa-bound chat provided by Anne and Nick. Dyke told Jones, 'Our news is crap. It needs sorting out. People watch our news and they don't believe it. It's got no gravitas.' Jones said he thought he could get Gordon Honeycombe, a highly distinguished newsreader who had just left ITN to concentrate on his career as an author. Dyke was withering. 'Naaahhh . . . You'll never get a *News at Ten* presenter to get up at five in the morning to read the news for a station that's got no viewers and everyone thinks is a joke. Forget it.' But Jones pulled it off, and Honeycombe arrived to give the required weight to TV-am's news bulletins.

Dyke told the news team to forget the original broadsheet approach to the news set up by Peter Jay. They had to adjust to the tabloid agenda, and he brought in a few Fleet Street hacks to help out. They were not always keen to come on board, but Dyke turned on the famous charm, often interviewing them over a plate of chips in the plush TV-am canteen. Dyke spent the whole of one interview with a potential newsdesk recruit deriding Peter Jay who, to Dyke's immense delight, had lately been exposed in the tabloids for getting the family au pair pregnant. 'That's the sort of story we want!' Dyke then pointed out that frogs' legs were available on the canteen menu – 'that's Peter Jay for you'. Dyke was particularly aghast that Jay had run *Farming News*, complete with the latest pig prices, as the first thing in the schedule: 'Pictures of cows' arses to watch while you are eating your breakfast – brilliant! If I don't do anything else here I'll have earned my wages just by getting rid of that.'

Dyke brought in one of his old mates from the *Newcastle Journal*, Peter McHugh, then working on the *Daily Mail*, to rough up the newsdesk a bit. McHugh lambasted the remaining 'luvvies' left over from the Peter Jay regime, telling them they wouldn't last 'ten minutes' in Fleet Street. But at first he had difficulty coping with the reduced budgets available at TV-am. At one editorial meeting he asked Dyke if he could take a camera crew to Heathrow to film Torvill and Dean's return from a tour of Canada. 'No,' Dyke snapped back. 'We can't afford it. Anyway, all we need to know is: Is he giving her one?' To underline the new tabloid approach, Dyke developed a relationship with Kelvin MacKenzie, the editor of the *Sun*. If TV-am had a sniff of a good (tabloid) story overnight, Dyke would tell the reporter, 'Phone Kelvin with this one. Tell him you are from TV-am and you know me.' And, to their astonishment, the reporters would get straight through to MacKenzie, who would run the story, giving TV-am the required credit. Another area of TV-am–tabloid co-operation was newspaper bingo. Dyke arranged for the numbers printed in the paper to be read out – an arrangement which suited both sides very nicely.

Dyke and Jones had made some running repairs in this way and had the outline of the new 'Birtist'-type editorial structure sorted out on paper. Getting people to work within the system was another matter. The team was still not quite right, and the odd pocket of resistance persisted. After about a month, the station officially 'relaunched' with its new schedule. Jones and Dyke would meet every day at 9.30, once the station was off air, to discuss how it was going. A few days after the relaunch, Jones staggered into one of these meetings, shell-shocked, and said, 'It's just not working . . . whatever I say, whatever I do, they are not following the plan.' Dyke turned to him and said gravely: 'You're right, Jonesy. The only way that we're going to get this fucking thing right is if one of us gets up at four o'clock in the morning every day and gets in here by five and produces the fucking programmes from the box hands-on.' He then paused and added: 'And I've decided it's going to be you.'

Jones signed up to a year of working twelve hours a day, seven days a week. Dyke rarely came in much before 8.30 am. In a way, this was a relief. The editor-in-chief was an absolute nightmare to deal with in the box, leaping about with his brain buzzing, directing camera angles and, thinking he was back at LWT, shouting instructions like 'Cue Telecine' when there was no such machine in the building. Dyke's main contribution was keeping the money men off the production team's back, thinking and rethinking the all-important editorial structure, recruiting talent and coming up with ideas for features, news slots – and stunts. These came in an endless torrent. It was a nice combination, and it worked well. Dyke the ideas man, touchstone of what the audience wanted, and inspired scheduler; Jones the inspired line producer, making it all happen on the screen hour by hour.

There was still a great fear, in the first weeks following Dyke's arrival, that the station's financial backers might lose patience and pull the plugs at a moment's notice. One Friday afternoon, Jones found himself chairing a forward planning meeting, lining up the features content for the next week's show, when the finance director stuck his head round the door.

'Clive – are you doing the forward planning meeting?'

'Yes, Roger.'

'Good. How far have you got into next week?'

'Tuesday.'

'Good. But I wouldn't go beyond Thursday because we've just had a million and a half pound bill from the London Electricity Board, and I can't pay it.'

And he shut the door. The story leaked to the editorial floor. There was anxiety as people rushed off to the wages office to make sure they would be paid. The crisis passed. But on the following Friday the ACTT threatened to go on strike over the redundancies needed to keep the station afloat. The union, concerned that any new agreements at TV-am could set precedents for other parts of the industry, was taking a hard line. When he heard about the dispute, Dyke's boss, Timothy Aitken, called the senior editorial team into his office and warned that if they had company cars they had better take them out of the car park and park them round the corner immediately. If the union voted the wrong way, he was going to have to call in the receivers.

But by the beginning of summer 1983, with Roland Rat in place, the ratings were up, the financial crisis eased, Dyke was enjoying life and TV-am began to turn the corner. Other key ingredients had, by now, been tossed

into the mix. At one ideas meeting Dyke announced that
the most important thing for TV-am was to find an
exercise instructor who had more appeal than the Green
Goddess, one of the main attractions of BBC *Breakfast
Time*. 'I want an exercise woman,' he demanded. 'She's
got to be a bit sexy, great figure . . . a bit mad, a bit crazy.'
Greg's PA, Jane Tatnall, who until this point had been
quietly and dutifully taking notes, piped up. 'Well, my
exercise teacher's completely bonkers!' Without skipping
a beat, Dyke said: 'Well, that's that then. Get her in. We'll
pilot her!' The result was Lizzie Webb, aka Mad Lizzie,
who rapidly became a minor celebrity. Another challenge
was to ensure that TV-am provided a relentlessly upbeat
show for its audience. With this in mind, Jones was told to
hire Chris Tarrant, then known to viewers mainly because
of hosting ITV's children's show, *Tiswas*.

Jones lined up the *Great TV-am Seaside Summer*. At a final
planning meeting he asked for some technical details
regarding the outside broadcast vans they would be using.
Jones knew that TV-am had no outside broadcast vans,
and had assumed that Dyke had made arrangements to
acquire one after deciding to base the summer schedule on
a non-stop, outdoor, seaside roadshow. 'Greg, you have
bought an OB van, haven't you?' Jones asked.

'What do you mean?' Dyke replied.

'Well, we don't have any OB vans, and that could be a
problem if you've told the advertisers that we are going to
be doing OBs all summer long.'

Dyke looked horrified. 'What are you talking about?
'Course you've got fucking OB vans.'

Jones exploded: 'No we fucking don't!'

Dyke became thoughtful: 'Oh fuck,' he said, adding,
after a pause, 'well you'd better get one then'.

Jones worked out that he could get a clapped-out,

secondhand OB van for about £17,000 and Dyke went to Timothy Aitken to ask for permission to buy it. Aitken just sighed and said, 'Well, we owe £2 million to the bank, so we may as well owe them £2,017,000.' And he wrote out the cheque.

TV-am's *Seaside Summer* was a great success. Combined with the ratings surge caused by schoolchildren plugging into the later and extended version of Roland Rat (slogan: *yeeeeeahhhhh . . . Number One Rat Fan!!!!*) it pushed TV-am's audience over one million for the first time. It also produced one of Dyke's own personal favourite TV moments. This was the sight of Blackpool's elderly Conservative mayor in full chain and regalia dancing to pop music with a man dressed in a gorilla suit on a deserted and windswept beach at seven o'clock in the morning. This was bettered, in Dyke's opinion, only by the sight of three stones of lard being pulled into the studio on a pallet as part of the 'Follow Diana Dors on her Diet' slot he had dreamed up. Dyke returned from a windsurfing holiday in Florida to find that TV-am had opened up a clear lead over the BBC with up to 1.7 million viewers compared with the 200,000 who were watching before he was hired.

Critics said that Dyke had taken the cheap and easy route of 'dumbing down' to achieve ratings. He was castigated in *The Times,* recently acquired by Rupert Murdoch, for destroying Peter Jay's worthy vision of an informative TV station by bringing in Roland Rat and other miscellaneous trivia. Dyke hit back by saying: 'That's rich, coming from a paper that's kept alive by the *Sun* and the *News of the World.'* Timothy Aitken's response was much more telling. 'It's not Roland Rat that's getting financial results. It's Greg Dyke and his grasp of the popular market.'

# Citizen Greg

In just two years Dyke had launched *The Six O'Clock Show*, a significant commercial success and a format that had reinvented current affairs as what would eventually become known as popular factual TV. He had followed that up by turning round a station that was on the brink of financial ruin. His track record and, importantly, his ability to work in the emerging cost- and profit-conscious world of modern television, had not gone unnoticed by people right at the very top of the TV business, and beyond in banking and finance.

# 10.
# The Beautiful South

Greg Dyke is sitting on the deck of a luxury yacht, decidedly not his own, looking out across the marina at Southampton harbour. His host, the starchy figure of James Gatward, controversial head of TVS, the ITV franchise catering for the wealthy and booming south and south-east of England, talks about the progress of the station, his problems with the regulators – and rival ITV companies – and his need to get his studios making programmes for the ITV network.

Dyke is edgy. He knows that Gatward is likely to offer him the post of director of programmes at TVS. But officially the meeting is not taking place. Dyke has not yet made up his mind about the move and he is keen to make sure that his bosses at TV-am know nothing about it. Gatward is nervous too. He has not told his existing director of programmes that he is for the chop. And so the meeting has been arranged in conditions of great secrecy – so much so that Gatward has dispensed with his usual assistants, preferring to make Dyke a cup of tea with his own hands, using the yacht's Calor gas stove.

The two conspirators are feeling pretty pleased with their security arrangements. Then the harbour Tannoy crackles into life and booms: 'Would Mr Dyke, who is meeting Mr Gatward, please report to the Harbour Master's office immediately.'

All around people look up. Their cover is blown. The reason is that Dyke had dropped his wallet somewhere on the way to the meeting and the police have tracked him down to the harbour. Dyke, a man who has an exceptional fondness for his wallet, in due course turns up at the police station, amazed at the degree of initiative they have shown.

Brian Tesler and John Birt, Dyke's old bosses at LWT, had watched Dyke's progress at TV-am with a growing sense of satisfaction. Tesler, in overall charge of LWT, and Birt, the creative chief, had always suspected that Dyke was a special talent or, more accurately, a man who had exactly the right approach to an ITV system that was just about to become much more commercial.

Dyke's performance at TV-am seemed to prove them right. The breakfast station was not yet making a profit, but Dyke had adopted a far more aggressive approach to TV, based much more firmly on analysing the schedule and giving viewers what they wanted, when they wanted, rather than the old approach of offering them whatever the programme-makers had come up with. He had even been prepared to play hard-ball with the over-mighty TV production unions, quietly lining up non-union camera-men and other production bods to be flown in from Ireland to keep the station on the air if his cost-cutting, mild as it was by the standards of what happened a few years later in the TV industry, caused a strike. But even that was not necessary. Dyke had kept the unions on side even though he was getting TV-am on to the screen at a fraction of the production costs anywhere else in the business.

Tesler had decided that Dyke might one day return to LWT in some capacity, if a suitable vacancy arose. In the meantime it was vital that Dyke was not lost to the ITV system by taking a job at the BBC, which, in the summer of 1984, seemed possible. Dyke's admirers included Michael Grade who, after his own stint as programme chief at LWT and stay in America, had returned to Britain to become controller of BBC1. Grade had asked Dyke to join him at the BBC on the promise of one day succeeding him. In the meantime Grade wanted Dyke to take on the job of running the *Wogan Show*, a crucial element in Grade's schedule and just the sort of thing to benefit from Dyke's experience in producing hours and hours of inexpensive studio-based material. Dyke was intrigued but wary. A mere verbal agreement that he would get the BBC1 job was not enough. 'Put it on paper,' he told Grade, 'and you are in business'. Grade could not do that and so Dyke turned him down.

At around the same time as Dyke was talking quietly to Grade, Tesler found what he thought was the perfect job for Dyke, a position that would suit both him and LWT – the position of programme chief at TVS.

The idea came up when Tesler and Gatward met at one of the endless round of conferences that were needed to run ITV, a profoundly federal system where companies holding regional franchises had to co-operate to produce a national service. In practice, ITV was dominated by the so-called Big Five companies, a group which was dominated by Granada and Thames but also included Yorkshire TV, Central and LWT. Between them these five companies controlled what actually appeared on ITV. The smaller companies, including Gatward's TVS, hardly got a look in. But even within the golden circle of the Big Five there were conflicting interests. LWT had always complained that the others in the Big Five did not always deal fairly with them, saving their best programmes for mid-week, when LWT was off the air, and leaving LWT with the tricky and expensive job of competing on Saturday night when, in a reverse mirror image of ITV, the BBC screened its most popular shows.

Over the years LWT's resentment of Thames, and

especially Granada, had grown to become a major problem for the smooth running of the system. LWT people complained bitterly about Granada's over-reaching arrogance and refusal to help them in the weekend struggle for ratings and revenue. The Granada view was that LWT was a cynical operation which produced cheap and cheerful end-of-the-pier showbiz material and fig-leaf current affairs programmes and was motivated more by ratings and money than any real commitment to public service.

LWT had the money but did not see why it should shell out a big chunk of its hard-earned revenues producing high-cost weekend entertainment for the benefit of the network. If Granada and the rest of the Big Five would not help out, then one solution was to turn to the smaller companies. TVS was identified as the perfect partner for LWT. Gatward – like LWT – was no friend of the old regime in ITV. And since TVS covered by far the richest part of the country, it was awash with money from advertisers. Gatward had already invested some of the money-mountain in new studios which, to his dismay, remained under-used because the Big Five would not take his programmes. An alliance between LWT and TVS seemed to be the ultimate marriage made in heaven – LWT had some shared access to the schedules as one of the Big Five, but was unwilling to spend all its money making the type of programmes it wanted, while TVS had the capacity to make the programmes, but could not get them into the schedule.

The problem was that TVS's creative strength was in areas such as science and nature documentaries and – especially – children's programmes commissioned by Gatward's existing ex-BBC programme chief Michael Blakstad. It was decided that if the LWT–TVS alliance, which made so much commercial sense, was to come to fruition, Blakstad would have to be quietly eased out and replaced by a man who would gear the company's output to the popular mainstream audience LWT wanted. That meant finding somebody with an unerring instinct for mass market tastes, with a track record of putting the ratings up . . . somebody not too bound down by being brought up in the old system, a leader who could shake things up a bit, turn round an organization that had gone off in the wrong direction. Somebody with a strong personality . . . very competitive . . . bags of attack and aggression – preferably a bit of a streetwise streetfighter with political nous who would take on the old system, who could get his elbows out and force TVS material into the schedules . . . and above all, somebody who LWT knew and trusted to ensure that TVS would, in future, use its millions to make *exactly* the sort of programmes it needed.

Which was why Greg Dyke found himself on a fine summer's day surreptitiously sipping Calor gas tea while sitting on the deck of Gatward's yacht in the bijou surroundings of a south coast marina.

Back at Egg Cup Towers, Bruce Gyngell is giving one of an endless series of media interviews marking his arrival from his native Australia to become the new chief executive of TV-am. The journalist is trying to get him to concentrate on the main point – is he going to support Greg Dyke's request for more money for programmes so that he can build on the momentum and keep the audience going up? But Gyngell, urbane, tall and tanned, and dressed as usual in his immaculately tailored suit and trademark pink shirt, keeps drifting off the subject.

'Do you know why men's and women's sexual organs

are so shaped?' he suddenly asks, apropos nothing. The journalist had to admit that she had not really thought about it, and so Gyngell's face lit up in triumph, enabling him to confide in hushed tones: 'Well . . . it is because women are earthbound while man's force comes down from heaven.'

Before the journalist can change the subject, he's off again.

'Pink . . . that's the thing. . . "The Power of Pink" . . . you should try it yourself. It is a positive energy channel. Wear a little pink and, I assure you, you will be much the better for it . . . '

By the time the interview was over, Gyngell had said very little about TV-am, but had given a fulsome exposition of New Age philosophy, plenty of praise for organic food and herbal medicine and, for good measure, a pretty comprehensive account of his own, personal spiritual journey. The main news, for those interested in his TV plans, was the observation that 'the medium of television is about Now-ness'.

People at TV-am reading the resulting article and wondering what it meant for their own jobs scratched their heads. What did it all mean? Greg Dyke had few doubts: 'He's fucking bonkers! . . . I mean, he seems nice enough . . . but he's barking. How can you work for somebody who's barking?' (Gyngell, for his part, would tell people, 'Greg's a nice guy . . . but he doesn't have a clue about business.') The two men were bound to clash.

Dyke had saved TV-am editorially, but not as a business. Losses had been cut from £600,000 a month to £250,000, but to move into profit TV-am would have to cut its costs still further. His own reputation in the industry and, more to the point, his salary, was linked not to profitability but to ratings (a £20,000-a-year bonus for every extra million). Understandably, Dyke was focused on pushing the ratings even higher which, he thought, would mean releasing more money to spend on programmes. In particular Dyke and Jones wanted to buy into rights to screen that summer's Olympic games, which in editorial terms would have been a brilliant move.

But Gyngell did not see it that way. He had been put into TV-am by the Sydney media mogul Kerry Packer, who now owned 20 per cent of the station. The Aitkens were not best pleased, warning the board: 'Watch out – Packer's hatchet man is coming.' Gyngell's mission was to cut costs to the bone, working on the well-known Australian principle that a station with modest ratings and very low overheads could often be more profitable than a high-cost operation with huge audiences.

Gyngell, claiming greater experience and a longer track record in the business, started interfering with the schedule, the very source of Dyke's power at TV-am and his soaring reputation in the industry. Dyke had taken to heart Sue's advice not to trust the financiers. They backed him when they needed him. But, as Dyke himself thought, once he had shown them it could work, 'The Money will re-assert itself'.

Dyke agonized for a little longer about the offer to go to TVS – at one point calling up Clive Jones during a reflective walk in Hyde Park, using an early version of a mobile phone, and claiming not to have known what to do. The indecision did not last for long. TVS was 'The Dream Franchise', as the advertising press put it. Nearly a quarter of the population were in the top (ABC1) earning and spending category, compared to the national average of 17.8 per cent. It had the highest percentage of people in work, the highest number of home owners, second car-owners and by far the highest percentage of affluent retired people. One of Gatward's lieutenants at TVS, Peter Clark, quipped that in the wake of the launch of Channel Four, 'catering for minorities is a fashionable topic in television . . . well, we are catering for a minority too . . . the rich'.

For Dyke the move to TVS was a way of escaping involvement in Bruce Gyngell's low-cost pink New Age ashram. He had completed a good and interesting spell at TV-am and was, anyway, looking for fresh challenges. With a careful eye to the future, Dyke knew that the close relationship he was supposed to forge with TVS meant that he would almost certainly return to his 'spiritual home' – LWT – one day. As director of programmes at TVS, he would be able to learn how television worked at the level of the board room and the network. He would get out of the ghetto of current affairs and studio-based 'factual' entertainment, meeting and working with a lot of very capable people in drama, comedy, light entertainment, children's programmes . . . all types of programmes, right across the board.

And so Greg Dyke said farewell to TV-am and accepted the position of director of programmes at TVS. Overnight it made him the most important figure in the creative management of television in the whole of Britain (South of Croydon).

# 11.
# Crossing The Line

Greg Dyke is kitted out in full dinner dress, complete with bow tie and cummerbund, his beard trimmed and neatly combed. Accompanied by Sue, elegant in an exquisite evening gown, Dyke has been pressing the flesh at the Glyndebourne Opera festival – the very pinnacle of the English summer social season – mingling with the elite of Hampshire society in the cause of TVS. At many operatic events the organizers ask patrons not to make a nuisance of themselves by coughing or rattling their jewellery during the performance. At Glyndebourne the management has instead issued a polite request that people should not drown out the strains of *Don Giovanni* by landing or taking off in their helicopters during the intermission.

The day has been onerous for Dyke, who is no great fan of opera, and he is pleased to be stepping into the roomy, air-conditioned interior of his chauffeur-driven Mercedes, settling down into deep leather upholstery alongside Sue. The car sets off, the wide tyres making a pleasingly crunchy sound on the gravel. Dyke cracks open a bottle of champagne and begins to pour a glass for Sue, disturbed only by a slight sway, thanks to the car's magnificent suspension. As he fills the glass and starts to loosen his clothes, Dyke becomes thoughtful. 'You know what?' he asks Sue, and pauses. 'We've become the people that we used to want to throw bombs at.'

It is the spring of 1986 and Greg Dyke is well into his second year as director of programmes at TVS. Dyke's appointment has started to pay dividends for TVS. The station is finally experiencing some long overdue success thanks to a couple of Saturday night entertainment shows. There's a new series from the young impressionist, Bobby Davro, *On The Box*, and *Catchphrase*, a spot-the-saying game show with state-of-the-art computer graphics. But all is far from well between Dyke and his controversial boss, the ambitious but paranoid James Gatward. The two of them are locked in a power struggle. Dyke is furious that in spite of his achievements Gatward refuses point blank to give him a seat on the TVS group board.

On the face of it, Gatward and Dyke had much in common. Gatward was a working class lad from Walthamstow on the borders of London's East End and, at a time when an Oxbridge background still counted for a lot in the television business, both should have been rank outsiders were it not for the sheer force of their personalities and other talents. Gatward was born in 1938 and started in TV in 1957 as a holiday cover scenery shifter after leaving South West Essex technical college. He had been turned down by a BBC production training scheme because he did not have a degree. He might have spent his entire working life as a studio carpenter and odd-job man had he not moved to Canada, where formal education and class were less important in establishing a white-collar career. In 1966 he returned to London to become a drama producer and director at the BBC. In 1979 he took a year off to work on a franchise bid against Southern TV, the incumbent station famous for children's programmes like *How!* and *Worzel Gummidge*.

People reckoned that Gatward had compensated for his unprivileged background by becoming addicted to the trappings of power. Unlike Dyke, he loved Glyndebourne and what it represented. He had made sure that TVS recorded some of the operas and was furious when the ITV network refused to give him a decent slot in which they could be screened. Everyone knew that he paid himself one of the biggest salaries in British TV. His *Who's Who* entry, in which he listed yachting and farming as his favourite pastimes, was a running joke inside the industry. Many of the ITV old guard, like David Plowright at Granada, regarded him as the upstart from hell. At TVS, much of his time was spent either flying above his domain in the company private jet or enjoying first-class flights to and from Hollywood, where he had ambitions to expand and position TVS as an international player.

Gatward was also derided for casting his own wife, the Scottish Sixties Hammer Horror actress Isobel Black, in a TVS drama series called *The Brief*. This was to turn out to be one in a long line of TVS drama flops. (Another embarrassment was Gatward's attempt to create a British version of the American glamour series *Charlie's Angels*. The result – *CATS Eye*, starring Leslie Ash as a paramilitary secret policewoman – was described by one critic as 'simply preposterous'.)

Despite these failures, Gatward liked to compare himself to Plowright, one of the most highly regarded men in ITV and his opposite number at Granada Television. Plowright, although an executive, had personally supervised the making of such distinguished drama series as *Brideshead Revisited* and *Jewel In The Crown*. Much to Dyke's irritation, Gatward told the trade press, and anyone else who would listen, that when it came to overseeing his station's drama, Dyke did not have much say in what went on. Gatward would claim that there was nothing wrong with that. His role was similar to Plowright's at Granada. No wonder Birt and Tesler had wanted to put Dyke in with a 'quality control' role before they went ahead with the plan to buy in more pro-gramming from TVS. They were much happier dealing with their man, Dyke.

In theory, TVS ought to have been Greg Dyke's sort of place. Southern TV had a reputation for stuffiness. The idea was that TVS would be different, less hierarchical, with programme-makers more involved in the business side. In practice, TVS was turning out to be something of a viper's nest – as one high-level departure followed another – and somewhat less egalitarian than planned. The original idea was that all the key executives would have exactly the same perks, including the kind of company cars they drove. But Gatward had demanded a Daimler Sovereign while the rest got Rovers. There were other problems related to Gatward's management style. As Dyke had begun to found out, Gatward could be irritatingly secretive, but did know a good business when he saw one.

On the day Dyke and Sue moved in to their new Hampshire home, Gatward drove round to wish the couple well. Surrounded by packing cases and half-empty boxes, Sue was in no mood to entertain Greg's new boss and her face froze when Gatward presented them with a bottle of champagne. Gatward took the hint and, forcing a grin, quickly sped off in his company Daimler.

By 1987 TVS – the 'dream franchise' – was really roaring on the back of the mid-80s consumer boom and the growing 'north–south' divide that followed the wholesale closure of the mining industry up north. Four years earlier, profits had been £4.5 million. They were now heading for an extraordinary £25 million. Money was flowing in in such quantities that even Gatward hardly knew what to do with it. He had invested some of it in building new, state-of-the-art studios in Maidstone, opened by Gatward's great hero, Margaret Thatcher. He had also put money into a company making satellite TV dishes. In 1984 Rupert Murdoch had launched the first version of Sky TV, a small-scale pay TV operation, now poised for bigger things.

Dyke would now attend board meetings and wield some power over what the majority of British viewers watched in their living rooms at weekends. In contrast to TV-am, TVS at the time was a well-run and conservative business (with both a small and capital C). But editorially, TVS left a lot to be desired. By the time of Dyke's arrival, the Independent Broadcasting Authority had warned Gatward that the station had 'some way to go before reaching its potential and the high expectations which accompanied the awarding of its contract. The company has enjoyed considerable success in expanding the business side of its operation . . . but the same energy and purpose have not always been fully matched on the programme side, where the record is uneven.'

At first Dyke's rough diamond approach, swaggering around the corridors and barging into people's offices with a torrent of four-letter words, led to a lot of unease among Gatward's team. Feathers were ruffled as 'the upstart from TV-am' slammed down the phone, leaving the air blue with the kind of language not usually heard in polite Hampshire society. Gatward rarely, if ever, swore in public, and Michael Blakstad – the man Dyke had replaced – had been a model of decorum and reserve. Sometimes Gatward would take a deep breath and suggest to Dyke that he cut down on the four-letter words. 'You're an intelligent guy with a good use of vocabulary. Is all this swearing really necessary?' Behind Dyke's back, staff would ask Gatward if Dyke was 'for real' and 'can he be serious?' None of this appeared to bother Dyke who, from the start, made no bones about the fact that he relied at least as much on his old mentors at LWT as anyone at TVS. It was soon being said that Dyke spent more time on the phone nodding in agreement with LWT's John Birt than he spent swearing at his own staff in Southampton. Some said TVS's new satellite relationship with LWT was a bit like being Bulgaria in the old Soviet Union-led eastern bloc.

At Gatward's regular Friday afternoon executive meetings Dyke's new colleagues were amazed at their new programme controller's unpolished and blunt behaviour. But as TVS's cost base was reduced and the shows began to improve and, according to plan, actually got shown at the weekend, any doubts that Gatward and his team had about their new programme controller began to evaporate. Dyke had won the respect of both his fellow senior executives and the staff. Gatward was so taken with Dyke that he was happy to sometimes shift his Friday board meetings so Dyke could return to LWT and play football with Birt and his old mates.

A key part of Dyke's strategy involved identifying the station's dead wood. Time-servers were singled out and got rid of as Dyke simplified the management structure and introduced a more streamlined look to TVS. Dyke even persuaded Gatward to sell the company jet because, in his opinion, the expense was not justified. Dyke's closest ally at the company was his old TV-am sidekick, Clive Jones, who joined TVS shortly after Dyke did. 'Jonesy' was put in charge of news, current affairs and sport. More than £6.5 million was ploughed into local news coverage, a huge investment but one that helped to keep the IBA off the company's back. When Gatward had first interviewed Dyke he knew that he had to bring up the question of his politics. Dyke assured him that his support of the Labour Party would not in any way affect his professional duties or judgement. The same question was put to Jones during his interview with Gatward and he had given the same answer. The region's politics posed a potential problem for Dyke and Jones. There were 73 MPs on TVS's patch, of which 72 were Tories. There was one Liberal Democrat – and he represented the Isle of Wight. They found it diplomatic not to wear their Labour politics on their sleeves.

Earlier Dyke and Jones, then still at TV-am, had looked on with alarm as Michael Foot's Labour Party ploughed the 1983 election. Politics did not play much part in the weekday output of TV-am, but Dyke naturally took an interest. People involved on the news side of the station at the time vividly remember him watching an especially dreadful Labour Party political broadcast featuring Gerald Kaufman in a studio pretending to lay a brick wall and banging on about unemployment in the building trade. 'It's total shit, completely boring,' Dyke raved. 'Why the fuck don't they ask me to do it for them? I'd do a much better job.'

The Tory landslide in 1983 had caused Dyke to start rethinking his politics. As director of programmes at TVS, Dyke was in a better position than most to see how the country's social makeup was changing and why the Tories were in the ascendant. He studied the ratings and the demographics – extremely accurate and up-to-date information on what people actually did for a living, how much they earned, what they spent their money on and other expensively gathered and hard-edged data of interest to TVS's advertisers. He could see how the population was being transformed.

The old 'working class' that Labour had tried to appeal to was beginning to evaporate. There were still poor people, of course, but most of these were concentrated on what remained of the council housing estates in run-down inner cities and the outlying areas of metropolitan regions. This new underclass was big enough to be a social problem, but too small and demoralized to have much impact on an election – and they were of no use to advertisers whatsoever. The scale of change was brought home to Dyke when he attended a twentieth anniversary reunion of former Hayes Grammar pupils in 1985. He had assumed that, like him, most would be Labour supporters if they were interested in politics at all. To his horror he found that most were rabid Thatcherites. All this con-vinced Dyke that the Labour Party had to 'modernize' or risk extinction.

The same was true, Dyke and his mentors back at LWT realized, of ITV – modernize and move in the same direction as the audience – especially the southern audience – or die. Mrs Thatcher, in power for a second term with an unassailable majority, was determined to take on ITV, identifying it as 'the last bastion of restrictive practices', held back by trade union power and a highly effective monopoly. Her attacks on the system were so extreme and her alliance with 'free market' media operators, such as Rupert Murdoch and Michael Green of Carlton, desperate to break into the protected British market, so close that some feared she might simply legislate to sweep it all away at a stroke.

It was against this background that Dyke and Gatward finally reached an agreement, and in June 1986 Gatward took the highly unusual step of putting out a press release to tell the industry that Dyke was staying put. Gatward had agreed to his board appointment, a head of drama would be recruited in due course and Jonesy was promoted to become Dyke's deputy. Also promoted were a number of ex-LWT people Dyke had originally brought to TVS. These included entertainment specialist John Kaye-Cooper, strategist Mick Pilsworth, who had worked closely with Birt at LWT, and Mike Southgate, who had helped to put the lavish production facilities at Southampton and Maidstone on to a more efficient footing.

Dyke had now cemented his power base, surrounding himself with a loyal group of executives who owed their allegiance to him. His new corporate status was now official. He had crossed the line to become one of the bosses, a suit, and not just any old suit. Earlier in his TVS career Dyke had crossed another line. He had suddenly become rich. A bundle of share options he had been given as part of his joining package at TV-am, previously assumed to be worthless, matured and delivered a windfall of at least £100,000 – a huge sum in the mid-Eighties. With his big wages at LWT and TV-am carefully invested in property, and his share money also invested, he was already far richer than LWT contemporaries such as John Birt and Barry Cox.

He was not a conspicuous consumer like Gatward, but from his new financial and managerial vantage points he was able to look at the financial side of TV in a new way. Before the move to TVS and the TV-am share pay-out, Dyke had experienced TV as a source of big salaries and, possibly, cushy contracts of employment. Now he could see that there was another class of people involved who were rewarded mainly by the movement of the share price and who drew ten – or a hundred – times more out of the business than even the most generously rewarded employee. Sometimes he would fix Gatward with an amused but incisive stare and say: 'You must be absolutely coining it.' The philosophy that Dyke's father had drummed into him was that nobody was any better or worse than him. That went for Gatward too.

If Gatward had managed to 'coin it', there was no reason why he should not also be able to do so.

# 12.
# The Big Bang

'Oi! Coppock! I bet you never thought this would happen!
. . . ' Dyke had just shoulder-charged into the office of
Peter Coppock, LWT spin-doctor-in-chief, banging the
door hard against its stopper. ' . . . You lot are going to
have to buck your ideas up . . . *I'm* back . . . '

Coppock said he was pleased and offered his congratulations. He knew that Dyke had returned from TVS
to be interviewed for the job of director of programmes at
LWT and, therefore, day-to-day boss of the entire creative
side of the company. Coppock also knew that it was
pretty likely that Dyke would get the £80,000-a-year job.
Dyke plonked himself down on the swivel chair, picked
up a piece of paper – as others might light a cigarette or
unwrap a piece of chewing gum – and began ripping it
into neat strips as he swung from side to side.

'I think we can get a bit of publicity out of it . . . what
about "how London Weekend put a man that a couple of
years ago they thought wasn't even worth giving a car to
in charge of the entire operation" . . . or, I know . . . I think
I've still got my leaving card where David Cox wrote
"Fuck off, Dyke, and don't come back" . . . Maybe we can
do something with that . . . '

There were plenty of angles to go at, starting with the
old 'washed up at 30, sitting on Wandsworth Common'
legend. Then there were one hundred and one variations
of the 'it's a funny old world – local lad makes good' story,
through to the obvious 'Chalk and Cheese' contrast with
the man he was replacing, the much less popular John
Birt. Dyke bounded off again and Coppock got to work.

Dyke had always thought that he might return one day

to LWT in a senior position. The opportunity had arisen when LWT's director of programmes, Dyke's old mentor John Birt, decided to leave LWT to become Deputy Director-General of the BBC. At the time Dyke was beginning to feel that he had pushed TVS as far as it would go, and had learned as much as he was likely to learn about the business from the backwater vantage point of the Solent.

The power to appoint Birt's successor was in the hands of the two most powerful people at LWT – Brian Tesler, the managing director, and Christopher Bland, the chairman. There were other, strong internal candidates, including Dyke's former boss Barry Cox. But Tesler was always likely to go for Dyke. It was Tesler who had steered Dyke into TVS, cementing the alliance between the two companies, allowing Dyke to learn about the system and life at boardroom level and to prove himself. As far as Tesler was concerned, Dyke had passed the test. He was particularly impressed by the way Dyke had fought his corner at ITV Network Controllers' Meetings, promoting the interests of TVS and LWT against opposition from the other Big Five companies, especially Granada.

Christopher Bland, an energetic multimillionaire former Tory politician and City financier, evidently needed a little more persuasion. Bland had first met Dyke when he was still at TVS. Bland's wife Jenny had invited him to a reception at the Blands' country mansion in Hampshire and Dyke remembered thinking: 'Blimey! This is a big house.' Later Dyke attended a dinner party and had been impressed when Bland turned up in a pair of dirty old jeans 'like I always wear', and decided that he must therefore be a more interesting person than Dyke had imagined. But the two men were not much more than passing acquaintances and they had not discussed the TV business in any great detail.

At LWT Bland's agenda was less about the programming side of the job and more about cost-cutting. In 1986 a government committee of inquiry, the Peacock Committee, had recommended that ITV franchises should be auctioned off to the highest bidder when they came up for renewal. The exact details of the auction plan were not known yet. But LWT, encumbered with expensive in-house production facilities and a large and highly-paid unionized workforce, was in severe danger of losing out to a more efficient, non-union 'greenfield' company which could afford to bid more.

And so Dyke got the job. One of his first duties as director of programmes was to attend an elaborate 'handing over' conference at a hotel in Kent. Birt had organized this event with characteristic meticulousness. There were sessions explaining how each of Birt's control mechanisms worked. The targets that had already been set were outlined and the importance of meeting them was emphasized. For Dyke's benefit, each manager had to describe what he did, how he fitted into the system and what issues he was facing. Birt also added his own pen portraits of key players in ITV, including the regulators, their strengths and weaknesses, analysing how they clashed with or complemented the plan he had devised for LWT. All present took copious notes in the customary style of an Oxbridge seminar. Dyke, in contrast, just sat there, apparently miles away, fidgeting about, doing his paper-shredding thing or doodling. What later amazed people was the fact that Dyke had soaked up every detail, sifting as though on autopilot the important and useful stuff from the blather before discreetly casting the LWT Bible according to John Birt to one side. Here was a man who could absorb the entire recent commercial history and management structure of a complicated operation like LWT at one sitting without any undue effort, and then summarize the gist of what Birt had been saying over a period of hours in two or three killer phrases.

Dyke soon had another encounter with 'Birtism' in the form of the vast compilations of TV industry data which the departing director of programmes liked to consume. Dyke knew that Birt was addicted to paperwork, but the reality was far worse than he had imagined. On the Friday afternoon of his first week as director of programmes Dyke returned to his office after lunch to find his desk piled high with several columns of documents, still warm from the photocopier. 'What the hell's all this?' he asked his PA, who explained that they were activity reports from managers and programme editors right across the board. It was further explained that Birt liked to take them home and read them in bed on Sunday night, ahead of the following week's round of management meetings. Dyke loudly announced that life was too short to spend half the weekend under a pile of paper and he had better things to do with his Sunday evenings.

(The end of the Birtist regime was welcomed at all levels of the organization and not least by Bill, Birt's personal driver, whose life had been dominated by a series of instructions written on Post-It notes. Birt loved these little yellow strips of sticky paper, praising them as one of the greatest inventions of the 20th century. It was said that he stuck them on to the headboard in the marital bedroom to remind his wife to do something or other if he got up and left the house earlier than she did. But the all-time humdinger Birt Post-It note was reckoned to be 'Bill – Jockstrap?' stuck on the steering wheel of Birt's limo, reminding the driver to make sure that the vital piece of equipment was ready and waiting when Birt turned out to play in the routine LWT Friday football match later that day).

For some in the middle ranks at LWT the first taste of the new regime came in the form of an unscheduled visit from the new director of programmes, who would barge into their office at any moment of the day and, affecting the style of an office boy or junior clerk skiving off, put his feet up on the desk, complain that he was bored, ask, 'What you up to then?', have a good moan about something or other, and make a few vital decisions before spinning off again for yet another informal visitation. It was all a bit different from Birt, who communicated with people in strict order of rank and mainly in the form of endless committee meetings and lengthy memoranda. In contrast, Dyke found it difficult to sit through a committee meeting, often feeling the need to jump to his feet and wander up and down as he was talking. A favourite Dyke trick was to walk down the fire escape in the middle of the building and enter people's offices by the fire door, thus catching staff off guard and engaging them with an opening gambit such as, 'This place is a bleeding mad house, innit?'

Dyke and Sue had sold their house on the bucolic outskirts of Southampton and moved back to the urban delights of Twickenham in west London, claiming to have missed the noise and graffiti. They bought a Georgian pile near the Thames for £500,000. Joseph, Dyke's dad, who had warned him and his brothers not to get too big for their boots, jeered that the estate agent had seen him coming: 'Half a million quid, and it hasn't even got a garage!' The move back to London plunged Dyke into the nightmare of commuting and traffic jams but, resourceful as ever, he turned the jams to his advantage by installing a battery-powered VCR and screen in the back of his chauffeur-driven Mercedes so that he could use it as a mobile viewing room. At weekends the kids liked to watch videos in the back of the car, but they had a habit of leaving the machine switched on, running the battery flat overnight. Another problem of allowing them access to the status machine was that they would leave toy guns on the back seat – difficult when Dyke would eventually have to drive into Whitehall car parks to represent the LWT case on broadcasting legislation.

With these domestic arrangements in place, and having abolished the worst excesses of 'Birtism' more or less overnight, Dyke got down to work on the main task facing him – breaking the power of the LWT trades unions and, thus, opening up the way for a huge reduction in staffing levels and costs. As an ex-union leader himself, Dyke knew the unions' tactics inside out. Importantly, there was also a degree of trust and respect on both sides, which might not have been present if anyone else had attempted the task. Dyke knew that the union people were not mindless militants who could only be battered into submission. They were intelligent people who were amenable to persuasion. In the late Seventies and early Eighties when Dyke had found himself on the other side of the table, he had stuck out for big pay rises and high manning levels because he knew that the company was in effect a protected monopoly which could afford it. With new broadcasting legislation on the horizon, and new players in the market including Channel Four, satellite and cable, that was no longer the case. LWT would shortly be fighting for its financial life. 'We've got to do this ourselves or wait and have it done to us,' Dyke told them over and over again. 'It will be far, far worse if somebody else comes in and does it.'

A couple of years earlier, Thames, prompted by the IBA and the fear of eventually losing its licence, had shown it was possible for the management to keep the station on air after finding itself in a strike over the introduction of new manning levels. But LWT, strengthened by Dyke's resolve, wanted to go further and took great care to carry out the groundwork so that the unions would be defeated once and for all. Dyke's ex-boss, Bruce Gyngell, had succeeded in reducing staff levels at TV-am after a bitter strike the previous year. Gyngell had outwitted the strikers by screening endless episodes of *Batman*. The union knew they were beaten when repeats of *Batman* drew 100,000 more viewers than the regular show that Dyke had helped to devise. Nominally Tesler, as managing director, was in charge of the plan, but it was Dyke who made the running and who oversaw detailed negotiations with the unions. The object was to sweep away the generous terms and conditions of service and, most important of all, reduce manning. It was decided to seek a confrontation with all the unions at one time. A key part of this strategy involved the staff knowing that management were prepared to run a management service if the unions refused to sign the new agreement and attempted to take LWT off the air.

By the spring of 1988 Dyke and his senior colleagues had completed their elaborate plans to wrong-foot the unions. Tapes were smuggled out of the building and hidden in garages all over London. An alternative broadcasting centre was set up. Managers could be seen walking round the corridors of LWT carrying teach-yourself Dutch books. They wanted the staff to think the management service could be run from Holland. In fact, although a scheme had been devised to run LWT from across the North Sea, Dyke and company had worked out how a non-union service could be broadcast from the station itself. LWT had shelved a long-running *Dallas*-style American soap opera that would fill up hours of airtime in the event of a strike. It would keep the audience happy and ensure that advertisers didn't defect to Thames. The series had been bought for the network, and other ITV programme heads wanted to know why LWT continued to put off showing it. Knowing that any walk-out would be ineffective gave Dyke a huge advantage in the talks with union leaders.

Then, on the last Friday in March 1988, without prior warning, all staff at LWT were presented with new contracts and told that if they did not sign them by the end of the day they should not turn up for work on Monday morning. They would, in effect, have sacked themselves. This was the Big Bang.

The unions, still reeling from Gyngell's much more hard-won victory at TV-am, capitulated at once and at a stroke the 'Spanish practices' that had led to stories of videotape editors earning more than Brian Tesler were abolished. Under the old system, technicians could earn up to sixteen times their hourly rate in overtime payments. The new maximum was double. It was not only Dyke's determination and his skill as a deal-maker that defeated the unions. The tide of history was against them, as the Government's anti-union legislation had shown. The Peacock Report, with its calls for a franchise auction and greater access for independent producers, was a signal that a more market-led, entrepreneurial broadcasting economy would eventually emerge in the Nineties. In this transitory phase, the broadcasting unions knew that they had got away with extraordinarily generous pay and conditions for as long as they could. They could see the way the industry was going, the prices charged by Soho facilities houses, and how independent producers had to be cost-effective or go out of business.

Over the next five years LWT's staff was reduced from around 1465 to 723, without any industrial action. Over the same period, the losses on the production facilities division were reduced from over £22 million a year to £2 million. Dyke insisted on large redundancy packages – expensive at the time, but worth paying to preserve the morale and self-respect of those who remained. He tried to sell the redundancy packages for what they genuinely were – or could be; a financial cushion that would enable people to take control of their own careers and work for themselves as freelances or by setting-up businesses. For some this really was an opportunity, a liberation. But for others it was never going to work out. It was pretty bleak being a freelance boom operator or lighting technician in a city that was full of studios and TV operations frantically slimming down to boost profits in the same way as LWT.

Other ITV bosses had dithered for years, but now Dyke, having gained an amazing degree of grip on the place within a matter of a few months, was playing hard-ball and acting with a degree of urgency and decisiveness that had rarely before been seen anywhere in British TV management.

And that was just for starters.

# 13.
# A League of His Own

In 1988, a year into his job as director of programmes at LWT, Dyke took on the ITV network responsibility for sport. This involved more clashes with Granada over the dumping of sports like rugby league, darts, all-in wrestling and crown green bowling. These had played well in the north, but were actively despised by much of the southern audience Dyke was trying to please. Dyke, who wanted to see more 'live and exclusive sport' on ITV, signed up the Rugby Union World Cup instead, but his chief priority in sport was football which, of course, was mainly a weekend activity and therefore suited LWT especially well.

Dyke had always been keen on football and had always played to keep himself fit, culminating in the ritual LWT Friday games. Dyke's family were avid Spurs fans, but as a child Greg decided to attach himself to Manchester United, which he later claimed was an exercise in pure perversity, designed to annoy his friends and relatives.

Football was unfashionable by the time Dyke became a student at York University in the 1970s but he played in a student team which was later remembered mainly as an excuse for drinking. Team-mate Phil Kerridge, who went on to become a librarian in rural Cornwall, later remembered one crucial game when Dyke had played with 'fire in his belly . . . but I think you can put that down to the quart of vodka he had drunk the night before'. Another team member said that they had to keep the ball on the ground because they were all too hungover to head it. Tactics seemed to owe more to *Monty Python's Flying Circus*, one of the few TV shows that Dyke bothered to watch at the time. When the other team was attacking, the York captain would shout 'dead ants' and the whole team would fall to the ground, roll on to their backs and wave their arms and legs in the air. The aim was to startle the opposition into making a mistake but, Kerridge later claimed, 'It didn't work. They always scored.'

Football played a smaller part in Dyke's life in the early 1980s. Clive Jones, his number two and great mate at TV-am, was a fellow fan and an experienced football reporter. Both Dyke and Jones had wanted to put more sport on the screen at TV-am. But football, since it did not take place in the morning, was never on the agenda beyond a bit of on-screen sofa-based banter. The first live football league match had been screened by ITV in 1983, just before Dyke left TV-am for TVS. But it was not seen as a great ratings success and mainly suited the northern and London ITV companies which, at the time, was where all the successful clubs and the majority of the fans were located. Worse than this, football was entering an horrific period which would, during Dyke's time at TVS, lead to the Bradford fire, the Heysel stadium tragedy and the banning of all English teams from European competitions. It seemed that football was part of the old northern Britain of Mollie Sugden, Jimmy Tarbuck, the Co-op and the pre-modernized Labour Party that Dyke complained dominated ITV – miles away from the aspirations of the younger and more affluent viewers that he had to look after at TVS.

But by 1987, when Dyke returned to LWT as director of programmes, football was beginning to change. A new generation of entrepreneurs were starting to eye up the clubs as undervalued assets, ripe for profitable development. On the football side, the attraction was often the value of the club stadiums – in many cases crumbling, uncomfortable and even dangerous Edwardian edifices sitting on prime development land in promising inner-city locations in the middle of a property boom. On the television side, it was being realized that football was one of the few 'drivers' that could persuade people to subscribe to the new cable and satellite services being developed.

Dyke's additional responsibility as head of sport for the whole ITV network inevitably led him into contact with the chairmen of the football league clubs. He became particularly friendly with Irving Scholar, the young and fun-loving chairman of Tottenham Hotspur, who was leading a campaign to modernize what would soon come to be called 'the football industry'. Scholar was quite unlike the combination of 'butchers, bakers and candlestickmakers' – the ageing collection of small-time businessmen and local worthies who had control of the clubs. He had made his money as a property developer and had then outmanoeuvred the dynasty of brown paper bag manufacturers to buy control of Tottenham for a couple of million pounds in the early 1980s. Under Scholar's control, Tottenham became the first club to be floated on the Stock Exchange. He then engaged Saatchi and Saatchi to advertise games, sell season tickets and merchandise and, most importantly of all, work out how football could make more money from television.

Dyke had been impressed by Scholar's lack of bullshit and the way he combined football fanaticism with the sort of 'East End lad made good' business acumen he had first encountered with Gatward. But, in contrast to Gatward's more reserved style, Scholar was more on Dyke's wavelength – a manic enthusiast for football, business and whatever project he happened to be involved in at the time. Like Dyke, Scholar talked non-stop in an unrelenting style which made it difficult for others to get a word in edgeways unless they waited for him to take a drag on one of his endless chain of cigarettes. His favourite saying was, 'Shhh – now listen to me.' Scholar would roar around London in his Range Rover with its flashy personalized number plate, FA H1T. His bachelor pad, a beautiful Georgian house in Regent's Park, was cluttered up with Spurs memorabilia. He had a place in Monte Carlo as well, and a deserved reputation for liking the high life. Scholar admired Dyke and would always say, whenever the ITV chief was mentioned, 'Shhh, now – listen to me – Greg Dyke is one of the few men in TV you can trust.' Dyke had earned this accolade for admitting that in the past the BBC and ITV had operated a cartel, refusing to bid against other for football rights and thus forcing the football authorities to sell the rights for next to nothing. Dyke had promised that ITV would in future treat them more fairly, paying much bigger fees for at least some of the games, sums much nearer what they were worth to ITV in terms of advertising revenue generated.

The deal that Dyke had inherited involved ITV and BBC jointly paying £3.2 million per year, which was shared equally between all 92 football league clubs, regardless of which matches and clubs were actually featured. It meant that the total annual income from television for a club like Manchester United or Tottenham, whose games were often shown, was less than £40,000 – the same as a fourth division club like Rochdale or Scunthorpe, who were never featured. The problem for people like Irving Scholar was that each league club had an equal vote, the small clubs having a massive built-in majority. Since the rights to their games were worth basically nothing, they would always accept whatever the BBC and ITV were offering without putting up a fight. They would then insist that all the money be shared equally on the increasingly implausible grounds that people only wanted to watch Manchester United on TV because they were playing in a league system that included 91 other clubs.

But in 1987 the football authorities found that they had another option. Dyke discovered that British Satellite Broadcasting, the soon-to-be-launched pay-TV operator, was ready to bid £9 million for exclusive rights to league football when the existing contract with ITV and the BBC ended in 1988. Even more impressively, BSB was prepared to put that up to £30 million per year – ten times what the ITV–BBC cartel was paying – if the satellite subscriptions went up according to plan.

Dyke countered by working up a plan with, at first, Irving Scholar and his Saatchi advisors to abolish the existing 92-club football league and replace it with a new 'superleague' based around the 'Big Five' clubs, who were followed by well over half the country's dedicated fans – Manchester United, Liverpool, Everton, Arsenal and Scholar's Tottenham Hotspur. To make things more interesting, and to give ITV a good regional spread of clubs, they added Aston Villa, Newcastle, Sheffield Wednesday, West Ham and Nottingham Forest. Such a league would generate more of the Arsenal–Manchester United-type matches that actually got a decent TV audience and cut out all the rubbish that TV had previously paid for but which nobody wanted to see, other than a few dozen local fanatics (eg Rochdale vs Scunthorpe). Scholar was the chairman most strongly in favour. He had always wanted Tottenham to play fewer games, each having 'an event-like quality' as the Saatchis put it, taking place less frequently and each hyped in advance like a cup final (with admission prices to match). It was an attractive proposition for the clubs. If they accepted the BSB offer they would get a maximum of £300,000 per year, since the money would still be shared between all the league clubs. But as members of the ITV ten, Dyke would pay them a round £1 million each and, since he was only paying the money to ten clubs, he would still be paying far less than the BSB offer.

Dyke unveiled the plan for the 'ITV Ten' breakaway league at a press conference in August 1988. He had backing from two important allies in the ITV Network – David Elstein of Thames and John Fairley of Yorkshire. Elstein and Dyke worked together closely, rallying the ITV companies to back the plan to set up and fund the ITV Ten. They managed to persuade the others that there was a real threat from the new British Satellite Broadcasting, although Dyke and Elstein were much more alert to the dangers of letting pay-TV off the ground. 'Multichannel television' was a danger to the whole of ITV, but the threat was greatest in wealthier parts of the country, including London, where take-up would be greatest.

There was an outcry when Dyke explained what the ITV Ten plan would mean in practice. Dyke was castigated, especially in the tabloids, as a 'hooligan' who was setting out to wreck the national game. The Football League Management Committee called an emergency meeting of all the 92 club chairmen. Of the 'ITV Ten' clubs, only Manchester United and Arsenal attended. The breakaway idea was voted down by a massive majority and the league said it was seeking an injunction to prevent the plan from going ahead. A few days later Dyke went to a meeting of first division clubs held at Aston Villa's ground. After much acrimony, a compromise was reached. Dyke and the 'Big Five' chairmen agreed to extend the breakaway to all twenty-two First Division clubs, and not just the ten at first selected. In return the twenty-two clubs agreed in principle to an exclusive contract with ITV worth £11 million per year and to reject the offer from BSB which, by now, had formed a consortium with the BBC. The first division clubs then decided to offer some of the money to the smaller clubs in the lower divisions who were told that if they voted against ITV the first division would break away, form their own league and leave them without a penny.

The rights to live games that Dyke had worked so hard to keep in 1988 became one of the building blocks of the weekend ITV schedule, with a live match ending just before tea-time every Sunday. Screened as 'The Big Match', the format soon settled down and Dyke was able to turn his attention to modernizing other parts of the schedule. This included an overhaul of the rest of ITV sport. Dyke had a long list of complaints in this department, nursed since the time of his 'Yuppie TV' campaign at TVS. Downmarket northern pseudo-sports like wrestling and darts were axed, earning Dyke the wrath of the *Sun*'s TV critic, who ran such an effective campaign that Dyke finally relented and reinstated darts. From now on, Dyke said, all sports programming – just like any other type of show – had to earn its keep in ratings terms. 'We have been criticized for not showing an interest in cricket,' Dyke complained. 'But who wants cricket? Nobody watches it on BBC2. It's got no audience.' As for crown green bowling, Dyke said, 'We only have it because some idiot paid for it in the past. Now there's great television for you – watching grass grow.'

Dyke had won the first round of his battle with pay-TV over football. The threat from satellite in the form of British Satellite Broadcasting had been nipped in the bud.

Without the football, and suffering from a host of management and other financial problems, BSB soon went under. But the threat had not gone away. The contract for televising football was due to run out in 1992, by which time Dyke would face a much more formidable adversary – Rupert Murdoch's Sky television.

# 14.
# Trouble Up North

Paul Bonner, the urbane and donnish chairman of the ITV Network Controllers' Group, a genuine TV heavyweight, is trying to stay calm. He has taken Greg Dyke to one side during a break in the routine horse-trading at the group's regular Monday meeting, where Dyke is representing LWT.

'Look, Greg,' Bonner sighs, 'I know there's a lot of tension between LWT and Granada. I understand all that. But – look – you simply can't call another controller "a motherfucker" in an open meeting.'

Dyke pauses, thinks carefully about what Bonner has said, and replies: 'But he is, isn't he?'

Bonner, now starting to grow a little irritated but struggling not to show it, says it again: 'Look, Greg. I've got to run these meetings and they are difficult enough without you winding people up.'

Dyke plunges into thought again. 'Well, what am I allowed to call him then?'

'Greg, I think you are missing the point . . .'

One of Greg Dyke's main jobs as LWT's director of programmes was to attend the regular Monday meetings of fellow ITV controllers at Knighton House, an un-distinguished office block that served as the headquarters of the Independent Television Companies Association, not far from Oxford Circus in Central London. The purpose of the meetings was to carve up the ITV national schedule which, at the time, was governed by an extremely complicated system of programme-making quotas. Each of the 'Big Five' ITV companies (LWT and Thames from London, Central from the Midlands and

Granada and Yorkshire from the north) was guaranteed fixed numbers of hours in the schedule to broadcast the shows they made, often regardless of quality or merit.

All would later agree that the system was deeply flawed and had to change as genuine competition for viewers finally emerged in the late Eighties. It could have been designed to create discord. All the companies used to fight each other – or moan about the amount of low-rating stuff - as they attempted to hammer out a network schedule that would ideally trounce the BBC, delight advertisers and win over the critics – and, of course, keep their own studios busy and bolster their own egos. The system was particularly infuriating for LWT which, unlike all the others, broadcast at weekends only. The other companies tended to reserve their best material for the weekdays, when the competition from the BBC tended to be weaker.

The man who Dyke had described as 'a motherfucker' was Steve Morrison, his opposite number at Granada. Dyke had disliked Morrison from the moment he first met him. Partly it was a clash of styles. Morrison was a loquacious Glaswegian with intellectual pretensions who was as long-winded as Dyke was pithy. 'He's the greatest bore of all time,' Dyke would say of Morrison. 'He gets his own way by boring everyone to death. You end up agreeing with him just to shut him up.' But then again Morrison was typical of Granada as a whole, or as LWT had long seen the company – arrogant, parochial, reactionary, self-interested. Granada saw itself as the very heart of the ITV network. Its track record included dramas like *Jewel in the Crown* and *Brideshead Revisited* – top quality drama that pleased audiences and commentators alike. It was the home of *Coronation Street*, Britain's most popular programme, and – more than that

– a national institution genuinely loved by millions. And Granada produced *World in Action*, the current affairs show that achieved ratings about which *Weekend World* could only dream. At the time, LWT's biggest-ever rating show was *It'll be All Right on the Night*. As Granada saw it, LWT's job was to provide the 'tits and tinsel', as Michael Grade put it – the froth for Saturday night. John Birt had admitted as much by adopting the slogan 'LWT – The Entertainers', in an attempt to rebrand the station.

The cold war between LWT and Granada had reached boiling point at the start of the 'eighties when John Birt and Mike Scott had been the respective controllers. Birt started bringing along reams of market research showing that Granada's programmes, with the exception of *Coronation Street*, did not play well in London and the south. There were cultural differences, a different sense of humour for example. Granada, he said, just was not pulling its weight by providing more southerner-friendly material, especially at the weekends. The conflict became public in April 1983 when Birt unilaterally refused to broadcast a Granada-produced series of 19th-century ghost stories called *Shades of Darkness*, claiming that Granada had made it to be screened during the week but had then dumped it on LWT when it discovered it was a creative and ratings flop. Scott had retaliated by threatening to put the low-rating *South Bank Show* and *Weekend World* on at 8am on Sunday morning in the Granada region, on the deliberately provocative grounds that the BBC was then showing the test card and this was the only time that these LWT gems would win the ratings battle. Matters got so bad that sometimes Birt and Scott refused to speak to one another during the Mortimer Street marathons.

Dyke had first become involved in network politics

when he was still at TVS, loyally pushing James Gatward's claim that the southern company should be given the same status as the Big Five, on the grounds of its growing financial power. As part of the LWT–TVS alliance which Dyke made flesh, he pitched in on Birt's side in the war against Granada and the campaign to emphasize the importance of the rich southern audience to the ITV network as a whole. ITV, Dyke complained, was like the Co-op, stuck in the past and catering to an idea of a traditional working-class audience that was years out of date. People, especially the young, were turning their backs on ITV in the same way as they were turning their backs on the Co-op in favour of Sainsbury's. Dyke was fond of quoting a rare example of a concise and pithy John Birt phrase: 'The south is moving north'.

A few years earlier, Dyke himself had put it more graphically at a TVS press conference, saying if he ever saw another old-fashioned sitcom featuring a professional northerner like Mollie Sugden, he would 'slit his wrists.' Gatward, sitting a few feet away from Dyke, winced. But everyone got the point. Dyke had followed up by getting TVS to produce more 'aspirational' and southern-friendly material for the network, including comedy shows from Bobby Davro and *The Ruth Rendell Mysteries*, a crime drama series that became a fixture of ITV's Sunday night schedules. In the papers Dyke was accused – or praised – for advocating the production of Yuppie TV. But Granada remained unmoved. Morrison's boss, Granada chief executive David Plowright, had been particularly scathing about TVS when Gatward and Dyke began to complain. And who was this Greg Dyke person anyway? All he had ever produced was Janet Street-Porter and Roland Rat.

Now, with his move from TVS to the big-time at LWT,

Dyke had a permanent seat at the network table and pursued his campaign for a modernized schedule with growing impatience.

Still, Dyke had injected a bit of life into the meetings. He couldn't do much, for the time being, about programme supply from Granada, but he did demand – and get – changes in the way the controllers' meetings were conducted. Until Dyke's arrival, the tradition was that the Big Five would take up their normal intransigent and defensive positions, lock horns on a range of boring and long-running feuds in the morning and then, as though exhausted by the sheer futility of it all, get reasonably well-oiled over a three-course lunch, exchange the latest gossip and recount a few funny stories. The wine would continue to flow all afternoon, when the clever ones seized the chance to drive through what they wanted.

Paul Bonner had arrived as chairman of the group just before Dyke joined in May 1987, and the two of them worked together to make the meetings more efficient. Dyke had a puritanical side to him, but more important was the fact that he wanted changes to the way the network operated and it suited the reactionaries if the controllers' meetings functioned as boozy awaydays. Dyke and Thames' David Elstein, known as 'Two Brains' because of his conspicuous cleverness, had upset everyone by insisting on a ban on smoking. This was soon followed by the abolition of lunchtime drinking and, eventually, the substitution of the traditional three-course lunch with sandwiches. People joked that Morrison and Dyke could now continue arguing and winding up one another from 9am to 5pm without a break.

Typically, Dyke began to ask some tough questions about what did and what did not deserve a place in the schedule. Like his predecessor, John Birt, he would back up his arguments with research based on detailed demographic analysis. He argued that it was shortsighted for ITV to go for the mass audience *per se*, particularly as the station's traditional audience, older and more downmarket, was beginning to change as society was changing. An editorial strategy that relied too much on appealing to the over-50s was asking for trouble, because ageing viewers were less attractive to advertisers and died off soonest. It was essential for ITV to regenerate itself by introducing shows that would also appeal to 16–24 year olds. Dyke believed that ITV must provide programmes that were popular with all the different demographic groups. This did not mean that he did not value the station's ratings juggernauts. Dyke campaigned to get an edition of *Coronation Street* (then a twice-weekly show) screened on Friday evening after LWT had taken over the London airwaves from Thames. As every other ITV company benefited from the ratings and extra ad revenue attracted by the *Street*, Dyke thought that LWT should have a slice of the action as well.

In private, Dyke thought the London companies should schedule the entire network, just as the BBC planned the viewing menu for BBC1 and BBC2, with companies like Granada providing regional opt-outs for local pro-grammes. Dyke won over John Fairley of Yorkshire TV to this view, but ultimately Thames's Elstein and his boss, Richard Dunn, rejected the plan. But Elstein did broker the extra Friday edition of *Coronation Street*. Traditionally Granada had always opposed the idea of a third episode, because they thought it would dilute the show's quality. But with the arrival of new channels, the company's pragmatic managing director, Andrew Quinn, realized that ITV needed to do everything possible to keep audience levels high, leaving Steve Morrison outflanked.

# Citizen Greg

Dyke's strong relationship with John Fairley helped him in his campaign to strengthen the weekend schedule by putting Yorkshire dramas on Friday and Sunday nights, starting with the comedy drama, *A Bit of a Do*, starring David Jason and Nicola Pagett, and leading to other Jason vehicles such as *The Darling Buds of May* and eventually *A Touch of Frost*. This new emphasis and investment in drama was the result of a large research project ordered by Birt before he jumped ship to the BBC. It showed that LWT was not serving the growing number of ABC1 high earners as well as it might and was therefore losing out on a lot of advertising revenue. Once again in his career, Dyke had struck lucky. Birt's early years as programme controller had coincided with a serious economic downturn, leading him to cut budgets in 1982 and go for less expensive light entertainment in the form of 'people shows' like *Blind Date*, and game shows rather than high-cost drama. But now the economy was booming, with consumer spending (and therefore TV advertising) leading the way on the back of cheap credit and soaring house prices (1988 was the year in which Harry Enfield's 'Loadsamoney' character became a national hero). Birt had built up a war-chest that was now made available for investment in drama. And, in a further stroke of luck, Dyke had Nick Elliott, the talented arts and drama producer he had beaten to the controller's job, ready to make it for him, and BBC1 in disarray after Michael Grade's sudden departure to Channel Four in November 1987. Dyke had a close relationship with Elliott but, as part of his puritanical approach, liked to wind him up by scheduling their regular meetings for 4pm on Friday as a way of preventing Elliott disappearing off to his Dorset residence for a long weekend.

Dyke's decision to more than double the amount of

LWT's drama led to a glut of stylish, but not too demanding series, including *London's Burning*, *The Charmer*, *Wish Me Luck* and *Poirot*. The policy helped pave the way for ITV's successful Sunday night 'double drama' policy. This involved scheduling two hours of drama 'back-to back' from 8pm to 10pm, with a fourth episode of *Coronation Street* added in the Nineties at 7.30pm to hook viewers in. 'Double drama' reaped huge dividends in the ratings, helping ITV to move up-market and appeal to the 'middle England' audience. Before long ITV's schedule would be dominated by drama, with high quality shows like *Inspector Morse*, made by Central, *Prime Suspect* and *Cracker* (both produced by Granada) all leaving the BBC gasping to catch up.

In entertainment, too, Dyke introduced a programme of reform also aimed at bringing ITV more up to date. Again the purpose was to attract a younger and more up-market audience. North of Watford end-of-the-pier entertainers like Jimmy Tarbuck and Cannon and Ball found that their contracts were not renewed. They were replaced by Hale and Pace, a more risqué act that went on to win LWT the prestigious entertainment award, the Golden Rose of Montreux. Their cat-in-a-microwave and 'penismobile' sketches caused outrage in the Home Counties, but Dyke was happy so long as the more affluent, younger audiences were switching on, thus keeping advertisers happy. 'Loadsamoney', appearing alongside his Greek kebab cove Stavros (Hhhallo peeps!), was himself one of the stars of *Friday Night Live*, a ground-breaking comedy show masterminded by LWT's new entertainment chief, Marcus Plantin.

Sorting out current affairs, the department where he had started in television as a researcher on *The London Programme* some ten years earlier, was to prove more difficult. Dyke's research showed that none of ITV's current affairs output really earned its keep. Within ITV only Granada's *World in Action* got ratings anywhere near what was needed to keep the accountants smiling. But it was expensive to produce and occupied a Monday night prime-time slot that, if given to an average drama or light entertainment show, would produce twice as many viewers. Eventually Dyke would declare that even *World in Action* was 'a luxury that ITV can no longer afford'. But if *World in Action*'s audience figures were small by the standards required by advertisers, the figures for LWT's *Weekend World* were microscopic. Dyke decided to so something about it, turning to Jane Hewland, the woman who had first harboured doubts about employing him at LWT.

Hewland's replacement for *Weekend World* was called *Eyewitness* and, according to plan, would have been shown at 6pm on Sunday in the traditional 'God Slot'. Dyke wanted to move ITV's religious show *Highway* to the old *Weekend World* 12 noon Sunday slot, arguing that the religious could watch it when they got back from church and could still look forward to seeing *Songs of Praise* on BBC 1 later in the day, instead of having to choose between the two. The move would free up the 6pm slot for *Eyewitness*, giving the non-believers an alternative to *Songs of Praise*.

Dyke was so sure of the strength of this argument that he went ahead with the planning for *Eyewitness*, only to find that the IBA, in one of its last potent acts, would not agree to the changes. Dyke had never really got on all that well with the IBA, although he had a lot of time for its generally mild-mannered head of programme services, David Glencross. Since leaving TV-am for TVS, Dyke had regularly attended all the IBA's major annual meetings and there had always been hostility. Dyke's very appearance in the IBA boardroom in Knightsbridge would send a shudder of distaste round the table. Their snobbery was palpable. It was clear to everyone present that Dyke was not the sort of person the members of the IBA governing council wanted to see running an ITV major. He was frank with them to the point of rudeness, telling them that they were 'talking rubbish' if he thought they were. But he never seemed to suffer much as a result until, finally, they refused to allow the replacement of *Highway* with *Eyewitness*.

When *Eyewitness* finally reached the screens, forced into the 12 noon Sunday slot, it was both a ratings and critical disaster. Designed to play in the early evening, it looked ridiculously upbeat for that time of day. It relied on fairly traditional 'investigative' stunts, but tried to apply them to 'serious' issues. So the Lockerbie story was dealt with by getting a cleaner to smuggle a box of chocolates – 'which could have been a bomb' – on board an airliner to show that airport security was lax. The fall of the Berlin Wall in 1989 exposed all the limitations of the show and its bitty, superficial magazine format. The Death of Communism would have been perfect material for *Weekend World*, which could have done all the major interviews and endless analysis. But *Eyewitness* could not rise to the occasion and Dyke was deeply worried that LWT's failure to do any substantial journalism around the biggest story of the second half of the century might be held against the company when it came to the 'quality threshold' in the forthcoming franchise round. A version of *Weekend World* was resurrected in the form of the super heavyweight *Walden Interview* in a somewhat desperate bid to impress the regulators.

Current affairs and religion aside, Dyke's return to

# Citizen Greg

LWT had been remarkably successful. He'd taken on the unions and won, and begun to modernize the schedule. Outside, the dark clouds of Conservative deregulation and the run-up to the franchise bid were gathering, but ratings were strong and revenue was buoyant. Inside the company morale was extraordinarily high, considering the number of jobs that had disappeared. Then one fine Monday morning Dyke walked into the controllers' meeting at Knighton House, ready for the customary slanging match with Steve Morrison, only to find that Central's Andy Allen, famous for his long lunches and even longer dinners, had some interesting news for him.

'Greg, I had dinner with your new boss last night,' said Allen, with a glint in his eye. 'You may be interested to know that he's a bicycle manufacturer.'

As a put-down, not even Morrison could top that. And for once Dyke had no answer.

# 15.
# Roland Rat's Dad

By now Greg Dyke, although not exactly a household name, was starting to be written about and profiled in papers and magazine supplements read by the chattering classes. A typical profile in the *Mail on Sunday* used the headline 'Mr Average' next to a picture of Dyke sprawling in a chair, an inane grin on his face, tie undone, suit crumpled to destruction, beard and hair all over the place . . . and talked about the way his 'meteoric' rise to within sight of the summit of one of the most important and glamorous businesses in the country had not changed his lifestyle or attitudes. Some journalists called him 'Reg' in tribute to his ostentatious ordinariness and to a *Guardian* misprint. The paper had omitted the letter G from the beginning of his Christian name while writing about his antics at TV-am.

His unpretentious style was already a legend in the industry. The story was told of how Dyke had visited the set of an LWT drama and, feeling peckish, had queued up with everyone else at the chuck wagon. 'Can't you read?' the caterer had said when Dyke reached the head of the queue – 'LWT staff only'. Dyke did not have an ID badge. 'But I'm the boss', Dyke protested . . . 'director of programmes'. The caterer gave him the once-over and replied: 'Yeah . . . and I'm Adolf Hitler.'

Dyke likewise often had difficulty being recognized as the boss when the management team attended out-of-town conferences. More than once he was mistaken for Christopher Bland's chauffeur. On another occasion during a dinner at LWT's favourite country hotel, Eastwell Manor (known to all as Eat Well Manor) in Kent, the refined wine waiter had at first refused to believe that the unkempt figure of Dyke, decked out in T-shirt and faded jeans, should be presented with the wine list, only to be told, for his pains, to take it away. Dyke gestured towards Mike Southgate, the production wizard he had brought back with him to LWT from TVS, on the next table: 'Eaarrr Mike! You're the bloody wine expert . . . you choose . . . ' After a reflective pause, Dyke caused the waiter to wince again by adding: 'And don't let's have that fucking Liebfraumilch either! . . . It's fucking 'orrible!'

At the same time Dyke was becoming an acknowledged master of the vital corporate art of the media interview, setting a lot of time aside to talk to journalists. 'I'm good,' Dyke would tell them, drawing upon a standard set of phrases he had by now developed for dealing with the press. 'I'm good . . . but most of all, I'm very lucky.'

But in private Dyke would tell people who he trusted that he sometimes wondered if he was really all that good. Maybe it was *all* down to luck. More than one close colleague, particularly those who Dyke himself had promoted or recruited into the business, would be told in a relaxed moment: 'You know . . . when you *fink* about it . . . the likes of you and me – we're just journeymen. We shouldn't be getting all this money. You wait! One day they'll find us out and throw us out of the door.' This feeling, which could sweep over Dyke at any time, would soon pass and his self-confidence would return.

Still, although never exactly shy and retiring, Dyke was an almost irritatingly modest man. Accidents of timing and circumstances meant that it had suited two of the most capable figures in the history of the industry to take him on as a protégé and show him the ropes. Dyke claimed that John Birt had taught him first how to make effective TV journalism and then, later, taught him about the politics and operations of the ITV companies and the network while he was at TVS. Dyke's second great tutor was Brian Tesler, the LWT managing director who had spotted his special abilities and had steered his rapid promotion in the business, even when Birt had entertained doubts. But by 1990 Birt had disappeared to the BBC and Tesler was about to retire. But not before giving Dyke a final and decisive push towards the top.

Tesler, in contrast to Dyke, was a dapper man with an all-year suntan who struck many as looking like the ideal TV chat show host. His management style was laid-back – appropriate to the original and declining role of ITV as the commercial wing of British public service TV. He had done much to turn the company around after it faced near-bankruptcy in the 1970s and another serious financial crisis caused by the recession of the early 1980s. But his greatest skill, as he saw it, was as a judge of character and a spotter of raw talent. It was Tesler who had appointed Michael Grade as director of programmes in the late 1970s, at a time when many in the business had thought Grade was just a 'song and dance' variety show promoter with far too little experience. The gamble paid off and the decision was to go down in telly-land folklore as one of the smartest appointments ever. When Grade left, Tesler replaced him with the more controversial figure of John Birt, which, despite a few problems, was also thought to have been an inspired choice.

Now Tesler was about to make the most difficult and controversial appointment of all – not just a director of programmes, in charge of the entire creative side of the company, but his own successor – the managing director, the man in charge of the entire shooting match. Tesler had always planned that John Birt would succeed him when he turned 60, the traditional retirement age for senior managers at LWT. But Birt had left LWT in order to 'save the BBC', citing Destiny. Tesler's birthday was rapidly approaching and it was vital that the company had the right leader at such an important time for the industry. The franchise round was fast approaching and the Government was pressing ahead with the most far-reaching set of broadcasting reforms in a generation.

Tesler decided that Greg Dyke, despite his lack of management experience, should probably be given the job. There were some rough edges, Tesler thought. But they could be rubbed off by sending him to Harvard Business School for a while – that was what he had planned to do with Birt anyway. But the decision was not entirely in Tesler's gift. He would have to persuade the LWT board and, most importantly, Christopher Bland, the company's rumbustious and increasingly dominant chairman. Bland liked and admired Dyke in many ways, especially for the hard line he had taken in pushing through 'down-sizing' and new agreements with the unions. As for making Dyke managing director . . . well that was another matter.

Bland was dead against the idea.

Francis Christopher Buchan Bland was born on 29 May 1938 in Yokohama, Japan, to Northern Irish parents. He was educated at Sedberg public school in Yorkshire and Queen's College, Oxford, where he read history, became active in Tory politics, won a fencing blue and became a member of the 1960 Irish Olympic Pentathlon team. After university, Bland returned to Northern Ireland where he joined the 5th Royal Inniskilling Dragoon Guards, rising to the rank of second lieutenant. He first moved into the commercial world at the age of 23, taking a job as an assistant advertising manager at Currys in 1961, moving on to become Marketing Manager of Singer Sewing Machines three years later. At the same time he became active in the Bow Group, a policy think-tank on the left of the Tory Party and edited the group's newsletter, *Crossbow*, for a time. He became a close associate of Norman Lamont, Michael Howard and Douglas Hurd who were then at the start of their political careers. They were to remain close friends.

In 1967 Bland began what was intended to be his own political career when he won the Lewisham seat on the GLC against the odds in a landslide swing to the Tories. Following his victory Bland tried to find a parliamentary seat and trailed around numerous Tory selection meetings. All of them turned him down. Instead, in 1972, aged 34, he was appointed deputy chairman of the IBA by Christopher Chataway, a former TV presenter who was a contact from the GLC. Bland held his position at the IBA for ten years, gaining an encyclopedic knowledge of the TV business including details of the finances and personalities of every ITV franchise operator. At the same time Bland had become a director, and then chairman, of the printing firm Sir Joseph Causton & Son. He steered the company from the brink of bankruptcy to become one of the most profitable printers in the country, gaining a deep understanding of the City in the process. In 1981 he married his teenage sweetheart, Jennifer May, a Viscountess, daughter of Ulster landed gentry and the former wife of the Earl of Strafford, thus gaining four stepchildren and, in due course, his only son, Archie. They set up home in grand style at Blissamore Hall, Clanville, near Andover in Hampshire.

In 1982 Bland joined the board of LWT, by which time he was already on his way to becoming a multimillionaire, since the value of his original £20,000 investment in Sir Joesph Causton had increased several hundredfold. By 1985, when the company was sold, Bland's stake was worth £5 million. His high-powered friends included fellow Conservative supporter Michael Green, the putative ITV mogul who in the mid-Eighties was humiliated when his takeover bid for Thames Television was blocked by the IBA. Undaunted, Green and Bland had worked together as part of an LWT–Carlton consortium to bid for the commercial satellite TV contract awarded by the IBA in 1986. The two men had been deeply disappointed when the contract went instead to a rival group, British Satellite Broadcasting, whose members included Granada.

In 1984 Bland had been made chairman of LWT at a time when Tesler was already grooming John Birt, then director of programmes, to take over as managing director in the future. Birt's departure for the BBC had been a blow, and both Tesler and Bland had agonized over finding a replacement. Tesler had told Dyke that he was in the running for the job – but the decision would by no means be automatic. But Bland, with his excellent contacts in the City and in the Tory Party, was in a better position than most to know that the Conservative Government was determined to force the ITV companies to become leaner, more efficient organizations. It was therefore vital, Bland thought, to make a statement of intent by appointing a known figure from the City rather than an existing TV executive – even one as effective as Dyke – to the top job at the company.

With Tesler's blessing Bland used a firm of head-hunters to trawl the City. Eventually he decided he had found the perfect contender in a city high-flyer who had been involved with the manufacture of bicycles. Bland could scarcely contain his enthusiasm, saying over and over that he was 'absolutely brilliant' – the 'ideal candidate' to manage the further slimming down of the company. 'He's forceful,' Bland gushed, 'he's dynamic . . . he's just terrific . . . far and away the best candidate.'

After interviewing Bland's hotshot candidate, Tesler told Bland that he could see the logic in appointing him, but added: 'It won't work. He won't be able to carry the staff – they won't follow somebody who's got no TV experience.' What was really needed was 'a programme man with a feeling for business'. Bland shrugged: 'Sure . . . but where are we going to find one?'

'Well, there's one right here in the company,' Tesler said.

'Who?'

'Greg Dyke.'

'Bollocks!' said Bland. He was still sure they could find someone better.

But Tesler persisted. The thing about Dyke, he said, was that he was a leader. He had a bit of 'business flair' about him. There were some rough edges, Tesler thought, but Dyke had coped well enough with budgets and even the fiendish complexities of the ITV network. He was an 'entrepreneurial character' who just needed a bit of polishing. A few months at Harvard would give him more confidence and 'burnish his business nous', as Tesler thought of it.

But Bland was still not convinced. He could see Dyke's potential, but it was 'too soon' for him to be put in charge of the whole shop. He had no City experience. Five years earlier he had been making *Roland Rat*. Tesler agreed to see Bland's man again. A few days later Dyke stormed into Tesler's office with the news that everyone at the ITV network controllers' meeting knew that some 'bicycle manufacturer' was to be the new managing director of

LWT and therefore his boss. Everyone, that is, except himself.

Dyke, understandably hurt by this humiliating turn of events, complained that he had been 'taunted even before the meeting began'. Tesler had assured him that he would be given serious consideration for the job and Dyke wanted to know why he had, first of all, been overlooked without even so much as an interview, and then not consulted or even told about the decision to appoint his new boss.

'What are you talking about?' said Tesler, astonished. 'No decision has been taken.' It was realized that news of the supposed appointment of Bland's candidate had leaked. Tesler got Dyke to calm down and then went to see Bland. He explained everything and ended up by saying that, as far as he was concerned, they couldn't possibly hire him now. Bland agreed: 'OK, let's go with Greg Dyke then.'

When the decision was later announced to the general public, the *Sun* ran the headline:

ROLAND RAT'S DAD GETS TOP TELLY JOB.

# 16.
# Golden Handcuffs

'Howdee maaah . . . yup it's yaaw boy Dwayne here, callin' frum lill'ol Har-Vard Biz-niz School . . . yup – I sayd Har-Vard . . . Jeeeze mama . . . ah sure am mighty sick of all these damn slick-tawkin' yankeees . . . How's thangs back they-yur in good ol' Texsus . . . ?'

Greg Dyke is on stage, the star attraction at the booze-soaked graduation party for students on an international course in Business Leadership. According to tradition, everyone has to do a comedy routine – a final role-play bonding exercise to round off the arduous 12-week programme. The Japanese have been on earlier – doing a sort of Karaoke routine which had, truth to tell, not been very funny at all. But Dyke, with his comedy routine based on a dim-witted Texan red-neck oil executive phoning home, is going down a treat.

'See maaa . . . y'all don't have t'git past sixth gray'd to git innta a fancy yankee bizniz school these days . . . no sir-reeee! . . . why I do declare, momma . . . Y'juss give the yankees thirty thousan' dollurs and they're just as pleased as punch t'give yer a fancy cer-tiffy-kate.'

It had been Bland and Tesler's idea to send Dyke to Harvard after they had appointed him managing director (elect) of LWT. The fact was that Birt had been lined up to go before he defected to the BBC and so Dyke, in a sense, inherited his place on the special 'leadership' course. Dyke was happy to go. He had by now become a devotee of modern American business thinking, an expertise gained mainly by reading the homespun works of authors like Tom Peters. At night Dyke would prop himself up and plough through books with odd titles like *The Three-*

# Citizen Greg

*Minute Manager* or *Thriving on Chaos* while Sue – the more intellectual of the two – snuggled up, more often than not, with a meaty tome dealing with sociological theory.

Dyke had not set much store by 'professional' managers who had done nothing in life other than, well, manage things. He often claimed, half jokingly, that the only theoretical knowledge about organizations anyone ever needed, he had gained as a politics student at York, where he had made a detailed study of Stalin's rise to power. Dyke was much more interested in people like Tesler and Birt, who had started off as programme-makers and then moved on to management later when they had some real life experience to work with. Then there was the example of one of his closest friends dating back to *The Six O'Clock Show*: Tony Cohen, who, after deciding he had gone as far as he could as a programme-maker, had left LWT to do a course at the London Business School where, naturally enough, he had chosen LWT as the subject for his MBA thesis. The upshot of Cohen's study was that if Dyke moved all the members of the LWT contracts department into one office, instead of having them dotted around the building, LWT could save thousands by eliminating all the time people spent walking along corridors and going up and down in lifts.

Dyke, who at the time was searching every nook and cranny for ways of eliminating hours wasted, was vastly impressed and hired Cohen as a business adviser, installing him in a tiny office across the corridor from his own more palatial chambers. Cohen then had to put up with Dyke wandering in ten times a day, showing him financial documents and asking, 'What the fuck does this mean?' Eventually Cohen said: 'Why don't you go to business school, like me? Then you'll know.' Dyke, who at first enquired whether you could do evening classes in the subject, took the point and so was happy enough to set off for Harvard.

The course itself was based around case studies dealing with what made particular companies either succeed or fail. The answer, according to Dyke's tutor, John Cotter, was the personality of the chief executive. This was great news for Dyke, who possessed personality in unrivalled quantities. Sue, who joined Dyke for the last few weeks of the course, had already worked out this simple central point, warning him, 'You have to be very careful with these people. You work best when you do things out of instinct. If you try to understand how you do it, you could lose it.' In the end Dyke found the course useful enough, claiming that Cotter had given him the self-confidence to 'be himself' – there was no need to ape the world of established businessmen and accountants.

Dyke returned from Harvard Business School at the beginning of 1990 and was typically self-deprecating, telling his mates that the only thing that his stay in the belly of the capitalist beast had taught him was that socialism was the better option after all. But in moments of greater seriousness he would say that at Harvard he had glimpsed the real nature of competition in business, and the degree of ruthlessness that was needed to succeed. Some of the others, seconded from American or Japanese companies, had blinked with incomprehension when Dyke mentioned his unease or attacks of conscience over his downsizing plans. All the bureaucracies of regulation, the high staffing levels, the luxury of being able to ignore consumer choice from time to time – all these things were only possible because British TV operated in more or less monopoly conditions and held a position in the nation's life guaranteed in the last analysis not by the market, but by politicians and regulators. A lot of that was about to change.

As managing director, Dyke started putting his thoughts about management into practice at once. The old management structure of departmental heads running and building their own departments and power-bases was largely dispensed with in favour of a sort of 'cabinet government' system in the form of a weekly meeting. Anybody with any authority in the organization was expected to attend and to support everyone else, and both feel and work as a member of a single team.

These meetings, later remembered by all involved as tremendously effective – and often very funny – always followed the same agenda. People would gather at 8.15am in the Westminster Room, the suite on the 18th floor of LWT's tower with a commanding million-dollar view of the Thames and the power centres of Parliament and Whitehall beyond. About forty people would be present, sitting around a collection of desks arranged in a U-shape, with Dyke and Bland at the head of the table and key advisors like Tony Cohen and director of corporate affairs Barry Cox sitting beside them, Last Supper-style.

Dyke would kick off the meeting at 8.30 sharp with what was called 'industry news'. This was sometimes a useful intelligence-sharing exercise about what other companies and the regulators were up to. But mostly it was an opportunity for everyone to come up with war stories and gossip – the ruder the better. They would all compete to tell funny stories against the opposition – rubbishing rivals like the self-regarding David 'Two Brains' Elstein of Thames TV, the fun-loving John Fairley of Yorkshire TV and, of course, the loathed and derided Steve Morrison of Granada. Dyke and Bland would banter away as a double act, fighting to finish off each

Dyke (circled) as a member of the University of York football team. He was a commanding figure as a student politician and journalist, and met and married Christine Taylor while he was there. (© Will Lack)

The success of LWT's *Six O'Clock Show* established Dyke's reputation as a programme executive. He was popular with the production team and is seen here at his uproarious leaving party.

After the catastrophic launch of TV-am, Dyke turned the station around and became known, ever after, as 'the man who invented Roland Rat' (pictured here with Jeffrey Archer).
(© PA Photos)

TVS boss James Gatward at the time Dyke went to work for him in 1984. At TVS Dyke had his first taste of the TV big time and plunged himself into the fraught internal politics of the ITV network. (© Universal Pictorial Press )

James Gatward at his 1969 marriage to actress Isobel Black, who he later cast as the star of a major TVS drama series. (© PA Photos)

Dyke inherited a strong position when he returned to LWT in the late Eighties, winning the ratings war with a weekend schedule built around top-flight football and quality-made British dramas like *Inspector Morse* (pictured). 'We are out-BBC-ing the BBC', he boasted. (© Rex Features)

Christopher Bland, chairman of LWT in the Eighties and early Nineties, pictured here as a promising young Tory politician in 1969.
(© Universal Pictorial Press)

Brian Tesler, managing director of LWT in the Eighties. (© Universal Pictorial Press)

BSkyB inflicted a humiliating defeat on Dyke by outbidding for the right to show the Premier League on TV. Dyke was to criticise BSkyB's effective owner, Rupert Murdoch, over a range of broadcasting and business issues. (© PA Photos)

The 'upstart catering manager' Gerry Robinson (left) soon after his arrival as chief executive of Granada – Dyke and LWT's traditional ITV rival. Dyke left LWT after a hostile Granada takeover and, although the move made him richer than ever, he described himself as 'unemployed'. (© PA Photos)

Channel Five went on air after a marketing campaign featuring the Spice Girls. The station was slammed by critics but was popular with advertisers and the City. (© PA Photos)

Marjorie Scardino who, to Dyke's dismay, was brought in as his boss, taking the post of chief executive of Pearson. The two executives got on well enough, but Dyke thought that she knew far less about the media than he did and decided to leave Pearson following her appointment. (© PA Photos)

Sir Christopher Bland at the time of Dyke's appointment as Director General. The 'winning team' of LWT were reunited.
(© PA Photos)

Public Service Man: Dyke's image makeover was designed to make him look more like a traditional BBC director general. 'I went in looking like Barry Gibb and came out looking like Henry Cooper,' Dyke said of his new, clean-cut image. (© Rex Features)

other's sentences, shouting 'bollocks' at each other – or anyone else in the room – if they did not agree.

Next up was the more serious business of the weekly ratings report, delivered by Susan Hately, the head of audience research. Each programme and the audience it had attracted would be discussed in turn, with Hately delivering the hard facts and Dyke quipping away constantly – 'See! What did I tell you? . . . I told you that one was a winner . . .' or, conversely: 'Christ, that's bad . . . which one of you fuckers talked me into running that one!' Dyke presided over this part of the meeting in the style of a football manager conducting a post-match analysis of last week's game, making them all feel that they were 'The Manchester United of the television world' – a great, close-knit team ready to beat the pants off all comers. Dyke would yammer on constantly. The only time anyone could remember him being stumped was when Hately did a special presentation on TV viewing habits in homes with satellite dishes. Hately said that Sky had nearly a third of the audience share in dish-homes. This immediately wiped the smile off Dyke's face. The whole room seemed to chill by several degrees. 'That can't be right . . . Are you absolutely sure?' Dyke asked, in the manner of somebody who had just been told that a loved one had been killed in a road accident. 'Are you seriously telling me that in satellite homes people watch as much Sky as ITV or BBC?' Dyke, brow furrowed, was reduced to muttering 'Christ!' and was miles away for the rest of the meeting as he mulled over the implications.

People also had the sense that Dyke and Hately could have had their weekly review of the ratings in private as, doubtless, their opposite numbers in other TV companies did, in order to 'privatize' the priceless information and bolster their own positions of power. But Dyke wanted all of them not so much to contribute to the discussion, but to see him in action, hear what the priorities were and feel included in the decisions. The 'inclusive' approach would then be extended to the rest of the staff. Dyke was always absolutely adamant that any major decision – such as the signing of a new star or the launch of a new series – should be communicated to the LWT staff – even the canteen hands and security guards – before it was released to the press.

After the Dyke–Hately double act, the legendary figure of Ron Miller, LWT's head of advertising sales, would take centre stage. Miller, who liked to roar around town in his top-of-the-range Lexus displaying the number-plate LWT-1, was more than a match for Dyke in the banter stakes. He would entertainingly complain and tease about low-rating shows, having them all in stitches with his salesman's patter, and regaling them with more war stories about the lavish lifestyles and wooden-headed antics of his opposite numbers at other ITV companies. Miller had been at the company since the early Seventies and Dyke would gravely tell people that it was Miller – much more so than even Tesler or – definitely! – Birt and Grade who had 'built' the station. He also had a fantastic network of (harmless and innocent) spies fanning out through the whole of ITV, and was thus reckoned by some to know more about what was really going on in the TV business than any other man on earth. After Miller's report on ad revenue, one of the other senior managers would, according to a rota, give a presentation about their own area of work. There would be questions and answers, with more jokes and hilarity, until the meeting ended.

Attendance at the Wednesday meeting was not compulsory. But nobody entitled to go would have dreamed of missing it (though arts chief Melvyn Bragg, in true Bohemian style, was often late). It was so funny. And you learned a lot. There was also the unspoken idea that this was 'the officers' mess'. The people at the meeting were the company. Through 1990 and 1991 the Wednesday meetings began to focus more and more on one thing – the impending auction for the ITV franchises, and the all-encompassing campaign by Bland and Dyke to make sure that LWT not only kept its licence but that it made the most out of the new and far more commercial ITV system that the new legislation would bring into being.

Thanks to Bland's financial acumen, LWT had come up with an ingenious capital reconstruction scheme. This involved borrowing a lot of money to buy back a sizeable chunk of LWT's shares and then, in addition, offering options to buy some of these shares at a favourable price to key members of the LWT management team. Bland had worked out that LWT could save about £7 million a year in dividend payments by buying back the shares, even after the cost of extra interest payments on the necessary loan had been paid. At the same time, the need to pay heavy interest charges would 'discipline' the company to cut costs and boost the bottom line. And most importantly, senior managers could be persuaded to part with some of their own money to obtain options on the bought-back shares. This would give them an incentive to make sure that the company held on to its franchise and, since they would not be able to cash in their share options until well after the franchise round, the deal would put them in 'golden handcuffs'. Bland had seen how in earlier franchise rounds competing companies had poached staff to bolster their bids. The 'golden handcuffs' would protect LWT from poaching. The locked-in executives would make a handsome profit only if they stayed with the company. If they defected – or if LWT lost its licence – they could lose everything. Dyke was enthusiastic and the deal at once caught his imagination. Here was a chance to take a gamble on his abilities and desire to win. He paid about £200,000 for his block of options – the second largest amount after Bland.

And so LWT's senior team, with Bland and Dyke at the helm, set out to prepare their bid to retain their right to broadcast. The stakes were high. If they lost, Dyke would lose his job, his reputation as a businessman and most of his family's life savings. If they won, he would become rich and LWT would emerge as one of the key players in a transformed ITV system.

Dyke was later to describe the months that lay ahead as 'pure poker'.

# 17.
# Doing the Double

People were beginning to notice that Greg Dyke liked nothing better than having to prove himself and coming out on top. He thrived on the ducking and diving and the deal making, but what really pumped him up was the desire to win, the thrill of actually winning and being hailed as a winner.

Eleven years previously, when LWT had last had its licence renewed, the process had been a breeze. The decision to allow the company to continue broadcasting was taken on the nod, behind closed doors by the IBA. At the time, programme-makers like Dyke were almost oblivious to what went on. It was little more than a formality. This time, though, thanks to Margaret Thatcher, the stakes were sky high and even the work-force worried if they'd still have jobs to go to in two years' time.

In theory, if a rival company outbid LWT and passed a subjective quality test, LWT could be out of business. When LWT's bid team of Dyke, Bland, Brian Tesler, now deputy chairman, Barry Cox, and financial wizards Peter McNally, Tony Cohen, Tony Kay and Neil Canetty-Clarke met for the first time on 2 February 1990, they decided to consider bidding for another franchise as well as doing everything possible to keep the present one. Dyke was convinced that Thames, TVS and TV-am were vulnerable. He had learnt to like and respect Thames' managing director, Richard Dunn, an elegant, statesmanlike figure. With his tall, lean frame, silvery hair and prominent cheekbones inherited from his Icelandic mother, he looked like a Nordic prince. In common with many in the industry, Dyke was won over by Dunn's obvious integrity, but his traditional Oxbridge public service view of ITV made him more suitable to running the BBC than to succeeding in the new market-led commercial world. Thames had not been as ruthless as LWT in cutting its costs and therefore the company was in a less strong position to outbid a rival. TVS, too, was vulnerable to a competing bidder because of Gatward's disastrous US expansion. On the other hand, TV-am under Bruce Gyngell had emerged as ITV's cash cow.

Although Dyke always denied it, some members of the board thought that Dyke had personal reasons for wanting to destroy TV-am and thus take revenge on Gyngell, who six years earlier had been the reason why he'd left the company. 'Of course we can do better than that Australian nutcase,' Dyke told colleagues.

Bland and Dyke had worked out that TV-am's huge profitability was not necessarily an advantage in the complex financial calculations of the franchise round. To maintain these profits, Gyngell would have to bid low. And he was unlikely to win against a higher bidder on the grounds of 'exceptional circumstances' (inserted into the rules to protect 'quality') as it was hard to see the Independent Television Commission rejecting a higher bid because of TV-am's lacklustre programme record and its predominantly low-budget sofa-based fluff. After considering all the various options, Dyke's bid team agreed to target TV-am. To avoid any chance of Gyngell responding by counter-attacking LWT, it was decided to put together a consortium that would apply as a group for the breakfast contract. In the next few months Dyke was in his element, assembling in secret a powerful alliance of media companies. They called themselves Sunrise Television. If the group won, Gyngell might be forced to return Down Under for good – and the press might finally allow Greg Dyke to forget all about Roland Rat. His reinvention as a successful businessman would be complete.

In doing the rounds of potential partners, Dyke's biggest coup was persuading the Disney Corporation to come on board. He had seen the mesmerising effect that Disney material had on his own children and knew from working at TV-am that giving children something they wanted to watch early in the morning was vital to the success of any breakfast TV station. Disney's involvement in Sunrise was especially valuable because the outfit had failed to sign an agreement for the Disney Channel to be carried on Rupert Murdoch's Sky. Dyke, more than most ITV executives, was worried that satellite could become a major competitor. So it was important that Disney should be locked into ITV. He knew that Disney could be a powerful 'dish-driver', persuading millions to subscribe to pay-TV.

Dyke had become friendly with a South African expatriate called Etienne de Villiers, who ran Disney's British operation. De Villiers had identified Dyke as the rising star of ITV and cultivated him and his commissioning budget. De Villiers was an impressive figure. Dyke enjoyed his laissez-faire, American approach to business, and his enthusiasm for the opportunities presented by cable and satellite TV, and beyond that, digital TV. De Villiers ate at the best restaurants, and wore fabulous suits paid for out of his US-style £300,000 a year salary. But Dyke's relationship with De Villiers failed to shield Sunrise from the notorious internal politics at Disney's HQ in Hollywood.

Dyke knew that pleasing the ITC was even more important than keeping the nation's kids entertained while their parents had a lie-in. Therefore it was essential that Sunrise could offer a credible news service, an obvious Achilles' heel at TV-am. For Dyke, the bad news was that ITV's news supplier, ITN, had agreed to join a rival breakfast bidder, Daybreak, which also included Bland's old friend from Carlton, Michael Green. Dyke was furious.

LWT was a 6 per cent shareholder in ITN, which Dyke regarded as a deeply inefficient operator. He resented how much ITV paid ITN for its news programmes, and for some time had wanted ITV to ditch *News At Ten*. This would give the network the freedom to show a more competitive, entertainment-based schedule after 9pm. The way things stood there was now a chance that LWT would end up, via the money it was pumping into ITN, subsidizing a bid against itself. But Sunrise needed to tie up a news provider. So instead of ITN Dyke signed up the next best thing, the news agency Visnews.

The bid's director of programmes was to be the relatively inexperienced Lis Howell, who had only recently taken over as managing editor at Sky News. But Howell's handling of Sky's Gulf War coverage had impressed the industry. The fact that she was a woman, and the first putative female programme controller in British TV, was thought likely to go down well with the politically correct ITC. The inclusion of the *Guardian*, via its TV subsidiary, Broadcast Communications, further strengthened Sunrise's clout as a news-based outfit.

Dyke and Bland had failed to persuade Green to join Sunrise, but an approach from Scottish Television and its leftward-leaning managing director, Gus MacDonald, had struck a chord with Dyke. 'If you are planning a breakfast bid, it would do you a lot of good to have a Scottish component – that way, it would look like a British breakfast bid.' Bland was not entirely convinced, but went along with the plan. Nevertheless he would sometimes remind his colleagues that Scottish was one of the smaller ITV companies. At one board meeting, Bland boomed: 'Who cares what STV think? They just want to piss with the big dogs.' These machinations were all carried out in the utmost secrecy. Many of LWT's senior staff were unaware that bid manager Hugh Pile, who Dyke had first met on the *Newcastle Journal*, was working on a breakfast TV application, codenamed Apollo, in his new 19th-floor LWT office.

With the consortium in place, the really hard part was crunching the numbers. LWT's new financial director, Neil Canetty-Clarke, had astonished colleagues by his brilliance. He had landed his current job while still in his twenties. His addiction to financial efficiency was such that it was said he even tracked his own mortgage for a few seconds every hour, moving the debt round from bank to bank around the world, depending on complex play-offs between tax, interest and exchange rates. He seemed surprised that others did not do the same.

Over the years Dyke had watched TV-am's profits surge ahead. Even so, he was aware that when it came to calculating the amount Sunrise would bid, he must be wary of not putting too much money into the envelope that would arrive at the ITC on 16 May. The regulator had the power to reject over-bidders. In any case, it was vital that the breakfast station would make a decent return and not be saddled by having to pay too much for the licence. One of the main reasons Dyke and Bland wanted to become involved in breakfast TV was because it would allow LWT to save money by using studios and facilities at the station's HQ on the South Bank, now hived off as

The London Studios and operating as a stand-alone business. But how much should Sunrise actually bid? Dyke and Bland would need all of Canetty-Clarke's financial dexterity, and more, to get their sums rights.

On the first weekend of April, Dyke and his Sunrise conspirators decamped to the Old Mill conference centre, Minster Lovell, on the edge of the Cotswolds. After hour upon hour of detailed number-crunching, examining revenue projections for the next decade, Dyke decided to veto the consultants' recommendation that Sunrise should bid £40 million. Instead they would go for somewhere between £32 and £36 million.

Dyke still needed to finalize the details of the main LWT bid. If the pressure was getting to him, most of the time he put on his usual Jack-the-lad act. Dyke told the story of how he was so distracted by working out the size of the LWT bid that one day he had left his Twickenham home to drive to Richmond Park to take his dog for a walk, only to find when he got there that he'd forgotten to bring the dog. It wasn't only Dyke's nerves that were beginning to fray. Tony Cohen, one of Dyke's most trusted strategists, had taken on the job of sweeping the LWT boardroom for electronic bugs. He used a hand-held box that contained a bleeper. One day the bleeper went berserk. The building was scoured for one of the few electricians who hadn't yet been sacked. Cohen was savouring the headline – 'Gyngellgate' – when the electrician explained that an unearthed wire from the air-conditioning system had set off the device.

Amidst all the paranoia, Dyke and Thames's Richard Dunn had negotiated a deal not to bid against one another and not to help any of their opponents. This was a sensitive area because when in 1984 Michael Green had attempted but failed to take over Thames, LWT had helped Green by providing him with valuable financial information about Thames. In return, Bland had received a written assurance from Green that he would not bid against LWT. There had also been talks between LWT and Carlton over running a joint news service if both turned out to be winners in the franchise round. Despite the considerable financial savings involved, Thames had always resisted forming a joint news venture with LWT. The prospect of collaborating with LWT on news appealed straight away to the commercially-driven Green. But winning was not yet a foregone conclusion.

It looked as if LWT would face only one rival. Put together by a group of independent producers under the name London Independent Broadcasting, the main mover in the bid was Tom Gutteridge, a former BBC programme-maker turned successful independent producer. He was a flamboyant figure whose doomed affair with TV presenter Anneka Rice was gleefully reported by the tabloids. In common with the breakfast contest and the way it pitched Dyke against Gyngell, the fight between LWT and LIB contained a personal dimension for Dyke. Gutteridge and Dyke had been contemporaries at York University in the early 1970s. Gutteridge, who ran the student TV station, was a luvvie, and Dyke the streetwise hack. (Dyke's newspaper, *Nouse*, complained that 'York Student TV has become virtually synonymous with Tom Gutteridge. He completely dominates the whole thing. Why should we be paying just so he can run his own TV station which only he and his mates watch anyway?') They had regarded one another warily then, and not a lot had changed in the intervening years. LIB was derided as 'The Groucho Club Bid', because it was there that members of its various constituents, who included film companies Palace Pictures and Working

Title plus entertainment giant Polygram, tended to congregate.

Dyke was tempted to regard LIB as a shambles, and it was not hard to see why. In contrast to LWT's high-secrecy approach, LIB leaked like a sieve and was prone to embarrassing accidents. One night they left the door of their Groucho Club room open and were burgled by a drunk who ran off with a couple of mobile phones, but failed to take any documents. But Dyke needed to avoid becoming complacent. For a week he dropped everything else and set out to find out everything he could about LIB. Assuming the role of the newspaper hack he'd once been was second nature to Dyke. He bashed the phones, ringing everyone he knew who might know something about LIB that he didn't. The strategy paid off. By the time LWT's bid team met for the final franchise strategy meeting on 12 April at Hever Castle in Kent, Dyke was confident he had discovered just about all there was to know about Gutteridge and company.

As the discussions progressed, Dyke and the others realized that bidding high for the licence would be unwise, because life afterwards would be one long uphill struggle. 'Who wants to spend the next ten years having nothing left to spend, scrabbling along, making a profit of one or two million?' There was, of course, another reason to bid low. If the 'handcuffed' executives were to reap the benefits of Bland's complex share option scheme, high profits were essential for the share price to reach the key figure of £2.78 in autumn 1993.

At Hever, Dyke and all the other senior executives had to write down how much they thought LWT should bid. The figures averaged between £21–22 million, with a ceiling of £28 million. Both Dyke, who went for £15 million, and Bland thought this was much too high. The team returned to London for further work. Dyke was still not completely certain that LIB would bid against them. Rumours suggested that TVS might make a play for LWT. Dyke wanted more information and needed to find a way of flushing out someone involved in the LIB group. He phoned Tim Bevan, head of Working Title, and offered him a £300,000 development deal in return for a promise that his company would not bid against LWT. Bevan rejected the offer.

Now Dyke and Bland could finalize their bid knowing that LIB would definitely go ahead. Sceptical of LIB's chance of passing the quality threshold, Dyke and Bland decided to bid low, but not so low that the sum would not look 'respectable' in the eyes of the ITC. The figure in the envelope was £7.58 million, personally sealed in wax by Bland with his father's signet ring. As for the Sunrise bid, at the last moment Dyke persuaded his partners to add more than £1 million to their bid because someone had told him that Daybreak would bid a fraction over £30 million. 'I was just talking to someone – someone who was not actually involved in their bid,' Dyke later said. 'The security of the Daybreak bid was not very good. Quite a lot of people knew.'

Up to sixty-five copies of each bid were required by the ITC. Nevertheless, LWT's bid documents had been lavishly produced. The final touch was the insertion of an erratum slip inside the front cover pointing out that the number of programme awards was incorrect: 'Since this document was written we have won one additional award.' Dyke, clowning around despite the gravity of the situation, had insisted on pointing out the 'error' as a joke. For once shunning the limelight, Dyke decided not to deliver the LWT bid in person. Instead he sent company secretary Graham Howell. It was just as well. A double bid masterminded by Richard Branson and David Frost, hoping to seize both the Thames licence in London and Anglia's in Norwich, almost came unstuck by nearly missing the noon deadline when they got locked in a traffic jam near Buckingham Palace caused by the changing of the guard. James Gatward, unlucky to the last, had to revise his plans to deliver TVS's bid in a fleet of heavy-duty security vans because they were too tall to clear the ITC's back entrance. The documents arrived instead in a convoy of Ford Escorts. One man who had deliberately missed the noon deadline was Sir George Russell, the ITC chairman. As the paper mountains had been driven in amidst unprecedented media attention, Russell had spent the morning fishing in Hampshire. He eventually arrived at the ITC carrying two trout.

In their hearts Dyke and his team never really thought they would lose, but it was an anxious summer as they waited for the ITC's verdict, due some time that autumn. From the City's point of view, LWT had never done better. Despite a recession, profits were up by seven per cent, leading the *Financial Times* to note that LWT was 'bucking the gloomy trend' in the economy as a whole. Thirty-six hours before the ITC announced the list of winners and losers, Dyke was in ebullient form at a West London party to mark the retirement of ITN boss David Nicholas. He was so confident of LWT's imminent success that he had already arranged for posters, badges and rosettes to be made proclaiming the station's victory. 'Honestly, Greg,' cautioned Bland, 'you can't do that, I'm too superstitious.' But Dyke was unrepentant. 'Look, if we lose, we are going to have a lot more to worry about that a few wasted poster sites.'

As the hours ticked away Dyke could hardly contain himself, restlessly zooming around the LWT tower, full of nervous energy. The ITC had arranged for all the bidders to be faxed the results at the same time. Dyke stood by the fax machine. Bland was in the building but was so nervous that the moment the fax machine burst into life he had to leave the room. It was later believed that he had been in the lavatory at the crucial moment. He emerged after the ITC fax confirmed that LWT had retained its licence and he heard the cheering. For Dyke it was a double victory. Sunrise had beaten the Carlton-backed Daybreak by less than one and a half million. It had been a close call. Gyngell's TV-am would soon become history. The pink panther had bid a ridiculously low £14.13 million, £20 million less than Sunrise's £34.61.

Dyke toured the building wearing a massive red, white and blue LWT rosette emblazoned with the slogan: 'The Best Showed'. He later said: 'When I die, and I'm looking back over the great days of my life – like the days when the kids were born – then that day is in the top ten.' Throughout the building a huge party was underway. Cilla Black and LWT's other stars posed for endless photographs alongside Dyke and Bland. The duo made a speech heralded by the theme music from *Rocky*. If a silver trophy instead of a document in the company lawyer's safe marked victory in the franchise auction, Dyke would have run a lap of honour with it, like the captain of a winning football team at Wembley. Better than that. LWT, just like Dyke's beloved Manchester United, had 'done the double' – winning two competitions – London Weekend and Breakfast – at the same time. That's how he looked at it.

But not everyone was so cheerful. Dyke's scheduling supremo, Warren Breach, couldn't help but wonder where the insane process of the auction was leading. He felt sorry for Richard Dunn and his staff at Thames who were the day's biggest losers, outbid by Carlton despite more than two decades of producing and broadcasting some of the best television in the world and operating as a profitable and decently run company. On hearing of Thames' humiliating defeat, he had sent a bottle of champagne to Dunn at his HQ on Euston Road, about a mile or so away on the other side of the river. Breach had enclosed a note saying: 'There but for the grace of God . . .'. The more he thought about it, the more he felt sick. Lots of people would now be looking for jobs; their whole way of life turned upside down, their children's future put in the balance because of what had been decided by a quango. It was unjust, it was stupid, spiteful.

Seeing that Breach looked out of sorts, Dyke bounded over and banged him on the shoulder. 'Why are you looking so miserable, you old fart? We've just won!'

Breach shook his head. 'I'm not sure we've won anything, Greg,' he replied. 'These are not good times we're heading for.'

# 18.
# Who Wants to be a Millionaire?

LWT emerged triumphant from the 1991 franchise round and took its place in an ITV system that had been turned inside-out. All around ITV there were changes that seemed to favour LWT, now routinely described by analysts as the 'powerhouse' of the ITV system. Dyke and Bland's manic cost-cutting had produced extra revenues of up to £40 million a year which, at one point, they had feared they might have to pay over to the Treasury to keep their licence. Now most of that money was flowing straight on to the bottom line, providing even more money for expensive programming – sports rights, big movies and home-produced drama – that Dyke knew was key to winning the ratings war with the BBC and keeping the threat from Sky at bay.

And so by the winter of 1991/92 Dyke found himself in an exceptionally strong position. Invincible, almost. Boosted by his strategy of running back-to-back 'double drama' on Sunday evening, ITV was thrashing the BBC in the weekend ratings war. The TVS-originated *Ruth Rendell Mysteries* were regularly attracting audiences of 14 million. LWT's own production, *London's Burning*, was getting 15 million. On some Sunday evenings ITV was winning almost 60 per cent of the audience, with the BBC down to well under a third. The BBC had counter-attacked with its own version of ITV's Dyke-inspired feel-good 'quality drama'. But the corporation's main weapon, a new drama called *Trainer*, set in the world of horse racing, managed an audience of only 8 million. '*Trainer* is dead!' Dyke boasted after the show's launch. 'We are ahead because we are out-BBC-ing the BBC.'

# Citizen Greg

In the summer of 1991 Dyke's growing importance in the business beyond the confines of LWT was acknowledged when he succeeded Thames' boss Richard Dunn as chairman of ITV's ruling body, the ITV Council. Not everyone had wanted him in such a high-profile and essentially political role. Some wondered how buttoned-up Whitehall civil servants and Tory broadcasting ministers – assuming he could get past security (since, with his beard and general dress style, he often looked like a stray terrorist or visiting football hooligan) – would take to Dyke turning up and, quite possibly, shouting 'bollocks' at them. Dyke's mother was horrified when one night she saw him on a TV news report filmed alongside the rest of ITV's top brass. They were all wearing immaculate suits and ties. Her boy, meanwhile, was clad in jeans and faded denim shirt, like some sort of labourer dragged off the nearest building site. But after his time at Harvard and, especially, after the great triumph of the franchise round, some of the other ITV managing directors showed him a little more respect, realizing that he could turn on the good manners and charm as easily as he could change his clothes – should the circumstances require it.

Unsurprisingly, Dyke's approach to getting ITV to work as one united front sometimes tended to be heavy-handed rather than diplomatic. The first people to complain about Dyke's forthright approach were the association's own staff. This was not surprising since he immediately moved to sack 120 of them, including the director, on the grounds that they were bureaucrats and therefore not needed. Dyke later explained that while previous ITV chairmen, including Dunn, had aimed for consensus among the constituent companies, he saw the job as being more about 'banging people on the head' until they were finally prepared to work as a single unit. In this ambition Dyke was helped by the statutory creation of an ITV Network Centre and Central Scheduler, which ended for good the horse-trading and rows about who should make what, armed with a £500 million annual budget provided by the companies. For the first time ever, ITV's programmes would be commissioned solely on merit, regardless of who made them.

Some people said that Dyke had been encouraged to take on the job of running the Network Centre himself, and he was believed to be keen until Bland told him bluntly that it was not on. He needed him to look after LWT, and anyway, if he left he would break the terms of the 'golden handcuffs' and, with the way the LWT share price was rocketing, stood to lose several million pounds. Dyke explained the situation by telling the papers he didn't want the job because 'I actually felt I'd enjoy myself more running a profitable broadcasting company'. Instead Dyke steered Granada's Andrew Quinn into the post of the Network Centre's first chief executive. Dyke had been impressed by the way Quinn had kept Granada on course during the convulsions after its much respected boss, David Plowright, was sacked by new chairman Gerry Robinson after a boardroom coup.

Dyke and Quinn's most pressing concern was to find someone who could become the Network Centre's first director. The rumour spread that Michael Grade, now successfully running a more commercial Channel Four, would be ideal. But Dyke had his own man – Marcus Plantin, his own successor as director of programmes at LWT. Despite the obvious accusation that it was an LWT stitch-up, the appointment went ahead.

But on another even more contentious issue, Dyke did not get his own way. For years ITV's more commercially-minded executives had wanted to move the network's flagship news programme, *News At Ten*, out of its eponymous 10pm slot. The reason was that *News at Ten* screwed up the whole schedule. The regulators' 'family viewing' watershed meant that most movies could not start until 9pm, which meant interrupting the film halfway through to show the news. Dyke and others thought the arrangement belonged to a time when there were fewer channels. Shifting the show to earlier or later in the evening would enable ITV to run non-stop entertainment programmes throughout prime time, opening up a slot to show more 'adult' movies between 9pm and 10.30pm. But moving it was bound to result in a run-in with the Independent Television Commission, the new and far weaker regulatory body which had replaced the old IBA at the time of the franchise auction.

When the new licences kicked in on 1 January 1993, Dyke immediately ditched the previously ring-fenced Sunday evening 'God Slot', bringing to an end the corporeal existence of Sir Harry Secombe's *Highway*. Despite much outrage, the regulators no longer had the power to stop him. Getting rid of *News At Ten* was the next logical step in making ITV's schedule more competitive, thus doing everything possible to keep revenue levels high at a time when rivals were beginning to erode ITV's dominance of the broadcasting market. Dyke and his opposite number at Carlton, Nigel Walmsley, were reported to be leading the campaign to move *News At Ten*. The plan was discussed at ITV's annual strategy meeting in June, with the change lined up for the autumn. The preferred time for the new bulletin was 6.30pm.

But Dyke and his colleagues had misjudged the impact that attempting to move *News At Ten* would have on the chattering classes. The politicians were furious. MPs hardly ever watched TV, but they loved appearing on it. They realized the huge value, particularly during election campaigns, of being able to communicate directly on a nightly basis with the ITV audience, many of whom relied on *News At Ten* for their daily updates from Westminster and Whitehall. Often key votes in the House of Commons took place at around 10.15pm, enabling *News At Ten* to report the story live. Prime Minister John Major protested in person to the ITC about the proposed change: 'I am particularly concerned that one of the strengths of the ITV network, the provision of authoritative news pro-gramming, may be seriously impaired if the main evening news is not part of the schedule,' he wrote. Labour leader John Smith also opposed the move. Even the Archbishop of Canterbury, not exactly Dyke's biggest fan after the dumping of *Highway*, joined in the row.

In July Dyke, as chairman of the ITV Council, was hauled before the National Heritage Select Committee, the parliamentary body that deals with broadcasting. The committee's waspish chairman, Labour MP Gerald Kaufman, accused Dyke and ITV of putting profits before programme quality. Dyke adopted the bull-in-a-china-shop approach. But faced with such united and wide-ranging opposition, ITV caved in.

Dyke felt bruised and betrayed by the row. He later claimed that Granada had driven through the proposal, after being pressured by Carlton. 'I know that, because I was lobbied,' he said during his Edinburgh Festival MacTaggart lecture in August 1994. 'In the furore that followed, both Granada, under their chief executive Gerry Robinson, and Carlton, under chairman Michael Green, disappeared without trace from the public debate. Both had PR men out their telling journalists and politicians that it wasn't their company's idea. Michael Green even went around telling all and sundry that the decision had been taken by low-level executives, which was an odd way of describing his managing director and director of programmes.'

The Brave New World of British TV, freed from old-style, paternalist regulation and mindful of its need to keep the City sweet, was turning out to be just as divided by competing factions as the old system. As Dyke was discovering, the network's new leaders like Granada's Gerry Robinson and Carlton's Michael Green were completely different from the kind of people who used to run ITV in the Seventies and Eighties.

If Dyke felt stitched up by his colleagues over *News At Ten*, the real battle for power in ITV was only just beginning – and it would have disastrous consequences for Greg Dyke and LWT.

In May 1993, the 'golden handcuffs' share option scheme which, according to some, had prevented Dyke from taking the job as head of the Network Centre, matured. Dyke had bought his block of shares in 1989 at 83p per share. The terms of the scheme meant that Dyke and the fifty-four other senior managers who took part could cash the shares when the share price reached 278p and stayed higher than this value for twenty consecutive working days. This happened on 7 May, by which time the value had risen to 385p – giving Dyke a profit of over £5 million, which he was entitled to cash later in September. As a union official, Dyke had played a part in winning a legendary 75 per cent pay increase. The share option pay-out was much better than that. It represented an increase of about 2500 per cent in the value of his original stake.

The implications of the deal had been lost on many

people at the time. Some had even refused to take part. But now that the scheme had performed better than even Bland had dared to hope, there was a tidal wave of criticism and bad publicity. The tone was set in the utterly sober and restrained columns of the *Financial Times*. The initials LWT, the paper said, now stood for 'Lottery Winning Ticket'. The paper thought that 'managers' rewards are out of all proportion to the risks they ran or effort they expended'.

One of the most heartfelt attacks came from Roger Bolton, one of the country's leading television current affairs journalists. Bolton had run BBC1's *Nationwide* when it had been in direct competition with Dyke's *Six O'Clock Show* for early Friday evening ratings in the 1980s. He had then gone on to head-up factual programmes at Thames TV and had found himself out of a job when Thames lost its licence in the same process that had now made the LWT top brass millionaires.

'I see former colleagues,' Bolton wrote in *Televisual* magazine, 'stalwarts of union campaigns for equal pay, reduced differentials and industrial democracy, becoming millionaires by cutting staff wages and sacking large numbers of their employees. It has become a matter of "how many people did you sack before breakfast today, daddy?".'

Inside LWT the atmosphere in many parts of the building was poisonous, made all the more dramatic because Dyke and Bland had always prided themselves on involving the staff and insisting that they were all part of one big happy family. Every summer Bland had laid on a garden party in the grounds of his baronial mansion near Winchester for all the managers, their wives and children. Granada might have put *Brideshead Revisited* on the screen, but this was the real thing – complete with lunch marquees, croquet, cricket and tennis. The wine would flow and Bland would mingle, a model of charm and hospitality (Dyke would spend most of the day flinging himself around as wicket keeper or looking after his kids, with Sue saying, not unreasonably, 'I've taken care of them all week – now it's your turn.').

Now, in some parts of the building, people could feel a sheer, cold hatred. Many understood the rationale for the handcuffs – helping to win back the franchise by giving managers an incentive to stay in place – but there was genuine astonishment that the pay-out was so big. Many incorrectly thought that the money was somehow being paid out of profits or company revenues, instead of the increase in stock market value. When this was explained, there was real anger that the workforce had not received a single penny from the soaring share price, linked as it was to winning the franchise back.

The case was summed up by Daniel Wiles, who had worked with Dyke as a director on *The Six O'Clock Show*. As elected staff representative, he claimed in the LWT in-house journal *Vision* that he had been 'besieged by outraged employees' who wanted to know the criteria for including the particular fifty-four people who were about to hit the jackpot. They had been told that the scheme was needed to lock in top talent during the period of the franchise round. But why then had people like finance director Peter McNally and Roy Van Gelder been included in the scheme when they were so close to retirement? They were now leaving the company with almost £4 million between them. And why had Mike Southgate, the managing director of the London Studios (and Dyke's Cost-Cutter General) been included when it was known that the main franchise rivals were not planning (or able) to set up studio complexes and would therefore not be looking to head-hunt him? There was little sense and no justice in it.

LWT had retained its franchise because its rival, London Independent Broadcasting, had bid more but failed to pass the quality threshold. In common with others, Wiles thought LWT had triumphed because of the programme-makers. Why had they not been included, especially people like features and current affairs editor Trevor Phillips and drama producer Jeff Pope, both mentioned in LWT's franchise bid document as crucial to the station's future plans? Dyke defended the scheme by pointing out the risks that people had taken. But he admitted that the cut-off point for inclusion was 'arbitrary'.

Eventually the staff organized a petition calling for a share of the spoils. Dyke was moved and suggested a voluntary scheme. This involved managers contributing a minimum of one per cent of their pay-out, rising to 3 per cent for those who had received more than a million. This created a pot of £2.4 million to be distributed as bonuses worth around £2000 each. Dyke personally contributed about £200,000.

Bland wrote a cheque for £250,000, making it clear that staff had absolutely no legal or moral entitlement to the money. Bland explained to journalists: 'I made it clear that if anyone put a petition on my desk I would not sign a cheque for tuppence ha'penny – the motive was generosity, not guilt.'

In contrast to Dyke's more shamefaced and slightly sheepish approach, Bland handled the criticism by confronting it directly. 'I'm a bloody good chairman and I deserve every penny,' he boomed at journalists.

# 19.
# Sick as a Parrot

In the early hours of Monday, 18 May 1992, Greg Dyke found himself in the living room of his Twickenham house stuffing letters into envelopes. Sue had gone to bed hours earlier and Dyke had only Trevor East of ITV sport for company. 'Now I know why I became chief executive,' Dyke said. 'So I can sit up all night folding up bits of paper and licking envelopes. Great!'

Dyke and East were exhausted. Three days earlier they had made a confidential bid of £235 million to secure rights to show the newly-formed football Premier League on ITV. It was a huge sum – ten times more than ITV had paid in the past for football. The arrival of Sky TV, which was also bidding huge sums, had put the price up, and it had fallen to Dyke, as ITV's head of sport, to decide how much ITV should offer to get the rights. Sky, owned by Rupert Murdoch and run by Sam Chisholm, a ferocious antipodean deal-maker, would be tough rivals, Dyke thought. But he reckoned he had the measure of them. In a way it was a re-run of the ITV franchise round of the previous year. The stakes were not quite as high, but it was another poker game. And Dyke was ITV's poker-player extraordinaire, the steely-nerved double-winner of the franchise round.

Dyke and East had presented their bid in person to a gathering of football club chairmen at White's Hotel in London on Thursday. They were confident and, some thought, a little too pleased with themselves, as they announced the £235 million bid. The sub-text, according to those present, was that there was no way Sky – which at the time was on the verge of bankruptcy, had hardly any subscribers and was regarded with derision by many in the industry – could compete with that. At the same time, some of the smaller clubs involved – the likes of Chelsea and Crystal Palace – thought there was an element of swagger in the way the ITV team presented themselves. Dyke and East were at pains to point out that they were paying a lot of money, but had a long list of things they wanted in return – changes in kick-off times to suit TV schedules, a lot of picking and choosing over which clubs would have their matches screened . . . it was, some thought, as though ITV was buying the football industry, making it just another subsidiary.

After the meeting, and despite these qualms, Dyke and East were pretty certain that their bid had been accepted. The chairmen of all the Premier League football clubs were due to meet at the Royal Lancaster Hotel the following Monday and vote for one of the two bids to be put before them. Dyke had got the chairmen of all the big clubs – Manchester United, Arsenal, Liverpool – on side. The only club thought to be predisposed towards Sky was Spurs, where Rupert Murdoch's commercial partner Alan Sugar had just beaten off the strongly pro-ITV Robert Maxwell in a takeover battle. But Sugar's involvement was only a slight worry. East even claimed to have shaken hands on the deal with Premier League chief executive Rick Parry, after taking him out to a boxing match in Manchester. East was so confident that the deal was in the bag that he had gone off on holiday.

Then on Friday afternoon Dyke found out that his bid had been leaked to Sky, who were prepared to offer more for a slightly different deal. There was a real chance that a majority of club chairmen, especially those in charge of the smaller clubs who stood to get more from Sky than ITV had ever given them, would vote for Sky unless Dyke added another £30 million to the ITV bid. Dyke phoned East and told him to return to London at once. The two men spent the weekend phoning round ITV chief executives and chairmen, trying to raise the extra money. Dyke had argued the case for spending heavily on football, backed up by ITV's new reliance on extensive audience research. But some still suspected that this was another instance of LWT leading the other companies by the nose or, more importantly, the wallet.

By midnight on Sunday, Dyke and East had raised an extra £27 million. They then revised their bid. To avoid another leak to Sky they decided to put the increased bid in the form of a confidential letter to be delivered personally into the hands of the club chairmen as they arrived at the Royal Lancaster at 8am on Monday morning. That was why Dyke and East were stuffing envelopes in the middle of the night and cursing whoever it was who had leaked their original bid.

Dyke had been one of the first executives in ITV to be alert to the danger posed to the existing system by satellite and cable TV. James Gatward at TVS had been interested in the commercial possibilities and had become involved by investing in a company that made satellite receiver equipment. A realization that ITV was unlikely to be able to hold on to its monopoly of TV advertising once cable and satellite had got off the ground had been the main reason he had diversified at TVS, buying US programme distribution companies and studios which, he believed, would grow rich supplying the hundreds – even thousands – of new channels that would come onstream around the world in the 1980s and '90s. Dyke had watched all this with interest, bolstered by his own experience of the US, where pay-TV was already well-established.

Sky and the cable TV operators had already been

sniffing around ITV, offering decent money to buy rights to repeat popular programmes on cable or satellite, in order to build a subscriber base. Some in the business had been delighted to discover this new source of apparently free extra income. But Dyke, as chairman of the ITV council, had urged extreme caution. He had seen how cable TV had taken away nearly a third of the American networks' audience not by making their own pro-grammes, but by buying and screening the networks' old programmes, building an audience, reaping extra subscription cash and coming back to the networks for more and more programming, bought on less and less advantageous terms. 'The American networks have been killed by their own products,' Dyke warned a conference. 'We are ten years behind them, so we can learn the lessons.' The most important thing was for the ITV companies to license their back catalogue instead of selling screening rights outright. The pay-TV operators would pay more money for total rights, but it was better, Dyke said, to take less money up front and get paid every time the show was repeated on one of the hundreds of new pay stations.

Dyke was also one of the first to realize that cable and satellite operators would need to buy the rights to live sport – and especially football – if they were ever going to get enough subscribers to build their business. After securing *The Big Match* for ITV, Dyke told a special session at the Edinburgh TV festival that he had paid 'about £5 million more than football actually merited' but that it was worth it to see off the threat from satellite TV. 'BSB wanted to show forty-four games a season, which is about the only reason why people might be persuaded to buy a dish,' he said. The satellite threat had then been nipped in the bud – for the time being.

But Dyke had made a lot of enemies among the chairmen of the smaller clubs, who had hated his plan to set up a new league in cahoots with a minority of rich clubs. The BBC was also furious, because Dyke's deal with the league spelled the end of *Match of the Day*. Industry sages like Paul Bonner later went on record to say that Dyke had injected an element of greed into the management of the game which he would later regret. But others said that Dyke had once again been years ahead of his time, spotting the way that television sports rights would go through the roof as pay-TV started to get off the ground. Analysts noted that rights to screen the 'ITV 10' would have been worth at least £100 million a year a decade after Dyke was proposing to pay less than £10 million to get it off the ground.

Without football, the loosely managed and free-spending BSB had failed to get anything like enough subscribers to become viable. It was soon effectively bankrupt and was forced into a merger with another and much more ruthless satellite operator – Rupert Murdoch's Sky TV. Sky had been around since the early 1980s but had failed to make much impact and was, like BSB, losing a fortune until Murdoch pulled off the masterstroke of hiring Chisholm to push through the merger with BSB. The merged company, British Sky Broadcasting, was formed in 1991 and immediately went on the attack, attempting to buy Hollywood movies and, most importantly, live football.

By 1991 Dyke's *Big Match* contract with the football league was coming up for renewal. There had been further upheavals inside the football league, where the first division clubs had decided to adopt a version of Dyke and Scholar's original superleague plan. But instead of the ten clubs proposed by Dyke, the twenty leading clubs resigned from the existing 92-club, four divisions football league and formed their own Premier League. The spur was the impending 1992 TV contract negotiations. The twenty Premier League clubs wanted to sign an exclusive deal with a TV company, keeping all the money for themselves instead of sharing it with the lower league clubs.

Dyke was very much in favour of the Premier League, since it was a step in the direction of the superleague he had always wanted. But it also offered opportunities to Chisholm and Sky. While Dyke started getting into detailed talks with 'The Big Five' on the future shape of the TV deal, Chisholm and his people began to lobby the larger group of small clubs, working a rich seam of resentment against the 'arrogance' of the big clubs and ITV.

Greg Dyke first met Chisholm over lunch at Langan's Brasserie in the West End of London in the spring of 1992. Chisholm was proposing a joint Sky–ITV offer to the clubs. ITV would keep *The Big Match* and Sky would show a second match, probably on Monday nights. If they competed with each other for all the rights, Chisholm reportedly said, 'these bastards in football will rob us' by organizing an auction. Dyke thought this was a sign of weakness on Sky's part. The broadcaster was desperate to get football, but was carrying massive debts, had hardly any subscribers and simply did not have the money to organize a bid even on the scale of the £40 million offered by the old BSB operation last time around. Dyke knew that Chisholm never made a move without the total approval of Murdoch. And sharing the rights to football was not Murdoch's style. If he wanted football and had the money to buy it, he wouldn't have sent Chisholm to see the head of ITV, pleading for a joint deal. He would just get his chequebook out.

# Citizen Greg

Murdoch was a standard hate figure in the UK TV industry, especially at LWT. Some still quivered when they remembered the time in the early 1970s when Murdoch had been on the LWT board as a minority shareholder. He would have bought the company if it were not for regulations that prevented newspaper proprietors from owning more than 25 per cent of ITV companies. Having to choose between giving up his stake in LWT or selling the *Sun* and the *News of the World*, he had decided to stick to newspapers.

Now he was again trying to get into British television, doubtless with a plan to dominate it as effectively as he dominated the newspaper scene, by the typically tacky back-door route of satellite television. Dyke shared the general revulsion against Murdoch's *Sun*, particularly intense in the football industry in the early Nineties after the paper's coverage of the Hillsborough football disaster, blaming the 92 dead Liverpool fans for their own deaths and, for good measure, accusing the survivors of pissing on rescue workers and robbing the corpses of the dead.

But at the same time Dyke admired Murdoch for his business acumen and even felt common cause with Murdoch's incessant criticism of British TV as being out of touch with the aspirations of the mass market. Dyke himself was on record as saying that the TV production process had been 'captured by an unrepresentative intellectual elite' – or as Murdoch put it in private, a bunch of 'prickly toffee-nosed pommie pooftahs'. A couple of years earlier Murdoch had given the MacTaggart lecture at the Edinburgh TV festival, castigating British television as uncommercial and in the grip of a self-serving Oxbridge elite. Dyke had responded by saying: 'It's quite flattering to think that anyone could describe me as part of an elite who doesn't give a toss about what the public wants, and that I run it just for my own gratification.'

Dyke told Chisholm that he would think about a joint bid. Sky was a nuisance – Chisholm was bound to put in as big a bid as he could manage, and that might put up the cost of renewing the contract. The alternative – a cartel with Sky to prevent a bidding war – would keep the price down. But if he went for it, ITV would be helping get pay-TV off the ground and that meant the long-term cost would be enormous, as the American networks had already found. The bottom line, Dyke thought, was this: 'Anyone who does a deal with Rupert Murdoch gets screwed in the end.' Eventually he told Chisholm that he wasn't interested in making a joint bid to get the football rights.

Rebuffed in this way, Chisholm got to work lobbying the smaller clubs, promising them more money than they would get from ITV and working on the resentment they felt against the big clubs and ITV. He soon had enough 'small club' votes in the bag to win a majority within the new Premier League. The big clubs, who needed exposure to a mass TV audience, were more of a problem from Sky's point of view. There was a danger that they would form a breakaway with Dyke and ITV and, as Chisholm knew, a Premier League without Manchester United or Arsenal taking part was next to worthless. But at least one of the Big Five – Tottenham – was likely to defect to Sky now that Murdoch's business partner, Alan Sugar, had bought the club.

Chisholm countered this danger by getting the BBC on board. Executives at the Corporation were still fuming at the way Dyke had brushed them aside in 1988, signing an exclusive deal preventing the BBC running its weekly *Match of the Day* highlights programme. Chisholm now offered the BBC the chance to get *Match of the Day* back as part of what was, in effect, a joint Sky–BBC bid against ITV. This was to prove a decisive move. The big clubs might not be keen to go with Sky, but the return of *Match of the Day* would give them the mass exposure they needed. If that was put together with a financial offer that at least matched ITV, then it would be an offer they could not refuse.

ITV and Sky were asked to make final presentations to club chairmen at White's Hotel, London, on Thursday, 14 May 1992 before they gathered to vote on the rival offers on the following Monday. ITV were offering £235 million for thirty live games a year for five years. The money would be paid to the Premier League, which was then free to share the money between the clubs. Sky made a presentation, but not a final bid. Somehow during the day of the presentation Chisholm got hold of details of the ITV bid and went away over the weekend to make arrangements to better it before the chairmen met again on Monday to take a final vote.

Dyke and Trevor East spent the weekend phoning round ITV chairmen to up their bid. ITV's 'federal' nature had been a handicap, especially when dealing with a ruthless competitor like Sky with its single controlling stakeholder – Rupert Murdoch – able to make a decision in seconds. But as Dyke set off for LWT – where he was due to open the refurbished staff canteen – and East set off to meet the chairmen at the Royal Lancaster, handing each a personalized envelope as they arrived in the hotel lobby, they reckoned they had done just enough.

A little later that morning East phoned Dyke to tell him that he had handed out the envelopes, that there was no sign of Chisholm's people, and that he thought that the deal was in the bag. What East did not know was that Rick

Parry, the chief executive of the Premier League, had immediately phoned Chisholm at Sky's headquarters, telling him there had been an unexpected, new and improved bid from ITV. Chisholm, in a panic, asked Parry for time to make a response. Parry delayed the start of the meeting for an hour while Chisholm phoned Murdoch in New York, rousing him from his bed at 4am local time, and got approval to add another £30 million to Sky's bid. This took the combined value of what Sky and the BBC were offering to £304 million over five years. Chisholm faxed the new offer to Parry, who put it to the club chairmen for consideration against ITV's offer of £262 million for a smaller number of live games and no highlights package.

Alan Sugar, of Tottenham, had meanwhile also seen the revised ITV bid and, apparently unaware that Parry had already tipped off Sky, rushed out into the hotel foyer where he was overheard yelping the phrase 'blow them out of the water!' into the receiver. When Sugar returned to his chair around the meeting table, he saw that the Sky bid had been increased. A vote was taken on whether Sugar should be allowed to vote on the offers as he had a vested interest in Sky winning, being the manufacturer of all the extra satellite dishes that were likely to be sold as a result of the rights going to Sky rather than ITV. It was agreed that Sugar could vote. The result of the vote on the offers was 14 to 6 in favour of Sky with two clubs abstaining. All of the 'big five' clubs voted for ITV, with the exception – as expected – of Sugar and Tottenham.

Dyke heard the result back at LWT headquarters. He went ballistic – firing off angry press statements against Parry for his supposed collusion with Murdoch, and against Sugar for his 'blow them out of the water' phone call which, it was at first assumed, was how and why Chisholm had upped his bid at the last minute.

But most of Dyke's fury was reserved for the BBC which, he said, had acted like 'Murdoch's poodle', enabling Sky to secure the rights by providing mass exposure for the clubs through the *Match of the Day* Saturday highlights package. 'They are fighting the battles of the Seventies, when they should be fighting the battles of the Nineties,' he said. 'They think that ITV is their main competitor, when they ought to be looking at their dropping audience figures in homes with dishes and then wonder why they are making a deal with satellite.' Dyke's theory was supported by ITC chairman Sir George Russell, who said: 'Had the BBC not taken the decision of going in with Sky, I don't believe the Premier League would have gone with Sky. On *Match of the Day* all the hoardings give major exposure to sponsorship. It would never have worked without the BBC.' Dyke later said: 'The single most important thing Sky did was football. It turned them round.' Between May and August 1992, when the season started, Sky signed up nearly one million extra subscribers, bringing in additional gross annual revenues of around £300 million.'We got sackfuls of mail arriving everyday,' Chisholm later remembered. 'It was like Christmas every day.'

Dyke and ITV were left with the distinctly inferior consolation prize of Nationwide League football, featuring the less well-supported teams who had not been included in the Premiership. Sky, booming on the back of its Premiership coverage, eventually hoovered up even that, along with the vast majority of the premium sports catalogue. Chisholm's personal victory over Dyke turned Sky from a loss-making disaster, which at one point threatened to sink the entire Murdoch empire, into a shining financial success.

For Greg Dyke it was the first really major setback in his career as a TV executive. In terms of the footballing analogies he liked to use in the boardroom, he had been to Wembley for the TV industry's equivalent of the Cup Final only to be completely outplayed by unfancied lower-league rivals. He was determined that if he ever had to tangle with Murdoch and Chisholm again, he would emerge as the winner.

# 20.
# Civil War

Every year at Christmas Greg Dyke liked to dress up as Santa Claus and hand out the presents at LWT's children's party. Some of his senior colleagues thought that someone as short as Dyke would realize how ridiculous he looked in a bright red Father Christmas outfit and allow someone else to play at being Santa. But Dyke, who loved being the centre of attraction, always insisted on his annual performance. Christmas 1993 was different. First of all, the golden handcuffs pay-out had poisoned the atmosphere and even Dyke realized that dishing out cheap trinkets from a sack to people whose work had enabled him to trouser several million pounds might not be the most sensible thing to do.

But there was another reason why Dyke was not in a position to play Santa Claus this time round. While his own kids were tucking into the mince pies and pulling crackers at LWT's children's party, Dyke was deep in conference at an emergency meeting with Cazenove, the stockbrokers. The crisis that was engulfing LWT had forced Dyke to put family life on hold. He'd even cancelled a family trip to Jamaica. A week or so earlier on 16 December, following months of speculation and financial manoeuvring, Dyke's old enemy, Granada, had launched a £660 million hostile takeover bid for LWT. Unless Dyke could come up with the deal of his life, he could soon be hanging up his LWT Santa Claus outfit for good.

Not that Dyke seemed unduly worried. He genuinely believed that financially efficient companies like LWT did not get taken over. 'I like a crisis. That's why I did so well at TV-am,' he once told a journalist. 'It sorts people out. I like a difficult time, then winning in the end.' Dyke and his equally confident boss, Christopher Bland, the LWT chairman, had been taken completely off guard by Granada's attack. Dazzled by their own success in the franchise round and their multimillion-pound bonanza in the 'golden handcuffs' share deal, they now regarded themselves as invulnerable. They'd played the system and come out on top. To some, it had started to look as if a degree of complacency had begun to creep into the LWT boardroom. Some thought that Dyke's newly found wealth had changed him a bit. There was even more of a swagger now.

Dyke had always been direct and fearless about offending people, but now he was more outspoken than ever. It was well known that Dyke had ambitions to take over Yorkshire Television, in which LWT had taken a minority stake that May, once the rules on ITV ownership were relaxed. Speaking at a Royal Television Society dinner in Leeds, attended by Yorkshire TV people, Dyke had badly misjudged his audience when, introducing the company's new chairman, industry veteran Ward Thomas, he quipped: 'And just to prove there is life after death, here is Ward Thomas.' The remark went down like a concrete duck. Then Dyke put more backs up by referring to another boss, Yorkshire's John Fairley: 'John has built up a tremendous company here, one of the great production centres of British television . . . and to have done it all from a box at York races is a truly remarkable achievement.' Members of the audience wondered if Dyke's success was beginning to go to his head.

Yorkshire, famous for its David Jason dramas and long-running soap, *Emmerdale Farm*, was considered vulnerable in City circles since it had bought Tyne Tees

Television in 1992 and now had to pay annual fees of £63 million for the two licences. Dyke had been thrilled when LWT had picked up 14.9 per cent of Yorkshire at what he thought was the knockdown price of £2 a share. 'It's a steal,' he gleefully told his managers at one of his regular Wednesday breakfast meetings. 'We've got one over on Granada. They've missed a real bargain and they don't realize it.' But when a few months later Granada had been put under the control of new chief executive Gerry Robinson, he spotted what LWT was up to and turned his sights on Dyke and Bland.

From the City's point of view, Dyke could still do no wrong as the station's share price ploughed ahead, despite a weak economy. This gung-ho mood was reflected at a company strategy weekend at the beginning of the year. A lot of discussion had been taken up with Dyke's desire to buy Yorkshire, but there had been a remarkable lack of talk at the conference over what might happen if one of the other big ITV companies mounted a bid for LWT. Also, little thought had been given to the legal implications of owning both Yorkshire and Tyne Tees under the current ownership restrictions. This blinkered perspective on what was taking place behind the scenes in an ITV where much of the running was now being made by people like Carlton's Michael Green, who regarded television as a business like any other, had been blown apart in the summer when Granada first pounced.

On 29 June Granada bought 14.9 per cent of LWT, the maximum it was allowed to buy at a single go without triggering a full takeover bid, paying the premium price of 500p per share. Robinson had acquired the shares from Mercury Asset Management, a big institutional investor that had large stakes in both LWT and Granada. LWT had just been subjected to the financial equivalent of Pearl

Harbor. On hearing that Robinson was stalking LWT, Bland immediately called Dyke, who was in Holland on a business trip. It was later reported that Dyke had been explaining to his Dutch hosts how LWT was set to become the powerhouse of a new 'national' ITV company at the moment Bland's call came through. His mood, it was said, had changed abruptly. Later that day Bland called in his senior managers to give them the news. He looked genuinely shaken as he explained what Granada had done.

Dyke and Bland wondered if Robinson's move was a strategic or speculative investment, an attempt by Granada to profit from LWT's soaring share price and buy representation on the LWT board, enabling him to keep an eye on things. The thought was quickly dismissed. The price paid – 500p a share – was too high for that. 'It was clear from the moment he bought his stake that Robinson would make a takeover bid the minute he was allowed to and that we would be fighting him off,' Bland later remembered. The national heritage secretary, Peter Brooke, was due to announce his decision on further relaxation of ITV ownership rules in November.

The minute Robinson's brokers had confirmed the purchase of the LWT shares, he phoned the LWT chairman. Bland simply said, 'Congratulations.' There was no question of Bland giving Robinson a seat on the board. A couple of weeks later, Granada bought another 5 per cent of LWT's stock, taking the total stake to 20 per cent – the maximum allowed by the regulators. The shares had been bought through an intermediary and Robinson phoned the next day to say, 'That was us.' Bland offered talks, but Robinson declined. Robinson was taking a gamble. Brooke had changed the rules to allow one company to hold two ITV franchises. But if Granada was to buy LWT further relaxation would be needed.

# Citizen Greg

If the expected changes did not take place Granada would have spent the best part of £100 million buying shares at well over the going rate to get a 20 per cent stake in a company he would never be able to control. But if Brooke would allow one ITV company to own two of the 'Big Five' franchises, then Granada would immediately launch a full takeover bid, offering whatever price, within reason, it took to obtain a controlling stake in LWT.

Bland and Dyke knew that they were in for the fight of their lives. A takeover would make them extremely rich – giving them in cash, rather than on paper, as much as double what they had earned when their golden handcuffs share options had matured a few months earlier. But they were determined to keep control. LWT was their baby – a company that they had totally transformed since taking control. The franchise round, as they saw it, had only been the start. Further deregulation offered all kinds of opportunities for growth and ever greater success and profitability. Dyke would have fought any takeover bid for LWT. The fact that it was Granada, a company he had always despised for what he saw as its arrogance and elitism, made it a needle match. The antagonism that existed between LWT and Granada was deep-rooted. It was not only about south versus north. Their two cultures were completely different. LWT was blatantly commercial and proud of it. Dyke and people like its legendary ad salesman, Ron Miller, thrived on its brash, Cockney wide boy image. To Granada, the oldest ITV company, having been on air since 1956, LWT was a southern upstart who couldn't hold a candle to their distinguished history of blue chip documentaries and dramas that outdid even the BBC.

For Dyke, the contest between LWT and Granada involved personal animosity as well. One of Robinson's first acts had been to sack the station's revered chairman, David Plowright. This had led to outrage in Britain's creative community as dozens of actors, writers and directors publicly denounced Plowright's ousting. Robinson was even sent a fax by John Cleese telling him to: 'Fuck off out of it, you ignorant, upstart caterer' (Robinson had successfully led a management buyout of Compass, Grand Metropolitan's catering and cleaning business), to which Robinson replied, 'Reading between the lines, I think I can safely say I am a bigger fan of yours than you are of mine.' Many of the old guard at Granada had left in disgust, but Dyke's old sparring partner, Steve Morrison, was thriving under the new regime. Some said it was actually Morrison who had persuaded Robinson to bid for LWT.

On 24 November Brooke made his announcement. For once Bland's finely tuned political antennae had failed him. LWT's move for Yorkshire was based on the assumption that individual companies would be able to operate a large number of franchises. The ban on 'cross-ownership' was lifted, as expected, but ITV companies would be allowed a maximum of two franchises, regardless of size. A further restriction remained in place. No single company would be allowed to operate both the weekday and weekend London franchises. This meant that LWT could not carry out its plan to buy the already merged Yorkshire–Tyne Tees, because it would end up with three franchises. Granada was allowed to buy LWT. The way was now clear for Robinson's hostile bid. The financial experts on every broadsheet newspaper except the *Sunday Telegraph* backed Granada to win.

Inside LWT there was fear of Granada, a feeling by some that Bland and Dyke would sell out. Neither of them had said anything in public after Robinson made his initial move. Many read this as meaning that they would grab Granada's money and run. Bland later claimed that he had not responded to Granada's official bid immediately because he was fearful of 'making silly statements'. In reality, Dyke and Bland met Robinson at his mansion in Holland Park, London, to see if they could agree a price. Robinson was offering under 700p a share. Bland and Dyke said they would consider offers above 900p and walked away, thinking that Robinson's bid was so low and LWT's share price performance so strong that they could easily see him off. The next day they got the backing of the LWT board to reject the offer and fight to maintain LWT's independence.

The strategy that Bland put together, and both Bland and Dyke attempted to sell, had two elements. One involved a further and even more brutal round of cost-cutting. This was designed to show the City that LWT really was a company that would do everything it possibly could to promote financial efficiency and keep the share price high. Bland's restructuring had left the company with significant debts that had to be paid back to a strict timetable. The effect left little alternative but to once again take a scythe to LWT's cost base. The other part of the survival package was designed to be offensive and was codenamed Operation Yeoman, because in geographical terms it resembled Oliver Cromwell's Eastern Association military alliance formed during the English Civil War in the 1640s. The idea was to persuade Norwich-based Anglia TV to come on board in a three-way merger. Anglia would take over Tyne Tees, leaving LWT free to capture Yorkshire. That way both LWT and Anglia would end up with two franchises and would therefore seem invulnerable to a takeover from a third. All four companies bordered England's east coast. It was an ingenious plan but, since it required the agreement of three separate groups of shareholders, Operation Yeoman was always going to be complicated.

In December Bland arranged for all the parties and their numerous entourages of merchant bankers, lawyers, consultants and assorted flunkeys to meet at LWT. As the massed ranks of financial and legal experts took their places alongside the TV people around the huge horseshoe-shaped table in the Westminster Room, Bland noticed that Anglia's team, led by managing director David McCall, was late. When they eventually arrived, Bland's short fuse got the better of him. In front of all those present, he gave the Anglia delegation a dressing-down for not being on time. Several of those present thought this an odd way of trying to persuade a commercial rival to join forces with LWT.

This kind of behaviour was all the more damaging to LWT's cause because of Dyke's own shortcomings as a diplomat. It would not be the only time Bland's temper got the better of him as the pressure began to mount. With his greater experience of the City, Bland was more aware of the gravity of the situation than Dyke, who always believed that LWT would triumph. Bland had a notoriously low patience threshold. He expected his staff to be able to produce any information he wanted at very short notice throughout the working day. One afternoon Bland told Dyke that he needed to see director of corporate affairs Barry Cox right away about a press release that needed urgent attention. On being told that Cox was working from home, Bland stormed into Cox's office and furiously went through Cox's files looking for the release, scattering paper everywhere. When Bland was finished, Cox's office resembled the aftermath of a particularly messy burglary.

As the takeover battle reached its final stage, there was some devastating news from Anglia. The company had decided to reject Bland's clumsy advances. Unbeknown to LWT, McCall had also been talking to Clive Hollick, owner of Meridian Broadcasting, which had replaced James Gatward's TVS on LWT's southern flank after winning the southern licence in the franchise auction. Like Carlton's Michael Green and Granada's Gerry Robinson, the ambitious Hollick was one of the new breed of financially astute ITV owners who would come to dominate the network as the decade progressed. Anglia had agreed to sell out to Hollick for a thumping £292 million.

Operation Yeoman was in tatters. In a reversal of the real Civil War, Bland and Dyke's roundheads had been routed and Robinson's cavaliers were advancing for the kill. Bland and Dyke retreated, forced to rely totally on their defensive strategy, the cost-cutting option. Inside the organization, the bitterness which had been felt at the time of the time of the handcuffs payout evaporated. The troops rallied round and prepared for siege warfare.

A specialist financial PR firm called Financial Dynamics was hired to quash the idea that Dyke and Bland were only interested in the money, and put it about that they would fight the take-over to the last breath. Nick Miles of Financial Dynamics later said, 'You only had to look into their eyes to see that they meant it.' The theme of LWT's defensive PR campaign was that, although Granada was offering shareholders a huge sum of money for their shares, LWT was so well run that they would make even more money if they hung on to them. The shares would be worth far more in the future.

Throughout, Robinson ran a clever campaign. He was only interested in one audience – the big City investment funds that owned chunks of shares in LWT and, very often, important stakes in the Granada Group – a much bigger company than LWT and which owned Granada TV as part of its overall leisure-based business. Bland and Dyke constantly emphasized the point that Granada was not performing as well as LWT, adopting the boastful slogan: 'Granada needs LWT but LWT does not need Granada.' This was true, but it did not help their case much. The institutions were, in many cases, more concerned about protecting their investments in Granada. Without a base in the south, and with no other alliances with major companies in the network, Granada TV might become isolated and even less profitable. Robinson encouraged the institutions to think what would happen if the takeover did not go through. Even if it were true that LWT shares would do better if Dyke and Bland got their way and remained independent, the institutions' shares in Granada would go down in value and overall they would be worse off.

Against this background Bland and Dyke launched a charm offensive designed to win over the City. Here both men handled themselves well, each deploying his considerable energies to maximum effect. But they were not always warmly received. Bland's restructuring of the company – the debt for equity deal which had involved buying back shares on a huge scale – had put some noses out of joint in the City. The bad publicity surrounding the golden handcuffs payout did not help either at a time when the financial community was being crucified in the media over its toleration of 'fat cat' remuneration and share deals.

One of their key presentations was made to Carol Galley, the head of Mercury Asset Management, LWT's largest institutional shareholder. Galley, regularly described in the press at the time as the single most powerful woman in the country, was in a position to almost single-handedly decide the fate of the company, and knew more about LWT, Bland and Dyke than many of her peers. She had worked with Bland and his team on the 1989 financial restructuring. Ernie McKnight, head of UK Equities at Scottish Amicable, said that the scale of the options package was 'excessive'. But Galley had been persuaded of the scheme's merits and voted through the changes.

Dyke and Bland now felt confident that Galley and MAM would support them once again. Those votes, on their own, might be enough to make Robinson back off. The value of MAM's 15 per cent in LWT had increased more than sixfold in just three years. The LWT management had a 15 per cent stake and so, together, LWT and MAM had 30 per cent of the shares. MAM's backing would not mean that LWT was home and dry, but it would be a formidable hurdle for Robinson to jump if he wanted control.

The deadline for Robinson to complete his takeover was set for 26 February 1994. His final offer was 748p per share, payable in Granada stock or 686p per share in cash – well short of the insurmountable 900p Dyke and Bland had said they were prepared to accept. The shareholders had to vote on the deal. From early in the morning the results began to roll in. After the franchise round and the news of the handcuffs payout, it was another day of high drama in the LWT tower. For nearly three months, since the launch of the takeover bid, they had felt themselves to be on a war footing, taking on the world and fighting for their lives. Robinson – 'the upstart catering manager' who had grown into a great ogre in people's imagination – was cast in the role of a heartless, cost-cutting bean-counter who would unleash another round of job cuts, clearing out LWT people and replacing them with people he wanted to move down from Granada's Manchester HQ, turning LWT into a branch office of the larger Granada Group empire. Dyke was on the internal PA system from the moment the votes started to come in, still not certain in his own mind which way it would go, but warning: 'If we do lose, don't walk out. Behave yourselves. It won't be so bad.'

Then, mid-way through the morning, there was a terrible blow. Carol Galley's MAM voted to accept the Granada offer. Dyke was later to imply that there had been some sort of deep and conspiratorial collaboration between Galley and Robinson. But there was a more straightforward explanation for her decision. At the time of Robinson's offer, MAM had a larger stake in Granada (17.5 per cent) than in LWT and agreed with Robinson that Granada needed LWT if it was going to thrive in the future. Although Dyke and Bland later criticized Galley, there was nothing personal about it, as far as she was concerned. She had merely balanced the likely damage to her investment in Granada which might result from the takeover not going through against Bland and Dyke's claims of the extra profits to be had from her LWT shares if they stayed independent. Galley calculated that she would be better off by going with Granada.

Even after the MAM hammer blow there still seemed to be a glimmer of hope. By mid-day acceptances appeared to be stuck at around 47 per cent – 4 per cent short of the overall majority of the shares Robinson needed. Dyke and Bland wondered what was going on. Then the most extraordinary episode of the whole day began to unfold. Bland took a phone call from an arbitrageur – one of the breed of high adrenaline stock market players who plunged into contested takeovers hoping to end up with a small but decisive block of shares which could be auctioned to the desperate adversaries. The arbitrageur had about 4 per cent of the stock – enough, it seemed, to represent the casting vote. He gruffly demanded 800p a share – a huge amount but, possibly, a price worth paying to keep control of the company.

Bland and Dyke, already incredibly tense and excited, went into a frenzy, working out whether they could afford to pay the arbitrageur what he wanted, always realizing that he would, in all probability, come back and demand even more if they came up with the cash. Bland was prepared to put a huge chunk of his family fortune on the line and ended up barking at Dyke that he should put all his money on the line as well. Bland later said that for a few hours he and Dyke had behaved 'like a couple of drunken riverboat gamblers'. Bland negotiated a £35 million loan with the bankers Samuel Montague and, with their own money in the pot, were ready to meet the arbitrageur's price. It was fortunate that they did not. At 2.30pm Robinson passed the 51 per cent mark, even without the rogue trader's 4 per cent. Talks with the arbitrageur were called off – he simply did not have enough shares to block the takeover, even if Bland and Dyke were prepared to pay his price. The game was up.

A couple of hours later, Bland took a call from the Granada chairman, Alex Bernstein, to confirm that Granada had 57 per cent of LWT's shares and now controlled the company. Bland conceded defeat and Dyke relayed the bad news around the building. The mood of disappointment was clear. After 25 years on air, LWT had ceased to exist as an independent broadcaster and, as of that moment, became merely a name, a plaque on the door of a building now owned and operated by Granada TV. Outside in the wider world of British TV the industry was dominated by ex-LWT people. The BBC's Director-General John Birt, Channel Four's chief executive Michael Grade and ITV network centre director Marcus Plantin were all former LWT people who had learnt their skills as deal makers and schedulers because they had had to tough it out as programme controllers at LWT.

Personally Dyke was devastated. 'I didn't cry – which was an achievement,' he later said. It was by far and away the blackest moment of his career. Publicly it was business as usual as he attempted to cheer up the troops. He told the staff that nobody would be sacked as a result of the change of ownership. He was considering staying on in some capacity himself. This was a source of comfort. Many people in the company had asked Dyke to remain as a manager if the takeover went ahead. He had become a father figure to many in the company, who imagined that he would somehow be able to protect them if he stayed and continued to work for Granada. In some parts of LWT there was relief that Granada had won. If the City had bought Dyke and Bland's latest bout of belt tightening, these people realized that economies on that scale would have made life extremely miserable at LWT. Dyke and Bland had laid on a drinks party, to be held whatever the result. There were speeches and attempts at jollity. But overall it was a mournful affair, made all the worse because it took the same shape as the ecstatic victory party after the franchise win. People came up to Dyke and congratulated him on putting up a brave fight.

At that week's Wednesday breakfast meeting Robinson turned up. On the surface everything was sweetness and light. Sitting in person at the U-shaped table where, week after week, the people he was now addressing had gossiped and gloated about Granada's shortcomings and internal convulsions, Robinson told LWT's senior management team: 'I have paid a lot of money for this company, but without you people LWT would be worth nothing, it would just be a name.' He said that he wanted them all to stay and assured them, of course, they had a bright future as part of a bigger ITV company with even bigger plans for the future. There was a dignified silence before, finally, Dyke quipped: 'Well, if you think we're so fucking good why are you taking our company away from us?' Robinson just smiled. In retrospect, people thought that Robinson had been brave and considerate in seeing them all in this way. He could have simply sent them their new job descriptions through the post if he had wanted to or, Big Bang-style, told the security guards to keep them out of the building.

There was speculation that Dyke might work for Granada. It was reported that he wanted to run both LWT and Granada's TV division, and report directly to Robinson. But once it became clear that Robinson's right-hand man, Charles Allen, would be put in charge of the TV business, the idea of Dyke staying began to evaporate. In any case, he believed that working for Granada would amount to 'sleeping with the enemy,' as he later put it. For Dyke and the old guard, working for a Granada-led LWT was a way to get nowhere fast – the operation was bound to end up as a satellite: London 'Weakened' Television.

Dyke did the round of press interviews, chat shows and current affairs programmes, trailing from sofa to sofa with his tale of woe. An interviewer on the BBC daytime *Pebble Mill* show asked him what he would do next – was he considering a move to the BBC? 'You must be joking,' Dyke replied. 'The way things stand, Saddam Hussein's got more chance of running the BBC than I have.'

The following Sunday Dyke appeared on BBC1's *Breakfast With Frost*. He bitterly denounced what he regarded as MAM's betrayal of LWT. 'What happened to LWT tells you all you need to know about Mercury Asset Management. The message they have sent out is, "It doesn't matter how successful you are, we will sell you out". It's no way to properly fund an industry.' He added the warning: 'If you wake up to find that MAM has taken an 18 per cent stake in your company – watch out'.

Dyke told the press that LWT had considered parading the station's stars as part of his campaign to save the station from Granada's clutches. He claimed that many had told him in private that they would not sign for Granada. 'I won't say who they were,' Dyke said, 'because I suspect they will sign in the end. What I have learned is that money buys everything in the end.' Dyke subsequently said that government policy on broadcasting had been catastrophic. 'Never,' he wrote, 'has a government done so much damage to one industry in such a short period of time.' He said that he was leaving the television business for the time being and 'perhaps permanently'.

In a parting shot Dyke quipped that he was now just another jobless statistic. He even said that he had registered at Twickenham job centre, describing himself as 'a bald, rich ex-chief executive keen to meet similar, prefer to avoid anyone keen on religious programming, regulators and Conservative politicians.'

At the age of 46, sixteen years after starting out in television, Greg Dyke, for all his millions, was right back where he started, taking long walks in the park, falling into bouts of what, by his own eternally optimistic and energetic standards, counted as depression, imagining that strangers could somehow see the word 'failure' stamped across his brow and once again wondering, 'Whatever happened to me?'

# 21.
# Lord Dyke of Hayes

A small group of ex-LWT film-makers – technical people, sound and lighting experts, cameramen, video editors – are enjoying a quiet pint, lolling around on benches on the wide pavement outside the Ailsa Tavern on the main road near the Thames embankment in Twickenham, staring aimlessly at passers-by. Suddenly one of them spots the familiar bearded and casually-dressed figure of Greg Dyke wandering along the street.

Dyke spots the group and approaches: 'Oi! What are you lot doing? Why aren't you working?'

The technicians, nonplussed, look at each other before one answers, matter-of-factly: 'Because you sacked us, Greg.' Dyke, looking momentarily guilty, dredged his memory before saying: 'Oh yeah . . . you're right . . . I did, didn't I?' And he sat down and had a beer with them.

Dyke had been devastated by the loss of his job at LWT. Just as winning back the franchise had been one of the greatest days of his life – a moment ranking alongside the birth of his children – leaving the South Bank tower had been one of the lowest. He had made a personal fortune of at least £7 million from the Granada takeover and now had wealth amounting to around £10 million. The money helped, but it could not really take away the pain of losing his life's work.

Friends worried about him, especially in the first couple of weeks after he left his office for the last time, on the brink of tears. He looked and felt guilty about what had happened. He felt responsible for the people he had left behind at LWT, many of whom would now lose their jobs. He knew that the whole culture of LWT was going to be destroyed. Dyke and others had sensed that on the very first day after the formal change of ownership. Suddenly the atmosphere was different, alien. In his darkest moments Dyke thought about the likes of Brian Tesler, Birt and Grade – as well as Bland; people who had built LWT into something. They had trusted and promoted him – taught him all he knew about the business – and in the end he had let them down.

That year Dyke's annual birthday gathering in May, a few weeks after his departure from LWT, had been a downbeat affair. He tried to be his usual lively, jokey self. But it did not quite work. He was no longer at the centre of things, no longer possessed of the latest insider news and scurrilous gossip about the TV industry. He was putting on a brave face. But anyone could see that the stuffing had been knocked out of him. At least this time round he had Sue and his family to turn to. At first Sue was delighted to have him around more – Dyke had become a virtual stranger when he was working all hours during the takeover battle. He was conscious of the way overwork had been one of the things that had killed off his first marriage and, anyway, was genuinely enthusiastic about seeing a lot more of his kids and playing the family man. Summer was coming and the whole family could be together for hours every day.

It was bliss – for about three weeks. Dyke's hyper-activity started driving Sue and the children up the wall. His daughter Alice had greeted her dad's departure from LWT by asking if *Gladiators* would still be on the screen on Saturday evenings. When he confirmed that it would be, she had said she couldn't see, then, what all the fuss was about. Now she had taken to asking any grown-up she came into contact with whether they could give her dad a job – anything just to get him out from under the family's feet. 'I left LWT in order to spend more time with my family,' he would later say, pausing for effect ' . . . only to discover that my family did not want to spend more time with me.'

Dyke had kept boredom away by spending some of his cash mountain. The problem was that after splashing out on a jukebox to play his collection of golden oldies, and already possessing an exceedingly posh house and flashy motor (and arranging in addition for his old LWT Merc to be sold cheaply to his brother Howard in a minor act of perfectly legal financial revenge on Granada), there was nothing much that he wanted to buy.

As a form of relaxation from the pressures of the Granada takeover battle, Dyke had been pursuing a long-running feud with Twickenham council over his plan to have a swimming pool built in his house. Final defeat by the planning committee prompted him to go house-hunting. But instead of buying a ready-made country residence, Dyke found a run-down estate near Upper Wallop in Hampshire, called The Barns, and was able to burn off some energy, getting busy with architects and builders doing the place up. He was soon insisting that, in addition to a swimming pool, a former ballroom in the main building should be converted so that he could play five-a-side football with his kids.

(Dyke was later persuaded to buy a golf course in Devon from Nigel Mansell as a form of investment. He quipped that the place was so posh that the only way he could become a member was to buy it. He took to golf with his usual manic determination to become a world champion at the game. A few years later the papers reported that an estimated 22,000 golf balls had been dredged out of the course's ornamental lake during repairs – 'most of them are believed to belong to Mr Greg

Dyke, the owner of the course'. Howard, who had retired early from his job in the insurance business, was highly delighted. He was installed as a director of the club and spent a lot of time in getting his handicap down.)

Dyke was adamant that the money would not change his personal socialist values. He might feel the odd twinge about all his cash but, apart from the big house, it did not change him much. He gave a lot to charity – supporting, in particular, a children's television foundation and various projects at his old college, York University. Dyke had revived the York connection when, just after the franchise round, he and Tom Gutteridge, the head of the rival LIB bid and another former York student, had been asked to form a fund-raising committee for the university's student trainee TV station. After his father's death Dyke provided the university with a new all-weather outdoor playing field, called 'The JLD'. A plaque on the chain-link fence read: 'This pitch was built with a generous donation from Greg Dyke, student in the department of politics 1971–1974 and is named in memory of his father, Joseph Leonard Dyke.'

Dyke had not gone into television in order to make millions. After LWT had won its franchise back, he told a newspaper, 'I'm going to end up rich, which is odd because I'm about the only person in ITV who really doesn't worry about being rich. The advantage of being rich is that you have "Fuck-Off Money". If you don't like it, you can walk away'. Now that his prediction of riches had come true, Dyke was determined that his children would use the local schools and would have to learn the value of money. Dyke was not keen on inherited money and said that his kids could only expect a modest inheritance and not millions. 'I don't want them to think money is easy. There are people like that in the TV industry and they are a rollover. I am competitive and I want my kids to be competitive too.' But at the time Dyke left LWT, his children were still too young for any of this to apply. One day he had been taking the kids to school when his five-year-old son Joe asked what he did for a living. 'I used to run a television station,' Dyke said. 'Oh,' Joe replied. He knew that his mother was a teacher. 'Is it you or is it mummy that is rich?'

Dyke's wealth had not diminished his attachment to the Labour Party and, now, with time on his hands, he decided to revive his interest in politics. In the summer of 1994, after the sudden death of Labour party leader John Smith, Dyke became involved with Tony Blair's campaign for the Labour Party leadership, which was being organized by ex-*Weekend World* researcher Peter Mandelson and Dyke's fellow ex-LWT millionaire Barry Cox. Dyke's old boss at TV-am, Jonathan Aitken, got wind of all this and raised the matter in parliament. Blair was being backed, Aitken said, by 'LWT hypocrites' who professed socialism but had become Fat Cat millionaires. He claimed that between them Dyke, Cox and Melvyn Bragg had given Blair £79,000 and that Cox had 'masterminded Tony Blair's £1.2 million fund-raising drive in the City'. Dyke later confirmed that he had given £15,000 to Blair personally and a further £20,000 to the Labour Party organization.

In a newspaper interview Dyke said that he had thought about going back into politics himself, but he would have to go in right at the top of the Labour Party; anything less would be 'too boring'. He reckoned as Labour Party leader he could 'put together a list of ten policies and get at least 80 per cent of the population to support them'. But he was not interested in serving time. He would make 'the world's worst backbencher'.

Mandelson had suggested that he could go into the House of Lords as a Labour life peer. But Dyke was not keen: 'Can you imagine it,' he told friends, ' . . . Lord Dyke of Hayes – it sounds like a bloody gay girls' pop group!'

Dyke's main ambition still remained in television. He claimed to have been 'swamped with offers' of consultancies for firms of City investors keen to gain from his expertise in the booming area of media stocks, but had dismissed them all as 'a bunch of whores'. Still feeling bitter, Dyke would regularly pop up to denounce the City which, he said, was one of the last redoubts of the old school tie and the class system. What he really wanted to do was run a TV station. A move to Sky in the wake of David Elstein, the former Thames director of programmes who had climbed out of the wreckage of the lost franchise to become a senior executive at Sky, looked unlikely. Dyke had clashed badly with Murdoch and his chief lieutenant, Sam Chisholm, during the lost battle over Premier League football rights.

The BBC looked like a better prospect in some ways. Dyke might be welcomed as controller of BBC1. But this would be a big step back down the pecking order, back to a status of director of programmes which he had held in 1987 before going to Harvard. The jobs he might be interested in – managing director of BBC Television or Director-General – seemed to be out of his reach, even if he wanted them. The BBC was certainly uppermost in Dyke's mind during the summer and autumn. In August 1994 Dyke was asked to give the annual MacTaggart memorial lecture during the Edinburgh TV festival – an accolade reserved for only the most celebrated movers and shakers in the industry. He chose for his main subject the threat posed to freedom of speech by the new commercial priorities of the TV industry and, as part of that, the vital need for strong and brave leadership of the BBC. Dyke strenuously denied it, but in the business it was assumed that Dyke's speech was his way of 'putting down a marker' as it was normally put – a very public application for a senior job at the BBC, should one become available.

Dyke limbered up for the MacTaggart by writing a long article about the future of the BBC in the *Daily Telegraph* to mark the publication of the Major government's White Paper on the Corporation's future. At one point it had been feared that the White Paper would propose the privatization of all or some of the BBC's services. In fact it turned out to be a very modest document, proposing hardly any change at all. The BBC had 'emerged unscathed', Dyke said, because of 'luck, good timing and John Birt'. Two years earlier Michael Grade had used the MacTaggart speech to lambast Birt, saying that the Director-General's introduction of an 'internal market', with its resulting redundancies, was in effect carrying out the government's policy of reducing the BBC's scale and importance by stealth. Dyke agreed that Birt had caused great 'pain' at the BBC, but he could see method in the apparent madness. Birt's changes had been carried out, Dyke said, 'at the expense of alienating a great many BBC staff. However, the government sees that alienation as proof that the BBC has changed.' Birt might be unpopular at the BBC and in the TV industry, but his apparent willingness to go along with the general direction of government policy had saved the Corporation from the high tide of Thatcherism. The political climate had changed, which meant that the BBC was now able to go on the offensive again. 'The biggest piece of luck the BBC had was the result of the 1992 election,' Dyke said. 'With a majority of less than thirty, there were always enough

Tory MPs who believed in a strong BBC to prevent legislation to privatize or dismember it.'

Dyke then picked over his own main practical bone of contention with Birt – the way the BBC had acted as 'Murdoch's poodle', lining up Chisholm and Murdoch in 1992 to ensure that rights to Premier League football were snatched from ITV. As Dyke had predicted at the time, football had been a huge success for Sky and it was more or less solely down to its brilliant marketing and exploitation of football rights that Sky had moved from the loss-making margins of British TV to become a serious threat. Football had worked so well for Sky that Dyke predicted it would hoover-up basically all British sport and put it into an even more profitable subscription service. 'The BBC probably won't have much sport in the future,' Dyke said, adding: 'It is difficult to have much sympathy for the BBC over this because it, as much as anyone, helped build Sky Sports by assisting it in a quite disgraceful way to get the Premier League contract.'

The lack of sport on the BBC, Dyke thought, would make the political job of justifying the licence fee all the more difficult. There were lots of people, like Dyke's own dad, who basically only watched sport on TV. Joseph Dyke had bought his family their first TV set just so he could watch Stanley Matthews in the 1953 Cup Final, and had come to rely on TV for sport. Forty years later there were still millions of viewers who were mainly interested in sport on TV. Now that they were shelling out around £300 already to Sky just to watch football, they might come to resent paying the BBC licence fee. And any threat to the BBC licence fee would be a threat to the entire TV industry, Dyke thought: 'By the year 2010 the BBC may well be the only organization in Britain able to finance much of the programming which has made British television so distinctive.' Dyke ended his article by wondering how 'brave' the BBC would be in the future. 'One of the roles of broadcasting,' Dyke wrote, 'is to act as a check on government.' The White Paper had given the Corporation 'a free run until well into the next century. It will be interesting to see what effect this has on programming'.

After this opening salvo in the *Daily Telegraph*, Dyke got down to work on the MacTaggart lecture itself, working from a small and unassuming office off the Strand in central London. He showed various drafts to David Housham, the producer of the lecture. Housham thought that the speech was surprisingly moderate and dry, coming, as it did, from Dyke. There were not many jokes, no shaggy-dog stories and much of it was written in the type of bland business-speak that John Birt might have used. Dyke explained that he didn't want to 'shoot from the hip'. Bizarrely, it was Housham who encouraged Dyke to pep the whole thing up with an opening joke or two.

The speech itself kicked off with the by now familiar attack on what the government had done to ITV. Dyke seemed to burn his bridges with Gerry Robinson by bitterly accusing him of proposing the abolition of *News at Ten* and then retreating to allow Dyke to take the political flak in order to protect Robinson's position with politicians who might be able to influence his purely commercial plans for takeovers and mergers. Dyke said that the new wave of businessmen who now ran ITV were much more likely to 'bend to political pressure' than previous ITV bosses like Plowright at Granada and Tesler at LWT, who came from a programme-making background. They had all seen what happened to Thames when the station had defended a controversial documentary called *Death on the Rock*, which had been singled out for criticism by the then Prime Minister, Margaret Thatcher. There were many in the industry who thought that Thames' robust defence of its programme-makers' right to criticize the government of the day had led directly to the company's loss of its franchise and, therefore, financial disintegration.

'If you look around the ITV system today,' Dyke said, 'in only four of the companies is the most important executive from a programming background, and two of them are from the smallest companies – Border and Channel. The rest are almost exclusively run by accountants or people with a financial background. There has been a significant shift in power.' The new model broadcaster, Dyke thought, was, above all, Rupert Murdoch. He had used his papers to get behind Thatcher – allowing hardly a word of criticism of her while his papers unleashed a tidal wave of bias against her opponents – and had been rewarded with all sorts of legislation and regulatory changes which directly helped him build up his business. 'Rupert Murdoch's priorities are clear,' Dyke said. 'Earlier this year he took the BBC off his Chinese satellite because of censorship pressure from the Chinese government. Will ITV go the same way?' Dyke wanted to know. 'What has happened to the duty to hold government to account?'

If the public could no longer rely on commercial television to check the power of the government, that made the role of the BBC all the more important. But here Dyke was worried that there had been too much cosying-up to the government. He mentioned an edition of *Panorama* attacking government economic policy which had been taken off the air in the run-up to the 1992 general election, and delays in running another edition of

*Panorama* which exposed alleged scandals in the running of Westminster Council – the Tory 'flagship' local authority.

Dyke repeated his call for editorial bravery at the BBC, especially now that the political climate had changed and the threat to its future was not so apparent. He had some specific proposals. The next government, which he hoped would be Labour, should set up a Commission of Inquiry to look at the whole broadcasting industry and 'clean up the mess' left by the 1990 Broadcasting Act. A new Labour Secretary of State, Dyke thought, would have to act quickly: 'The Blair government will be elected on a programme of open government but might after a couple of years decide that open government was not such a good idea after all – like many governments – and then there will be pressure again.' The Commission, Dyke added, would have to look at the BBC's constitution, coming up with new suggestions for the appointment of BBC governors. 'We must never again be in a position where the government of the day can fill the BBC's board of governors with their friends and placemen as the Thatcherites did. Nor should the chairman be the government's man, as the current chairman, Marmaduke Hussey, plainly is. It is also important that the Governors' role should be clearly defined. They are either regulators or managers. They can not be both.'

The speech was popular enough, castigating as it did all the principal bogeypersons – Gerry 'Catering Manager' Robinson, Michael Green of Carlton, Thatcher and Murdoch. But it was strangely downbeat and plodding by Dyke's normal standards. Many present were disappointed that he had not let rip in the sensational style of Michael Grade. It was a good, clearly thought-out speech, and pretty much an accurate reflection of what most of the people in the audience had thought. But one or two complained that it had not really 'caught fire'.

Afterwards Dyke was remarkably unstarry, trotting off to dinner with a group of friends. As an aside, the *Observer* media journalist Emily Bell got hold of Sue who, after the speech was over, had been denouncing Murdoch in far stronger terms that Dyke had allowed himself on the platform. Bell asked which paper she and Greg read on a Sunday. Sue said they got the *Sunday Times* – a Murdoch paper. 'Well, if you hate Rupert so much, why don't you buy the *Observer* instead?' Bell asked. Sue thought this was a great idea and yelled across the room: 'Greg – why don't we buy the *Observer*?' Dyke's brow furrowed. It was clear that he was against, but he was at pains to show that he was taking the suggestion very seriously. Dyke said they could probably afford it (a buy-out of the *Observer* as a publishing company would, at the time, have cost around £50 million). He would think about it, he said, but he wasn't sure it was a good idea.

Others present immediately read Dyke's speech not so much as an application for the BBC Director-Generalship, but more as giving public notice that he was interested in doing the job one day – perhaps after a new Labour government had come to power and changed the nature of the Governors. The chances of Dyke becoming Director-General were slight while the Tories remained in charge of Whitehall and Marmaduke Hussey, the Tory nominee as BBC Chairman, and the current crop of Governors remained in place.

# 22.
# The Comeback Kid

Greg Dyke is standing in the men's lavatory in a drab-looking sports and leisure centre just outside Leeds, watching a fit and athletic young man swab the floor.

'Bit different from last year innit, Justin?' says Dyke. The athletic young man is Justin Lanning, a professional ice-skater, who in 1994 had won the British Championship. Dyke is interviewing Lanning for a 'behind the scenes' Channel Four TV sports series called *On The Line* – Dyke's first – and almost certainly last – outing as an on-screen television reporter.

Dyke had taken on the job in the autumn of 1994, around the time of his MacTaggart lecture. The decision to plunge back into programme-making was a way of killing time and burning off excess energy while he waited for another big job in TV management to fall vacant. Other assignments for the series had included an investigation into the use of psychologists in sport, during which Dyke had found himself accidentally put into a trance by a hypnotist. There had also been a headline-grabbing interview with Will Carling. The former England rugby captain got himself into trouble by describing the governors of the Rugby Football Union as '57 old farts'. Dyke had also investigated the controversial placing of Torvill and Dean in the previous year's Olympics.

The exercise had allowed Dyke to see what it was like in the newly cheap and not very cheerful world of hands-on TV production. Dyke was a great enthusiast for technical innovation in television. The latest thing was digital editing. This had replaced the old system of video editing he had been used to as a programme-maker at LWT. Digital editing speeded-up things by a factor of ten. A programme could now be put together by one person using a computer for a few hundred pounds, instead of a massive team of unionized tape editors costing many thousands. Dyke was impressed by the speed and efficiency with which the series had been made, even though his own involvement had left him 'knackered'.

If Dyke's interest in *On The Line* waned towards the end of the series, he could be excused. In December 1994, halfway through the production process, he had begun work on his first really serious TV job since leaving LWT – becoming managing director of Pearson Television. For a couple of months Dyke had to divide his time between rushing around the country interviewing bent jockeys and shady referees for *On The Line* and establishing himself in his new position as chief of the TV wing of Pearson, the blue chip media and leisure conglomerate whose portfolio included the *Financial Times* and Penguin books.

Pearson's boss, Frank Barlow, had first met Dyke thirty years earlier when he had been running the newspaper group where Dyke had started his career as a reporter. Back then, Dyke had led a revolt of junior reporters demanding more money. Barlow had been the hard-nosed, tight-fisted manager who had reportedly turned them down, saying – this being the swinging Sixties – that Dyke and his fellow militants would only waste any extra money on buying transistor radios and other rubbish. The newspaper group had been part of a national chain of local papers, Westminster Press, and Barlow had worked his way up through a series of boardroom coups to become head of Pearson. He had watched Dyke's career with interest since he emerged as a figure on the national media scene during the saga of Roland Rat and TV-am.

Pearson was a conservative company. It had absolutely rock solid assets. But the City was impatient. It wanted the company to follow the example of Rupert Murdoch and diversify from printed media into television, so Pearson had started to build a broadcasting business and already had a minority stake in Yorkshire TV and Sky. The stake in the satellite outfit was left over from a badly misjudged investment in the catastrophically mis-conceived British Satellite Broadcasting venture in the late Eighties. BSB had gone bust, its assets bought out by Sky for next to nothing and its shareholders, including Pearson and Granada, locked into a minority, and somewhat humiliating, position on the new Murdoch-controlled board of British Sky Broadcasting. Now, after the successful flotation of BSkyB on the stock market with a multibillion market capitalization, there was near hysterical clamour from the City for newspaper-based companies like Pearson to become 'multimedia'.

Barlow, as chief executive of Pearson, saw his chance when Richard Dunn, the head of Thames TV, suggested that Pearson should take over the former broadcaster that, after losing its ITV franchise to Carlton, had been reorganized by Dunn to become an independent pro-gramme producer and supplier. The deal was facilitated by Dennis Stevenson, the chairman of the Tate Gallery. Stevenson, who had impeccable contacts in the City and the political establishment, was on the boards of both Pearson and Thames.

Pearson paid £100 million for Thames, which was later thought to have been a cracking bargain. Within a few years Pearson was to get all its £100 million back, plus a profit of £40 million simply by selling the stake in the Astra satellite that came with ownership of the company.

On top of that, Thames had a vast back catalogue of vintage comedy and drama series, including *The Benny Hill Show* and *Mr Bean*. These were bound to keep increasing in value as the thousands of new 24-hour cable and satellite channels being set up around the world started crying out for something – anything – to show. Thames' investments in the cable stations UK Living and, particularly, 'golden oldies' channel UK Gold were also certain to increase in value.

The deal was done on the clear understanding that Dunn who, after all, was a former Chairman of ITV and one of the most experienced and respected broadcasting executives in the country, would take charge of Pearson's growing interests in TV. But it was not to be. Dunn did not know that Barlow had been courting Dyke after he had walked out of LWT and wanted him, and not Dunn, to be in charge of Pearson TV. Barlow had worked hard to steer Dyke into the company. Dunn was popular with the blue-chip members of the Pearson board who liked his refined style, aristocratic good looks and gentlemanly approach to business. In contrast, Barlow was a blunt northern grammar school boy. As far as he was concerned, Pearson had spent its money to obtain Thames's back catalogue and residual production expertise and facilities. Dunn and Barlow had never really got on. In his secret talks with Dyke, Barlow had assured Dyke that Dunn was happy enough to stay on as head of Thames. Dyke and Dunn's relationship would be presented to the world as one of formal equality, with Dunn in charge of Pearson's UK television operation and Dyke concentrating on international expansion as head of Pearson TV.

Just before Christmas 1994, Barlow at last told Dunn that he wanted him to continue as managing director of Thames TV, which would henceforth operate as a subsidiary of Pearson's new TV division to be run by Greg Dyke. Dunn was aghast. In some ways Dyke was a more junior figure in the industry than he was. There was still mistrust left over from the days when Thames and LWT were rival broadcasters, and resentment that Dyke was a big winner in the franchise auction that had destroyed Thames and wrecked Dunn's career as a broadcaster.

Dunn was awarded the CBE in the 1995 New Year's honours list and on 2 January attended a scheduled Thames senior management meeting. Champagne had been laid on to celebrate Dunn's award. After the initial round of congratulations and back-slapping, Dunn lifted his champagne glass to his lips, took a tiny sip, put the glass down carefully on a desk top and said: 'Well, chaps, there's something I've got to tell you. I'm leaving. Greg Dyke has been brought in over my head.' The implication was clear. Dunn was being forced out.

It was a hell of a shock. At first some thought it might be a kind of complicated self-deprecating joke connected with the award of the CBE. After the trauma and mass sackings that had followed the loss of the franchise, things had stabilized following the link-up with Pearson. For the first time in years there was a feeling of genuine optimism. Most thought, given the circumstances, Dunn was doing an effective job. Dyke, on the other hand, came from LWT – the 'tits and tinsel' Saturday night entertainment station, the detested Carlton's partner in the new ITV. But it was no joke. Dunn was perfectly serious. He was leaving the company to which he had given the best years of his life. By the end of the week his staff would be working for the man many had previously thought of as 'the enemy' – Greg Dyke.

Dyke sympathized with Dunn's predicament and both men loyally toed the official PR line that they were looking forward to working with each other as equals, hoping to maintain this fiction until Dunn could leave quietly after a decent interval. In the event the PR line held for less than twenty-four hours. The day after the announcement of his appointment, Dyke came into Pearson's offices to be told by a press officer that 'the whole world' was running the story that Dyke had been brought in over Dunn's head. Dyke decided to deal with it by giving an exclusive interview to *Broadcast* magazine. The head of press, Roy Addison, was the first to witness the change in leadership style. Dunn tended to choose his words carefully when talking to journalists. Dyke simply plonked himself down on the edge of a desk and was overheard saying: 'Yeah, yeah . . . I lied . . . so what? . . . you fucking well have to – sometimes – in this business.'

Thames was the largest independent production company in the country and Dyke's basic salary of £275,000 (with bonuses he was to earn more than double that during his time at Pearson) placed him on level terms with an ITV managing director. But it had nothing like the same status and, for a few years, Dyke was to find himself out of the public eye, deprived of his role in the national soap opera of public life. Dyke's place of work seemed to emphasize his reduced importance, with depressing effect. Thames had already disposed of its corporate headquarters in Euston Road as part of the inevitable cost-cutting process after losing the franchise. Activities were consolidated at the company's studio complex in Teddington, about ten miles to the west of central London. Dyke felt uncomfortable and unhappy working there. At the best of times it had been old-fashioned and ramshackle. Studios and offices had been bolted together over the years of Thames' expansion with no apparent logic. It was all very different from the highly rationalized 'television factory' Dyke had been used to at LWT. Walking from one part of the complex to another was difficult, involving turning in and out of blind corridors, across connecting bridges and up and down flights of stairs. It was confusing and, now that Thames was no longer a broadcaster, depressing and lonely.

The whole place was like a ship after everyone had been evacuated, leaving the captain and the senior officers on the bridge. The car park was full of flashy cars but nothing much was going on inside. Thames' biggest continuing production, *The Bill*, was made on location. Dyke desperately missed the buzz of LWT and would wander the echoing corridors, wiping the slowly gathering layers of dust from the pictures of old Thames stars like Eamonn Andrews, Des O'Connor and Kilroy, feeling thoroughly spooked and desperately searching for somebody to talk to.

Dyke set about making a few cosmetic changes, starting with the office he had inherited from Richard Dunn. Dyke announced that it was far too big and only added to his feeling of being locked up in a vast and deserted television morgue. He wanted it partitioned. He brushed aside technical objections and ended up in a partitioned office which was alternately freezing cold or boiling hot – the heating and air-conditioning had ended up on the other side of the partition. This minor disaster merely made Dyke more determined to move the whole company out of Teddington, away from the sleepy suburbs and back in the buzzing heart of media-land in central London's west end. Eventually the operation was moved to a gleaming post-modernist edifice just to the north of Soho in central London, complete with vast designer reception area and crowned by a gigantic atrium. The Teddington complex was sold off, and with the move all physical traces of Thames were finally buried, the old company's 'intellectual property' wrapped up into the aggressively-promoted and brand new identity of Pearson Television.

And so Greg Dyke began to lay the ghost of the Granada takeover to rest. He was once again utterly focused, working on a corporate comeback on a grand scale. His plan was to build Pearson into the biggest private sector TV concern in Europe and perhaps – eventually – the world, through a series of high-powered business deals.

# 23.
# Wheeler-Dealer

Greg Dyke and his LWT scheduling chief, Warren Breach, are relaxing alone in the executive dining room of Walt Disney Corporation's headquarters overlooking the valley, just outside Los Angeles. The building, done out in typically over-the-top Palladian Disney-fantasy style, is one of the most famous physical landmarks in corporate California.

Breach gets up and wanders over to one of the huge, strange circular windows, attracted by the unbelievable shade of the cloudless blue sky and the view of purple-topped mountains in the distance. At the window, Breach tilts his head to peer at the massive statues of the Seven Dwarfs which support the roof with their outstretched arms.

'Here, Greg! See that one . . .' Breach gestures toward the pot-bellied figure of Grumpy, surreal in its enormous scale, '. . . it looks a bit like you, mate!'

Before Dyke can reply, Disney's chairman Michael Eisner bustles into the room, surrounded by a gaggle of bag-carriers, clean-shaven with flashing white teeth and decked out in identical suits as part of the company's cult-like and strictly enforced dress code. Dyke, dressed in jeans and trainers as usual, joins in the round of muscular handshakes and back-slapping.

For Dyke, one of the greatest attractions of becoming a senior TV executive had been the chance to visit America, and especially California, on a regular basis to set up programme deals with the big American studios. Dyke loved everything about California, starting with the

climate. As an outdoor type Radical Rambler and dedicated windsurfer, the place was paradise. Then there was
the unrelenting can-do, no bullshit and workaholic
attitude of the people, especially in the TV and movie
business. Eisner himself typified the style. In 1994 he
underwent quadruple by-pass heart surgery and was back
at his desk within two weeks, hardly batting an eyelid.

By LA standards, Britain was a relatively small market,
and British TV companies like LWT and Pearson were
pretty small beer. But that did not stop Eisner turning up
to meet the Brits in person, making them feel that their
money was as good as anyone else's. Dyke liked that
approach – all very different from the stratified world of
British corporate life, where a chief executive in Eisner's
position would be much more likely to send a deputy. In
LA, if you had the cash you went straight to the top, did a
deal with a minimum of fuss and went to the beach to
celebrate. Going to LA was a glorious escape from the
British TV business, where the regulators, banks,
politicians, critics, professional grumblers and the City
were on your back all the time. In California Dyke could
concentrate on the creative side and, above all, 'do deals'
– morning, noon and night.

Now, as head of Pearson TV in the mid-1990s, Dyke
was determined that the company should become a
player in the world TV market, which meant breaking out
of the constrained and confined world of British television
and establishing a presence in LA and other media centres
around the world. It would mean buying up existing TV
production companies. The aim would be to create a
collection of programmes which could be produced for
local markets with local talent on both sides of the camera,
and then understood and watched with equal pleasure
(or, more likely, mild interest) by anybody anywhere in

the world. Pearson had already made a start by acquiring a 10 per cent stake in a company called Television Broadcasts of Hong Kong for £108 million. The City, which had been urging stodgy old Pearson to do something exciting for years, was impressed. The consensus of the analysts was that Dyke had bought entry into the booming Chinese TV market – one which was destined eventually to become the biggest in the world – at a very low price.

Then Dyke pulled off his first really big deal – buying the Australian-based production company Grundy Television – makers of *Neighbours*, *Prisoner Cell Block H* and owners of the format and licence to make *Sale of the Century*. Grundy had been built up by its eponymous founder Reg Grundy, who had started as a jobbing TV producer, created *Neighbours* and turned it into one of the first ever truly 'global' television programmes. It had become a sort of televisual equivalent of Coca-Cola or McDonald's – simple, universal, bland and cheap to produce. It could be shown in every country in the world and so in an age of worldwide multichannel television and slashed programme budgets it could be sold cheaply, beating locally-produced material on price and yet still providing vast profits for its owners.

Buying Grundy made sense for Pearson. But Dyke was the key to pulling off the deal. He knew Reg Grundy personally from meetings at programme-buying jamborees and the two men were friendly, sharing a similar approach to life. Dyke had once accepted a lift in Grundy's personal Learjet on his way to a programme-buying gathering, drinking champagne all the way and living it up. As it happened, Grundy, who was getting on a bit, had put his company up for sale just at the time Dyke had taken the job of running Pearson TV. Reg

Grundy was already fabulously rich and so could afford the luxury of choosing a purchaser who he thought would look after *Neighbours* and keep the production team together. He was open to offers, but definitely disinclined to sell out to a faceless American corporation. Grundy was therefore delighted to find that his old pal Greg Dyke was in the running and – even better – had the money to make him a decent offer. Dyke came up with an offer of £175 million for the company and flew in Concorde to New York to sign contracts and shake hands. The deal was done in the departure lounge of JFK airport, with Reg flying up from the Caribbean, where, as usual, he was organizing business from a satellite phone on the deck of his yacht. Dyke returned the same day with the paperwork in his briefcase, the proud owner of a format library based on serial drama and game shows.

More triumphs were to follow, including, eventually, the purchase of All American – another company with a vast back catalogue of highly exportable material. The company was best known as the maker of *Baywatch* – a show which did useful business around the world and which Dyke and Warren Breach had already run on LWT. The attractions of *Baywatch* were well known, but Dyke was more interested in All American's vast back catalogue of game shows, including *The Price is Right*, *Family Fortunes* and many more. All American was to be acquired for £233 million, allowing Dyke to claim that Pearson TV had become 'the biggest producer of TV drama and entertainment in the world.' 'As the TV market fragments, building brands will be harder,' he said at the time. 'Whoever owns historic brands will be at a tremendous advantage. You just couldn't make *EastEnders* today.'

Within the space of a few months Pearson TV had been

transformed from being not much more than a name on a piece of paper to become a thoroughly modern international media company with offices in London, Hong Kong, LA and Sydney.

Dyke was mainly interested in building Pearson into a global TV business. But there was still the problem of what to do with the company's original core – Thames. The company's back catalogue of shows such as *The Sweeney* and *The Bill* were not much use on the international market – nobody in America, or China for that matter, could understand why it was that the cops did not have guns. But an opportunity to use some of the Thames back catalogue and ownership of 'formats' to hit programmes such as *Wish You Were Here* presented itself in the form of the franchise to run Channel Five, which was to be auctioned in 1995.

The Channel Five franchise was the last piece of unfinished business left over from the 1990 Broadcasting Act. It had been a sop to the advertising industry which, for years, had complained about ITV and Channel Four's monopoly over advertising slots. The new channel was conceived as a sort of national ITV or 'ITV-2' but, screening out all the usual cant about increasing consumer choice, its main purpose was to increase the number of advertising slots available every day on British television and, therefore, drive down prices.

Preparations for the channel had not gone well. A first round of bidding ended in farce when the ITC disqualified the sole bidder – a consortium of Thames, Pearson and Thorn EMI. For Dyke, then still at LWT, that bid's failure was a triumph. He and his ITV colleagues had lobbied hard against a fifth channel, fearful of the damage that a new commercial broadcaster would do to

ITV. Two years later invitations to apply for Channel Five were issued once more. This time the competition was fierce. The bids included a consortium led by Rupert Murdoch, one involving the the Mirror Group and another put together by Virgin. Pearson had formed an alliance with Lord (Clive) Hollick's United Media group in a joint bid led, in practice, by Dyke.

It had been known from the start that Channel Five would be very hard to get off the ground. It would be in competition with the existing channels, especially ITV and the increasingly populist Channel Four, and in competition with the new force of satellite TV and even the Internet. There was also a technical nightmare lurking in the background – the waveband allocated to the new channel would cause interference on existing video recorders and, in addition, computer games consoles. The ITC was insisting that whoever won the franchise had to retune the nation's video recorders at their own cost. This would involve a personal visit to 9.5 million households. The cost was bound to be vast and, more worryingly still, unpredictable. All would depend on how quickly a vast army of video retuners could be recruited, go into people's homes and get out again. Dyke himself had six TV sets, four video recorders and a satellite dish, as well as a computer games console, in his Twickenham house. If everyone was like him it would take them fifty years to complete the retuning job. Dyke then made matters worse by saying that the retuning requirement was 'a burglar's charter' – the perfect excuse for the nation's criminals to gain access to any house of their choice. The remark, made off the cuff while Dyke was still at LWT, led directly to the imposition of all sorts of expensive ID, prior notification and training arrangements. Dyke later said that the quip had been the most expensive words he had ever spoken.

But with all these problems, and despite his 'focus' on Pearson's international expansion, Dyke still thought it was worth giving Channel Five a go. At Pearson he was tremendously well paid and, increasingly, was an important player in the international TV business. But he was well away from the spotlight, with little influence over what people actually got to see on their TV sets in the evening. Running Channel Five, if it could be made to pay as a business and win the franchise auction, would move him back towards the centre of national life.

The key to Channel Five, Dyke was convinced, would be an aggressive form of scheduling known in the trade as 'striping and stranding' – which means running the same programmes in the same slots every night. Channel Five would attack one of the weakest parts of the ITV schedule – News at Ten. Channel Five would run a movie every evening at 9pm. The idea was that, with a proliferation of channels, the audience was thoroughly confused as to what was on and when. Striping and stranding, linked to a massive pre-launch publicity campaign featuring the Spice Girls, meant viewers knew where they were with Channel Five. And through Pearson's international acquisitions and a further series of programme deals, this would be relatively cheap to do. It made no sense for Channel Five to set up its own studios – everything could be made more cheaply by independent production companies, including those owned by Pearson.

Channel Five would have to keep its costs down so that enough could be bid in the franchise auction while still leaving some money left to, eventually, show a profit. Dyke insisted that everything should be done as cheaply as possible, evening at the bidding stage. A team of about ten people worked in a single big room off Warren Street in Bloomsbury. Junior people in the operation immediately warmed to Dyke and were highly amused by his constant frustration with life, stripped of much of the infrastructure of Big Shot corporate life. Once they saw him hail a taxi and get in, only to be decanted back on to the pavement a few moments later. It was explained that Dyke was so used to being in a chauffeur-driven limo that he had got into the taxi and asked to be taken to some advertising agency or other without realising he had to give the address. (Dyke was so physically inept that he once spent an entire day trying to put together a flat-pack desk for his office. At 6pm he was still sitting in a heap of empty boxes, covered in sweat and cursing. Once his desk was set up, it turned out that Dyke had little idea how to use a computer and, like many dads at this point, often turned to his teenage children for instruction.)

As with the ITV franchise round, the rival consortiums would have to make a cash bid in addition to presenting programme plans. The financial equation was basically the same – the more cheaply you could make a viable schedule, the more money you would be able to bid. The difference this time was that the quality threshold was much lower and, since it was an entirely new service, there was no 'special circumstances' clause to favour an incumbent with a 'quality' track record.

The rival consortiums all had their strengths and weaknesses. To begin with, a consortium put together by the *Mirror* newspaper group, the European arm of the American NBC network and SelecTV – one of the country's biggest independent production companies – looked like the most serious opposition. NBC could put up a lot of money; as makers of *Birds of a Feather*, SelecTV had a vast back catalogue of British light entertainment; and the Mirror Group would promote the channel for free (a major cost for all the bidders) and supply much of the daytime programming. But Dyke destabilized this rival bid by the clever means of bidding to buy SelecTV in order to add its programmes to Pearson TV's portfolio. The Pearson buy-out of SelecTV was not completed until after the franchise auction, by which time NBC and the *Mirror* had withdrawn from the bid, having been scared off by the cost and risks involved in the national video retuning requirement.

The closest competitor was to be Virgin. The Virgin bid was being organized by Jeremy Fox, another York student and former member of the LIB team which had bid against Dyke and LWT in the ITV franchise round. After the bids had gone in, Dyke had met Fox at a Disney children's party and started teasing him, saying that he and Pearson had seen to it that the bid was 'stitched up' with the regulators in advance and that Virgin had 'no chance'. He also let slip that the ITC had asked for clarification on some details of the Pearson bid. This was a legitimate request, but Richard Branson subsequently attempted to use it against Pearson in a court case that sought to overturn the success of the Pearson bid, causing much fear and loathing all round.

At one point the main threat seemed to come from Rupert Murdoch, who was interested in acquiring a terrestrial outlet for the material he was already showing on Sky One. Murdoch's involvement naturally made Dyke nervous for a while. 'If Murdoch wants it,' he told members of his own bid team, 'he will stop at absolutely nothing to get it.' But Dyke thought that public opinion would force the ITC and parliament to prevent him owning a 'terrestrial' TV channel in addition to Sky and his newspaper empire. But Murdoch's team put in a 'token' bid of just a few million which, some thought, was the financial equivalent of putting up two fingers to

Channel Five and its chances or, others surmised, was an accurate reflection of the commercial value of the channel once retuning had been factored in. In reality Murdoch had pulled out of the bid, Dyke later learned, after coming under political pressure. Michael Grade, head of Channel Four, had run an effective press campaign, arguing that Murdoch should be stopped at all costs from getting his 'tentacles' on Channel Five. If he did get the chance to run the channel, Grade had said, there would be a 'nightmare scenario' in which Channel Five, Sky and the Murdoch newspapers would cross-promote each other. With Murdoch's money behind it and access to the vast library of Fox TV studios, also owned by Murdoch, Channel Five would corner the market for programmes. Channel Four would find it difficult to compete and might be crushed 'like a nut between the nutcrackers'. He had urged parliament to pass a one-line bill giving the ITC discretion to ignore the largest cash bid which, Grade thought, was 'certain to come from Rupert Murdoch'. In the end Murdoch was personally 'phoned by a minister in the Conservative government, Dyke believed, who had told him to pull out. The decision had caused uproar in the Murdoch bid team. They believed they had put together the winning bid.

In the end Pearson won the right to run Channel Five with a bid of £22 million – exactly the same amount offered by Virgin. Dyke won out because Virgin failed to meet the minimal quality requirements imposed on Channel Five, just as the company had failed to get over the quality threshold in the 1991 ITV franchise auction.

It was always nice to win, but putting one over on Murdoch was especially delicious.

# 24.
# M-People

Nick Evans, Dyke's old mate from the *Newcastle Journal* and his early programme-making days at LWT, had been delighted by an invitation to appear on a Channel Five daytime chatshow to talk about his multimillion-grossing, bestselling novel *The Horse Whisperer* and the resulting Hollywood movie. The new channel, partly owned by Pearson and directed by Greg Dyke as chairman, had been launched in March 1997 after a Dyke-led consortium had won the franchise to run Channel Five eighteen months earlier.

The chatshow was not much use as publicity. Channel Five was watched by only about 5 per cent of the population – and this small band were not reckoned to be the world's greatest fans of Evans's particular brand of literary fiction. Still, it would be a chance to visit Channel Five headquarters and say hello to Greg. And to Gloria Hunniford, one of Channel Five's main daytime TV presenters and a person who had been with him at LWT when she was a presenter on Dyke's *Six O'Clock Show*. And to Mike Southgate who had been Dyke's production manager at TVS and then moved with him to LWT as studio manager. And Alan Boyd – Dyke's ex-LWT light entertainment specialist. And ex-*Six O'Clock Show* and LWT stalwarts like Michael Attwell, Hugh Pile, John Longley, Tony Cohen . . . 'Christ!' Evans thought to himself. 'This is like going back ten years to the mid-Eighties glory days of LWT. Greg has brought them *all* with him.'

Dyke's tendency to surround himself with people he knew and trusted was natural enough. But it did not go unnoticed by those on the inside track in the TV business. Janet Street-Porter had lately been involved in a rival, and ultimately abortive, bid to run Channel Five, and fingered Dyke's mates, among others, in her MacTaggart speech at the 1995 Edinburgh TV festival. 'British television managers have always been "M-People" – that means middle-class, middle-brow, middle-aged, Masonic in their tendencies and fairly mediocre.' After delivering the speech Street-Porter marched up to Dyke's chief money man, Mike Southgate, and rasped: 'You're the fucker I was referring to. And what annoys me is not only that you are a Suit, but that you've made a lot of money out of it.' Street-Porter, like Birt, had left LWT for the BBC and thus missed out on the chance of being included in the golden handcuffs bonanza.

One of the key players in the Channel Five bid was another ex-LWT executive – Warren Breach, Dyke's scheduler and the man who had often accompanied Dyke on his programme-buying trips to California. Breach had made just under a million from the golden handcuffs deal, but he had stayed on at LWT after the Granada takeover. Dyke had phoned him one day about six months after the takeover and asked 'What the fuck are you still doing there?' Almost all the other senior managers had walked out, and Dyke seemed to think it was disloyal of Breach to stay on board. What was he playing at? Breach said mournfully that he had nowhere else to go, but agreed things were getting a bit grim under Granada's Mancunian yoke and said he was planning to leave at the end of the year.

Dyke told him that the worst thing he could do after leaving a great company like LWT was 'sit and stare at four walls – it will drive you mad'. And although Breach did not come to work for Pearson, Dyke signed him up to the team which was looking at the feasibility of a Channel Five bid. Breach was delighted. They were again their own masters and, fairly soon, Breach even found that he could walk across Waterloo Bridge, with its view of the LWT South Bank tower, without wincing with pain.

As Dyke and Breach got down to detailed planning, they realised that Channel Five was going to have to be a very different animal from LWT. Dyke had once bowled into Warren Breach's office demanding to know what could be done about Channel Five's late night schedule. 'I can tell you, but you won't want to hear it,' Breach had said. The latest research showed that Channel Four was doing exceptionally well after 11pm when the pubs shut. They had developed shows like *Eurotrash* which had a lot of 'tit and bum' in them. Breach set out his case. The regulators were less powerful these days and now had cable and satellite to worry about. The American production houses were making special, and reasonably tasteful, versions of TV movies and mini-series with a lot of sex scenes added. They were cheap to buy. 'The only way to go, I'm afraid, is soft porn. It's what people . . . or young men, which is your audience at that time . . . want.'

Dyke thought about it. 'OK then . . . go away and research it . . . but this is definitely *your* idea, right? . . . Not mine . . . I'm dead against it, but you are *demanding* that we do it, OK? . . . Sue will go potty when she finds out. But, OK, test it out . . . ' Breach got the dirty job of watching hours and hours of soft porn movies to see what might lure the target *Loaded* audience away from Channel Four.

Once the franchise had been won, attention turned from Dyke to Dawn Airey, the former Channel Four executive who had been hired to actually run the channel under the overall direction of Dyke and David Elstein, the ex-Thames programme chief who had been recruited from Sky to become Chief Executive of Channel Five television. Airey's appointment was in some ways a gamble. Dyke was skipping a generation and going for a woman of tremendous ambition, but relatively little experience. She could rely on Dyke's help, but some wondered if Channel Five would end up like GMTV, the breakfast channel part-owned by LWT that had replaced TV-am after the franchise round.

Getting the GMTV franchise had been one of the great triumphs of Dyke's career, but things had gone less well when the station went on air. GMTV's ratings collapsed within weeks of the launch in January 1993, and within a month it had lost 15 per cent of its audience. The crushing lead over its rivals had been lost and Channel Four's *The Big Breakfast* was drawing level. Worse than this, the rate of decline seemed to be accelerating. The station's morale evaporated as Lis Howell, the director of programmes brought in fresh from organizing non-stop coverage of the Gulf War for Sky News, began to flounder. The trouble was that the original consortium that owned GMTV – LWT, Scottish TV, the *Guardian* and Disney – had concentrated on putting together a convincing bid to win the franchise. Their thinking about the direction the service would take had not gone much beyond putting Howell's name on the headed paper.

Members of the bid consortium began to fall out with each other almost as soon as the station went on air. Disney were not at all helpful. They refused even to provide a decent feature film for launch day. Although Harry Roche, the head of the *Guardian*'s TV wing, was formally in charge of the consortium as chairman, the real power lay with LWT chairman Christopher Bland, who would put him under a lot of pressure, especially when the scale of the impending potential disaster was realized.

Dyke's first move had been to get station chief Christopher Stoddart to sack Lis Howell. Dyke seemed to hate doing it. He had head-hunted her himself and, in his usual way, left her to get on with it. A story later circulated that Dyke had spotted Howell in a supermarket near his Twickenham home and had been so horrified by the idea that she might confront him that he dropped all his groceries on the floor and ran away.

Dyke replaced Howell with his former colleague Peter McHugh, the tough-minded ex-*Daily Mail* news reporter who had headed up the news operation at TV-am. The two men had known each other since they both worked for the *Newcastle Journal* in 1970s. But there was to be no repeat of Dyke's early Eighties breakfast TV triumph. Despite all sorts of changes, GMTV continued to struggle and, although it enabled LWT to 'pour money down its own drain', because it kept an otherwise empty studio busy, it was crippled by its huge annual franchise payments and was only to make a profit years later when the ITC agreed to reduce its licence payments.

Running the similarly low budget Channel Five in a broadcasting environment which, if anything, was now even more competitive was going to be a big challenge. Dawn Airey would have to make do with a programme budget of only £110 million, compared with the £600 million or so available to ITV. Dyke and Elstein had already decided that the channel should aim for a 'young ITV audience' pitched somewhere between ITV and Channel Four. In the marketing blurb the editorial formula was to be described as 'modern mainstream'.

Dyke and Airey were in many ways soulmates. They were both famous for being boisterous and outspoken. Her inclusion in the bid as director of programmes showed that Pearson was serious about having programme-makers and not just entrepreneurs in charge of the channel and was reckoned to have helped land the franchise, as was the fact that she came from Channel Four and that she was a woman. Against the high tide of feminism, Dyke might have been criticized for his preference for working mostly with men. In his defence he could claim that he had done more than most to promote women. Lis Howell had been his choice to run GMTV and, even though things had not worked out, she had been one of the first female programme controllers anywhere in British television. LWT had even won an award for its exemplary equal opportunities record and policy of promoting women whenever possible (though Dyke, slightly missing the point, had insisted on going to the awards ceremony and collecting the trophy himself, brushing aside objections that a woman should go by saying, in wounded tones, 'Bollocks! I promoted them, didn't I? So I should get the award, shouldn't I?').

Then, just after the Pearson TV–United Media consortium won the Channel Five licence, another woman was about to enter his professional life. Marjorie Scardino, the Texan former chief of *The Economist* magazine was brought in over Dyke's head to replace the ageing Frank Barlow as chief executive of Pearson. Dyke was both astounded and outraged. He had thought that he might get the job or, at least, somebody would have been brought in with at least as much stature in the media business as himself. Scardino, by all accounts, was a highly effective executive, but Dyke thought that she was nowhere near experienced enough to be his boss. The same night as the appointment was made, Scardino called Dyke at home to talk things over. Dyke told her that there was no point in talking about the future because he was leaving at the first available opportunity. All that remained was to work out the terms and timing of his departure.

Warren Breach, hearing the news of this setback sent Dyke a little note to mark the occasion. 'This,' Breach wrote, 'is carrying equal opportunities *too* far!'

# 25.
# Fuzzy Monsters

Both Greg Dyke and Marjorie Scardino loyally toed the official Pearson PR line that they were getting along just fine and were perfectly happy in their respective roles at Pearson. There was much talk from Scardino of giving Dyke a lot of autonomy to run the TV side of the business. At the same time, for the sake of maintaining the City's confidence, she had to make it perfectly clear that she was the boss. In fact Dyke was looking for a way out and Scardino accepted that he would leave Pearson sooner rather than later.

The PR line wobbled seriously only once. In the summer of 1997 Pearson spin-doctors planted a story in the financial press suggesting that Dyke was on the point of being sacked after supposedly mismanaging an aspect of Pearson TV's move from Teddington to the West End. The new building boasted a splendid and extravagantly built central atrium, said to have bust the budget by £300,000 and known to all as 'Dyke's Folly'. In reality, Dyke had simply disappeared on a family holiday for 24 hours, going straight from his office to Heathrow without telling anyone. Fearful that Dyke had walked out in a huff after a disagreement with the board, the spin-doctors had decided to get their retaliation in first.

They need not have bothered. Dyke was soon back in contact. In fact, at a personal level, Dyke and Scardino came to like each other. They had a mutual distaste for the stuffy, upper-crust conservative world of the Pearson board. When she arrived and first met Dyke, she had said: 'Hello . . . you're the one I am supposed to be like.' And it had been Dyke, more than anyone else, who had pushed for Barlow's retirement and an injection of new management blood into the company. Dyke had been told that he was one of a group of executives in with a good chance of becoming the Pearson chief executive. From that position he had planned to pull off what was to have been the next step in the series of TV megadeals with which he had built Pearson TV. Dyke was talking to Lord Hollick, Pearson's partner in running Channel Five, about buying the Meridian and Anglia ITV companies. The deal would, at a stroke, Dyke thought, make Pearson by far the biggest private TV company in Europe. Failing his own elevation, Dyke would have backed the appointment of Dennis Stevenson, the most energetic and politically connected member of the Pearson board. But Scardino? No. All she had done at a senior level was run *The Economist*. She had done well enough with that, Dyke thought, but that experience was not enough. Dyke began looking for a new job and it was Scardino, he told others, who first suggested that he make a bid to become Director-General of the BBC.

John Birt was due to step down in April 2000 and the appointment of a replacement would take place in the summer of 1999. In public, Dyke's name had first been linked with the top job at the BBC as early as April 1996, well before Scardino's arrival at Pearson, when Christopher Bland had been appointed Chairman of the BBC's Board of Governors. Unlike Dyke, Christopher Bland had walked away from the TV industry after the Granada takeover, investing part of the £12 million he gained from the merger in a hi-tech medical instruments company. At the same time Bland was chairman of the Hammersmith Hospital Trust, which funded some of the leading cancer hospitals in the country. (The bond between Dyke and Bland had become even more close when Bland had used his medical contacts to help Dyke's dad Joseph during his fatal illness a few years earlier).

Bland's hospital work had brought him into contact with Virginia Bottomley, the Tory health minister who became Heritage Secretary at the fag-end of the Major government. In this capacity she had the responsibility of appointing a successor to the retiring BBC Chairman, Marmaduke Hussey, a man so out of touch with some of the realities of modern broadcasting that he had been accused by a former BBC Director-General of thinking that FM, as in FM radio, stood for 'Fuzzy Monsters'. She chose Bland. Dyke marked the event by telling the papers, 'The governors will learn that his greatest weapon at a board meeting is to shout, "Bollocks!"'

One of Bland's first acts as the BBC's new Chairman had been to appear as an after-dinner speaker at the annual Pearson TV management think-tank, held over two days at the Lucknam Park Hotel near Bath and arranged before his appointment. Bland made a funny speech saying that he had just received the BBC internal telephone directory. There were so many departments and sub-departments and such a vast number of people employed by the Corporation that it was all 'a bit like becoming Mayor of Basingstoke'. He noted that Dyke, through his acquisition of ACI and other American studios, had decided to take Pearson TV into the movie production business. 'The only way to make a small fortune in the movie business is to start off with a large one,' Bland said. It was an extremely old joke but, since it teased Dyke over the way he was spending Pearson's cash like water in his acquisitions campaign, it went down very well.

After Bland's speech there was a question-and-answer session. People asked politely probing questions about where he thought the BBC was going, could the licence fee survive – the usual stuff – and Bland gave off-the-cuff answers until one of the diners asked: 'Would Greg Dyke make a good BBC Director-General?' There was a sharp intake of breath and Dyke looked sheepish. 'I am talking, of course, in theory,' the questioner mumbled into the silence. Bland composed himself and said with great seriousness that John Birt was doing an excellent job and intended to stay for many years yet, adding: 'But yes, Greg would make a very good Director-General and, if he's ever interested and the post was available, I'm sure he would make a very good candidate'. A couple of months later Bland told Ray Snoddy of *The Financial Times*, in what was his first big interview after becoming BBC Chairman, that he 'would want Greg Dyke in any organization. I love working with him. I miss the guy and I had terrific fun working with him'.

Since leaving LWT, Dyke and Bland had continued to meet regularly, perhaps once or twice at month, over breakfast at Bland's favourite London restaurant. After Bland became Chairman of the BBC they had plenty to talk about. Dyke had been involved in unstitching what was planned as a series of joint channel ventures set up by Richard Dunn of Thames and Bob Phillis, the BBC Deputy Director-General. The aim was to give both the BBC and Pearson an international presence and had been hyped as the BBC's most important international initiative ever. Dyke went over the deals in person and tried to push things to some sort of conclusion. But nothing ever seemed to get resolved. 'Parts of the BBC are commercially inept and complacent,' Dyke would say, mad with frustration, 'and we *are* paying them and they *still* can't fucking do it!' Eventually Dyke stopped all joint projects with the BBC and wrote off £25 million to bring it to an end.

Neither Bland nor Dyke entirely blamed John Birt, their former colleague, for the fact that parts of the BBC were in a mess. Dyke would often wonder what the Corporation had been like before Birt had arrived. At least he had put some sort of management systems into the place. He had been fought almost to a standstill by the old guard at the BBC. His attempts to grab complete control of the place had been bitterly resented and Birt had not always played the internal PR game very well. His critics were definitely right about one thing. The BBC was no longer a fun place to work. An internal survey showed that 95 per cent of BBC staff didn't like the way the place was run and no longer trusted its senior management.

Many BBC people thought that Birt's most disastrous move of all had been his decision to divide the place into two sprawling divisions, Broadcast and Production. Birt attempted to sell this reorganization to his senior managers and staff by explaining it as the next logical step in developing the BBC's internal market. Birt had always believed that the BBC gave too much power to programme-makers. But this new scheme effectively reduced producers to second-class citizens, because they now had to sell all their ideas to the extremely powerful people in the Broadcast division who controlled the budgets. Producers were furious that the Broadcast people could buy in programmes and services from outside the BBC while they could not sell their ideas to anyone else.

The complicated scheme involved another painful round of internal restructuring as BBC Radio and the internationally respected World Service both lost their traditional autonomy. There was outrage in Britain's radio community and from those who, like its former boss John Tusa, thought the World Service was being devalued. Birt and Bland were accused of 'cultural vandalism'. The row led the government to set up a committee to monitor the impact of the changes on the World Service.

Inside the BBC, the restructuring caused anger and dismay. Senior people like Birt's head of TV, Will Wyatt, and BBC1 controller Michael Jackson were upset that just as the BBC's ratings were finally beginning to improve, John Birt had forced the BBC into another lengthy period of upheaval and uncertainty. The way the changes had been made also got people's backs up. Birt's secretive tendencies had got the better of him. He had not consulted even his deputy Bob Phillis about the plan. Phillis and others felt Birt had hijacked them. Not long after, Phillis departed the BBC to run the Guardian Media Group.

A much bigger blow to Birt was losing Jackson, who left to run Channel Four. Jackson's biggest coup in his new job caused further embarrassment to Birt and the BBC. In October 1998 Jackson announced that he had stolen the rights to Test Match cricket, held by the BBC for more than fifty years. Sport had become a black hole for the BBC. The cost of sports rights had soared since the days of the old BBC–ITV duopoly. Meanwhile Birt was investing heavily in new digital channels, including several commercial ventures that would not begin to see a return for some years and public service stations like the problematic News 24. The BBC had already lost England home rugby union matches, Formula One, the FA Cup, and the TV rights to the Ryder Cup. And now cricket. To many viewers, especially people like the late Joseph Dyke, sport was what the BBC ought to do best. If the BBC couldn't afford to screen great national events like the Test and the Cup Final, what was the point of having the

BBC in the first place? When a few months later Des Lynam, the face of BBC sport, announced he was leaving to join ITV, it looked like the end of an era.

A lot of people agreed when the Culture Secretary Chris Smith said the BBC's priorities should be sport, comedy, drama and natural history programmes. When, during the autumn of 1999, BBC1 scored a much-needed hit with the hugely expensive computer-generated science documentary *Walking With Dinosaurs*, critics said the programme was a reminder of what BBC1 should be doing much more often – putting on quality shows that were too risky for commercial rivals to make. The trouble was, argued the critics, that with wall-to-wall docusoaps and endless shows about cookery and gardening, it was virtually impossible to distinguish BBC1 from the 'dumbed down' commercial stations. Investing in digital activities was all right provided that 'core services' like BBC1 had enough money to give audiences something special in return for their licence fees.

That summer Noel Edmonds had left the BBC after thirty years, claiming that the BBC was 'no longer committed to quality programming'. He said he was 'heartbroken'.

# 26.
# Things Can Only Get Better

It is 5am, just after dawn on a beautiful spring morning at the start of May 1997. The sun, low in the sky, is reflected off the modernist plate glass of the South Bank arts complex and causes the River Thames to sparkle.

Along the wide pavement overlooking the river – all the way down from Hungerford Bridge to the LWT tower – people are gathering. Many are drunk and all are extremely pleased with themselves. There is laughing and cheering. Outside the Royal Festival Hall there is the sound of thudding pop music. *Things . . . Can only get better . . . Get better . . .*

The music fades and Tony Blair takes to a platform in front of the Festival Hall. He quietens the crowd and then makes a carefully prepared speech accepting victory in the General Election.

'The British people have put their trust in us. It is a moving and a humbling experience. We have been elected as New Labour and we will govern as New Labour,' he said. There is mad cheering at this soundbite, even though people are not all that clear what it means, exactly.

Inside the Festival Hall a select band of invited guests are mingling with Labour activists, enjoying the party. Gerry Robinson of Granada-LWT turns to Clive Hollick of Meridian, the ITV successor to TVS, and says with a gnomic smile: 'Now it begins'.

Greg Dyke is wandering about in the company of Melvyn Bragg and Helena Kennedy, the radical lawyer, beaming from ear to ear. The three friends had watched the close of polls and early result on TV at a party in Kennedy's house and had then spilled out on to the streets, loaded up on champagne, laughing and shouting and making their way to the South Bank . . . *Things . . . Can only get better . . . Gedbetter . . . from nowwwwwwonnnnnn . . .*

Dyke had not been active in the campaign beyond coming out in public as 'a fan' of Blair and New Labour. In a newspaper interview he explained that his trip to Harvard Business School had taught him that 'it was possible to run capitalism with a social conscience'. He added: 'You can be in business and make money and still put something back into society.' His main contribution had been financial. In 1994 Dyke had donated money to help finance Blair's campaign to become leader of the Labour Party. In the same year he joined a Labour fundraising scheme called The 1000 Club, which involved pledging £1,000 a year to the party. He had topped this up with contributions of £5,000 each to help finance the private offices of Jack Cunningham and Mo Mowlam and a £25,000 donation to the Labour 1997 election campaign. With a further donation after Blair was elected, Dyke gave the party about £50,000 over a period of four or five years. Other LWT millionaires also made contributions or helped out in various ways – but their importance and influence had, over a period of years, been far greater than that of merely financial backers. To an extent that was not widely appreciated at the time a network of journalistic, academic, political and business contacts centred on LWT had been crucial to transforming the party through the late Eighties and Nineties.

By the time of Blair's election, the LWT current affairs show *Weekend World* and its successor, *The Walden Interview*, were distant memories. But the influence of the people who had made them lingered. The creation of New Labour and its 1997 election victory had, in a way, been a

# Citizen Greg

triumph for 'Weekend World-ism'. The programme had hired a large number of intellectuals over the years and, in many ways, had functioned as the British equivalent of the policy 'think tanks' which are so important in the American political system. The British Labour Party had always been notably hostile to intellectuals and theorizing. Such policy-making forums as the party had tended to quickly degenerate into sterile battlegrounds. Supposedly right-wing and left-wing factions would fight over basically empty slogans, rather than think through the complexities of policy. *Weekend World*, with its vast budgets, large staff on big wages, general glamour and prestige and access to politicians and other powerful persons eager to appear on TV, had been able to act at times as a sort of unofficial Labour think tank.

There had never been any pretence that *Weekend World* was anything other than left of centre and almost everybody associated with programmes was a Labour or – more fashionably for a while – SDP supporter (the main exception was the conservative commentator Bruce Anderson, who always stuck out like a sore thumb). But they were not just any old sort of Labour supporter. Taking a lead from Peter Jay, *Weekend World*'s original presenter, and John Birt who set it up, *Weekend World* was determinedly 'Atlanticist', taking its leftism not from intellectual European socialism or old-fashioned British trade union power but from the agenda of the US Democratic Party. While the traditional left was more interested in trade union rights, nationalization and economic planning, the *Weekend World* agenda was more to do with racial equality, monetarism and individual freedom. Tony Benn in his diaries described *Weekend World* as 'a weekly party political broadcast for the right wing of the Labour Party'. Television critics and reviewers noted that presenter Brian Walden 'fawned and drooled' over 'Atlanticist'-type right-wing Labour and SDP politicians like David Owen and Roy Jenkins. In the late Seventies and early Eighties the right vs left battle for control of the Labour Party had brought to an end all civilized, let alone intelligent and original, discussion of what the party might actually do in office. And so *Weekend World* became a place where Labour supporters could 'think the unthinkable' – and get handsomely paid to do so.

Ten years later many of the policies first aired on *Weekend World* were central to the way the Labour Party presented itself to the public. The triumph of LWT-style 'Atlanticism' inside Labour was such that the party had to a large extent remodelled its organization and policies on those of the US Democratic Party. In addition to ideology, people like Peter Mandelson, who was at *Weekend World* for a while shortly after Dyke left the programme, and Barry Cox, had helped Blair to the leadership of the party. They brought with them the LWT house-style addiction to audience and market research, demographics and focus groups. Birt had pioneered modern (American-derived) audience research, and understanding the importance of audience research had been one of the first lessons Dyke had learned as an LWT executive. Birt and then Dyke were the first in ITV to see the extent to which the British population was changing, what their preferences were, how they saw themselves and what their aspirations were for the future. Birt and Dyke had done all this for the commercial reasons of preparing a winning schedule and helping advertising sales. But they appreciated the political significance of the research. It showed that Labour had absolutely no chance of winning so long as it tried to appeal to an idea of 'the working class'. No such group existed any longer, at least not in London and the South East, if it ever had.

When Dyke arrived at LWT in 1977 he was very much on the traditional left of the party – a journalistic collaborator with Chris Mullin, the editor of *Tribune* and one of the main organizers of Tony Benn's campaign to become leader of the party. His experience first at LWT and then at the LWT 'satellite' TVS, especially the demographics, had made him rethink his politics. For a while, in the mid-Eighties – when Dyke was busy making his pile of money – his interest in the national political scene waned. A few years earlier, when Dyke was editing *The Six O'Clock Show*, he had been to a dinner party at Barry Cox's house in Hackney and found himself sitting next to the Blairs, not knowing who they were. Cherie Blair revealed that she was a fan of *The Six O'Clock Show*. Dyke had not returned the compliment. He spent part of the evening complaining that the Labour Party was being taken over by yuppies and that it was being 'destroyed' by lawyers and barristers.

But Blair had embraced the whole modernizing American agenda and Dyke was genuinely enthusiastic once again. Most importantly, Blair had turned out to be a winner and with his election victory had ended almost twenty years of Tory rule which had coincided with the best years of Dyke's life. Through most of this period the Conservative Party had been led by Margaret Thatcher, a woman Dyke despised with particular ferocity. This, others noted, was in a way a paradox, since Dyke – more than almost anyone else in the TV business – had directly benefited and risen to power on the back of changes that she had personally unleashed on the industry. But his loathing knew few bounds. Years later he could still remember with relish where he had been at the moment of her downfall – driving along the motorway with Sue, listening to the radio with rapt attention as she announced that she was standing down after failing to get the support of enough backbench MPs to stay on as Prime Minister. Shortly afterwards, in the run-up to the ITV franchise auction, he had denounced her approach to the television industry by saying: 'It's time we told the old bat what's what. Anyway, she's gone, finished. She can't touch us any more.' The splenetic outburst was widely reported in the press.

Now Thatcher was long gone and, despite Blair's personal homage to the 'old bat' delivered during the election campaign, the change of government also meant a change of policy towards the broadcasting industry in general, and towards the BBC in particular. For Dyke personally it opened the possibility of becoming a serious contender for the job of BBC Director-General – utterly impossible until Bland became BBC Chairman and still extremely unlikely under a Tory government. But the first practical result for Dyke of Labour coming to power was not in broadcasting but in the slightly surprising area of the National Health Service, where he agreed to chair a committee charged with designing a new patients' charter.

Dyke was hyperactive in this odd role as in any other, and was soon being accused by fellow review panel member Claire Rayner of having 'hijacked' the process, forcing through his own views and ignoring all the others. He eventually wrote much of the report himself and it appeared under his name. The most important part of the document, Dyke later said, was a passage which, he said, was the essence of the 'philosophy of management', which he had learned years before on *The Six O'Clock Show* and had never really changed. Dyke wrote:

'I believe that most people are capable of achieving outstanding performance – well beyond what many have been led to believe they can achieve – but that can only be brought out by an inclusive management style. I do not believe that people are best motivated by fear but by being involved in the decision-making process, by taking part in the setting of goals for an organization and by being able to celebrate achieving them.'

While he was writing his NHS report, Dyke happened to have lunch with John Birt and told him the same thing in more succinct language. 'They've lost the staff,' Dyke said, 'and when you've lost the staff, you can't do anything – nothing works.' All the people he had met who worked in the health service, Dyke elaborated, thought that whatever success they had achieved was despite the managers, not because of them. As long as the doctors and nurses felt like that, any kind of programme of modernization was bound to fail. Birt responded in an edgy, guarded fashion. The parallels with the BBC, famously in the grip of a 'climate of fear' under Birt, were blindingly obvious. Exactly as Dyke had intended.

# 27.
# Glory, Glory, Man United

'Greg! If we lose this deal because of you . . . I'll sue!'
Martin Edwards, the chairman of Manchester United plc,
is reaching the end of his tether. Edwards and the rest of
the United board are keen to accept a takeover offer made
by Rupert Murdoch's Sky TV, which will earn most of
people in the room millions and, in some cases, tens of
millions.

It is 1am, on an insufferably humid late August night in
1998. The board have been locked up in an anonymous
London hotel meeting room arguing over the offer for
more than eighteen hours without a break. Dyke, who
had joined the United board two years earlier, mainly to
advise the club on its burgeoning TV activities, shrugs
and smiles: 'I told you . . . he's not offering enough.'

Edwards, with a final howl of frustration, adjourns the
meeting. Dyke heads off home to Twickenham. In many
ways it is a straight rerun of the LWT takeover by
Granada. Dyke is on the job for up to twenty hours a day,
running on pure adrenalin, fighting off a rapacious
predator with bottomless pockets and City backing, who
is moving to snap up Dyke's pride and joy at a
knockdown price, planning, in all probability, to inflict all
sorts of damage once in control. But there are differences.
This time Dyke has the chairman and the rest of the board
against him. And, despite this huge disadvantage, Dyke is
determined that he will not be beaten again. The next
morning he is up at 6am, ready to resume battle.

Dyke's business dealings with Martin Edwards and the
Manchester United board dated back ten years to the mid-

Eighties when he was head of ITV sport and was working on a masterplan for an 'ITV 10' football superleague. Edwards and United had then been key allies, along with David Dein of Arsenal, in Dyke's failed battle to prevent Sky buying the rights to screen the Premier League in 1992.

Dyke had lost in 1992 because all twenty clubs in the Premier League had acted as a cartel, selling rights to screen football matches in one take-it-or-leave-it bundle. United, Arsenal and most of the other larger clubs had wanted their games to be on ITV. But they had been outvoted by the smaller clubs who, after much skullduggery, had been persuaded they would be better off doing a 'bundled' deal with Sky. Dyke had reacted by saying that Sky's deal was probably illegal, because the Premier League had acted as a cartel. If the big clubs decided to challenge the deal in the courts, Dyke believed, they would almost certainly find that they were entitled to sell the rights to their home games to the highest bidder, match by match: ITV for instance. But the case was never put to the test.

When Sky's 1992 deal with the Premier League came up for renewal in 1996, Dyke was at Pearson and was thus forced to watch events from the sidelines. This time there was to be no formal bid from the ITV network. Football had been such a financial success for Sky that ITV could not now afford anything like the money Sky was able to put up. Dyke's partner in Channel Five, Lord Hollick's United News and Media, had offered £1 billion to fund a plan to set up a Premier League channel as a 50/50 venture between the company and the League. But Hollick wanted a ten-year deal to protect his investment and the Premier League was not interested. Dyke considered Pearson bidding for the rights, with the idea of acting as a wholesaler, selling the rights match by match to any channel who wanted them. But the outlay needed to beat Sky would be enormous and, at the time, he was already spending heavily buying American and Australian studios and programme catalogues.

Sky renewed its contract with the Premier League. The £600 million the broadcaster paid for the rights showed how dependent Sky had become on showing Premier League football. The broadcaster's own internal research showed that the clear majority of subscribers were signing up for dishes mainly to watch the Premier League. As Dyke had always maintained, without football Sky would have found it difficult to make a big impact on the British market. Football was Sky's jewel in the crown and the key to its £1 billion a year revenues. But such dependence on a single type of programming from a single source represented the broadcaster's Achilles' heel.

Straight away after the 1996 deal Sky sensed a new danger – that the larger clubs, and especially Manchester United, might break free of the Premiership cartel, quash the deal with Sky in the courts and sell their rights individually, as Dyke had always advocated. With the change of government in 1997 there was also the danger that the Office of Fair Trading and Restrictive Practices might act to break up the Premiership in the interests of consumers. These were troubled waters for Sky, and Greg Dyke decided to start fishing in them.

Ominously for Sky, in the summer of 1996 the board of Manchester United starting looking at the possibility of launching its own TV channel. 'MUTV', as the channel was to be called, would not be able to show any of United's live home games so long as Sky had exclusive rights to show these as part of its deal with the Premier League. The threat of Manchester United developing into an independent and, in fact, rival broadcaster to Sky, owning the hottest property in the pay-TV market, was itself a terrifying prospect for Sky. When United started talking to Flextech, the specialist 'channel creation' company, about the development of the station, Sky immediately put in a counter-bid to help create and run MUTV on very advantageous terms.

Then, just as ominously for Sky, Dyke joined the Manchester United board with a specific brief to advise on broadcasting. Dyke had settled in at Pearson, where things were going well, and he had enough time on his hands to help out the club he had supported all his life. He bought a block of 80,000 shares. It was said in the gossip columns, especially after Marjorie Scardino had arrived as his boss at Pearson, that he was thinking about becoming the chief executive at United when the incumbent, Sir Roland Smith, retired in 2000. All went smoothly for a couple of years, with Dyke taking an interest in MUTV, waiting for the day, probably some time after the existing Premier League deal with Sky expired in 2000, when the channel might show all United's home games and therefore become by far the most valuable single property in British pay-TV. If that happened, Sky would be mortally wounded, if not destroyed altogether.

Then in August 1998 Sky TV moved to protect its position. The broadcaster's chief executive, Mark Booth, concluded in secret the outline of a deal with United chairman Martin Edwards which would have given Sky control of the club (and thus removed the threat of an independent MUTV). Booth was offering 217.5p per share, which valued the club at around £600 million and would have guaranteed Edwards a personal pay-out of at least £80 million (Edwards' father, Louis, had bought control of the club only twenty years earlier for about £30,000).

Dyke was in a minority of one in opposing the takeover, at least at the price Sky was offering. Dyke now found himself in a replay of the Granada–LWT takeover bid, right down to the fact that the nominal chief of Sky was Gerry Robinson of Granada. On the face of it he was in an even weaker position in resisting Sky than he had been in resisting Granada at LWT. He knew that the City institutions would sell out if their advisors told them the price was right. At least the board and management of LWT had been opposed to the takeover. The United board, in contrast, wanted to sell out. And the management, including Alex Ferguson, knew nothing about it. Edwards and Booth were keeping everyone in the dark.

The United board had been assured by its advisors, HSBC, that Sky's offer was a good one and that it fully reflected their own valuation of the company. But Dyke did not agree. Dyke had a low opinion of HSBC. He had dealt with them during the Granada–LWT takeover where, he thought, they had undervalued the TV company, advising their institutional clients to sell and thus enabling Robinson to buy it very cheaply. The United chief executive, Sir Roland Smith, wanted the board to be unanimous. But Dyke would not accept the offer or even recommend that it be put to shareholders until the board got a second opinion on the club's value. Dyke's own choice of consultants, Merrill Lynch, thought that United shares were worth a minimum of 240p each – a much higher figure than the Sky offer.

The first round in the battle went to Dyke. He persuaded the board to reject the offer or, at least, hold out for a much better price. Smith, Edwards and Booth negotiated in secret until on 28 August a Manchester United board meeting was called in London to discuss an improved offer – 230p per share. Dyke still thought this was too low and, to the increasing annoyance of Martin Edwards, wanted to hold out for more. It was then, at 1am, after listening to eighteen hours of Dyke solidly stonewalling, that Edwards had issued his half-serious threat to sue for compensation if the Sky deal did not go through.

The board meeting resumed the following morning and continued arguing and negotiating in secret. By now they had an open phone line to the Sky board, also in permanent session, meeting on the other side of the City. Murdoch was present and handling the talks personally. When Roland Smith told him that only Greg Dyke stood between him and the unanimous acceptance of his bid, Murdoch reportedly said Dyke was the 'traditional enemy of Sky'. He warned the United board that Dyke was a man who they 'should watch out for'. Dyke later said that Murdoch had behaved like a 'thug' during the takeover battle. At one point Dyke was called by his advisors Merrill Lynch, who said they had been talking to their New York office. Murdoch had apparently threatened to withdraw the extremely lucrative contract to organize the multibillion stock market flotation of Fox if their London office did not stop supporting Dyke.

By 2pm on the second day of the marathon board meeting there was still no agreement, but Roland Smith contacted Sky and said the board might be able to accept a bid of 240p or more. This was angrily rejected by Murdoch who pointed out that he had previously been assured that the club was for sale at 217.5p. He said he would pay 230p and not a penny more. Roland Smith said that he could not get unanimity at that price. Murdoch, reportedly replied: 'We don't care. We'll do a deal at 230p and let Dyke vote against you. Let there be a director who is against you.' Smith said that was not acceptable. It had to be unanimous.

Eventually Murdoch and Booth cracked and offered 240p. Dyke considered putting them through the winger again, pointing out that this price was the lowest value in the range suggested by Merrill Lynch. But he gave in. The price valued United at about £625 million. Dyke agreed to drop his objections. He signed a letter of acceptance so that the board could unanimously recommend acceptance of Sky's bid. Dyke's intransigence had cost Murdoch perhaps £100 million. But this was not to be the end of the drama.

The Murdoch papers, led by the *Sun*, hailed the deal as 'a great day for football and for Manchester United' under the headline GOLD TRAFFORD. The paper pushed the implausible line that, having shelled out £625 million for United on top of the £600 million paid for the Premier League rights two years earlier, Sky was planning to spend further tens of millions buying star players for the United team. The *Sun*'s triumphalism was premature. Amid a huge political outcry and effective lobbying by an anti-Murdoch 'fan power' group, the takeover was referred to the Monopolies and Mergers Commission. The day after the deal had been made public, Dyke phoned Mark Booth, Sky's chief executive, and told him that the deal would not be allowed on competition grounds. Booth later told journalist Mihir Bose, 'I said "nonsense" and we had a bet that if he was right I would buy him lunch.'

Dyke then pulled off his own PR masterstroke. He announced that he would donate any money that he personally stood to make from the takeover to charity. In fact the sum involved (unlike the fortune he made from the equally detested Granada takeover of LWT) was only about £30,000. But it was a stunningly effective move. The *Daily Express* ran the headline:

DYKE TELLS DIRECTORS:
GIVE AWAY YOUR ILL-GOTTEN GAINS

Dyke's continuing opposition to Sky's bid ensured that a deal which had been designed to go through quietly remained in the spotlight for months. In the summer of 1999, to Dyke's huge satisfaction, the MMC outlawed the takeover on competition grounds, just as Dyke had predicted. Without control of Manchester United, Sky's domination of British football looked like it might have a limited future. And without that domination the vast profits Sky had made for Rupert Murdoch were under threat.

Which was why, in the summer of 1999, Greg Dyke was the last man on earth that Rupert Murdoch wanted to see as Director-General of the BBC, the most powerful rival broadcaster in the country.

# 28.
# Citizen Greg

It had seemed like a good idea at the time. Pearson's director of communications, Roy Addison, had booked Dr David Starkey, the historian and professional controversialist, to give the traditional after-dinner speech at the opening night of the biennial Royal Television Society Cambridge conference taking place amid the ersatz gothic splendour of the King's College dining room. Pearson had taken over the sponsorship of the dinner as a way of underlining the company's growing importance in the British TV business.

Starkey is coming towards the end of his talk. The audience, comprising the entire top brass of the British TV industry, listen in horrified silence. On the platform next to Starkey, Greg Dyke and Jeremy Isaacs, the chairman of the society, fidget uneasily, their faces showing increasing embarrassment.

'Sorry, this has all been very solemn,' Starkey says, sensing the discomfort. He turns briefly to Dyke, who has his arms tightly crossed and is staring at the ceiling. 'I'm not just a media entertainer, you see. I still have that residual notion that was taught in this university all those years ago that real academic work – that thinking the unthinkable is important – even in front of an audience that doesn't like it, is the thing to do. . . thank you very much for having me. I hope you don't regret it too much.' One person, towards the back of the room, starts to clap like mad. But otherwise there is a stunned and deathly hush.

David Starkey's speech at the conference would later be remembered by everyone who was present as one of the most embarrassing moments in British TV's corporate history. Dyke had personally introduced Starkey as a 'provocative and, above all, entertaining' speaker. It had started well enough, with Starkey producing a couple of witty, gossipy put-downs, as expected. 'Casting my mind forward two years into the future,' Starkey said, 'I can see myself attending the same event and being hosted by Sir Gregory Dyke, shorn of his beard and introducing me to you in front of Lord John Birt.' John Birt, who was due to retire as Director-General in less than three years, shouted: 'Oh no he won't!' Starkey, his voice already betraying cold contempt, rather than the trade-mark waspish sophistication he was hired for, replied: 'Well, yes . . . there's a Shakespearean word which all of us here are very familiar with which I won't use.' That was as funny as it got. Starkey then launched into an astonishing, unrestrained and highly personal attack on all those present.

He began by saying that TV had exploited the emotion surrounding the death of Princess Diana a few weeks previously to the point of creating mass hysteria. Television had stopped just short of inciting lynch mobs, egging on a dangerous and irrational minority who might easily have marched on parliament and created an electronic version of the French Revolution and The Terror. During the Diana crisis the BBC had relied on vox pop interviews with the uninformed: 'One of these people,' Starkey said, by now practically spitting out each word, 'said, "Oh yes, me wife died a year ago but this affected me much more badly" – that is a direct quote.'

Then Starkey began to get more personal. 'Regulation of the media,' he said, 'began in the age of Lord Reith. It was based on the assumption that those on top knew that they were different from most of the audience.' But now,

Starkey continued, 'all the talk is of "the people",' of pleasing the audience and pandering to the ignorance and prejudices of the masses. The people running TV were no longer educated and cultivated and responsible conservatives like Reith. They were the modern-day equivalent of the demagogues of the French Revolution.

'Let's now come really close to home,' Starkey said, appearing to take a sadistic pleasure in the discomfort of all present. Birt, the man picked out as the modern-day TV-version Robespierre, shifted uneasily in his seat. On the platform sat Citizen Greg, the People's Tribune, looking mortified.

The executives before him, Starkey said, had turned the news into 'a continuous form of entertainment, not designed to encourage thought or criticism, but to provoke the emotion of anger. Ideas don't matter any more – sensation and personality are now the only things that matter.' The trend for 'People Shows' and fly-on-the-wall documentaries (which, at the time, were much in evidence in the BBC, ITV and Channel Four schedules) were 'travesties which fit reality into the conventions of drama'. The people who ran television, Starkey said, had embraced the Californian approach to TV which, he said, was now 'all about car smashes'. Starkey told a story of how he had seen a Californian TV reporter at the scene of a car smash, excitedly inviting his viewers to imagine the horrific pain and injuries of a burning corpse trapped inside a wrecked car. That was where the self-regarding people assembled in their dinner jackets and bow ties at the RTS were heading.

The speech finished, and there was much rolling of eyes and muttering before Dyke made his way to the microphone. 'Ladies and gentlemen,' said Dyke gruffly. 'I have just discovered that it is my role to thank Dr David

Starkey . . .' There was faint laughter as Dyke turned nervously toward his tormentor.

'All I would say is that you are very different to Rory Bremner, who we had last time . . .'.

Dyke had started to think actively about a move to the BBC when Marjorie Scardino had been put in over his head as chief executive at Pearson. Before that he would have been content to stay, building up Pearson TV and perhaps ending his career as chief executive of a greatly expanded Pearson media group. But Scardino's arrival in 1996 had made him determined to move on.

After his tussle with Murdoch over Manchester United in the autumn of 1998, Dyke began to turn his attention increasingly towards the BBC. Everyone knew the race for John Birt's job was wide open. There was no obvious outstanding internal candidate and it was being widely said that senior jobs in British TV were becoming increasingly difficult to fill because of a lack of top class home-grown executive talent. But many key people in the TV industry and in the chattering classes beyond believed that Dyke would get the job because he enjoyed powerful patronage. Despite his wholly commercial background, people figured that New Labour's ascendancy and Christopher Bland's increasingly dominant position as BBC Chairman gave Dyke a huge advantage over any rival candidate, including Birtists like news supremo Tony Hall, World Service boss Mark Byford and ex-Radio 1 controller Matthew Bannister, best known for his headline-grabbing clashes with Chris Evans.

It became clear to many who attended Richard Dunn's memorial service at St Martins-in-the-Fields in November 1998 that Dyke was thinking seriously about the Director-Generalship. Dunn, the former head of Thames and the man who Dyke had beaten to take control of Pearson's TV interests, had died suddenly, drowning in the swimming pool at his Berkshire home after suffering a heart seizure, a month before his 55th birthday. He had always been a tremendously fit man and many said that he had never really recovered from the trauma of losing the Thames franchise. Like a lot of people in the TV industry, Dyke was devastated by Dunn's death.

After the service, at a reception held for mourners at the Garrick Club in nearby Covent Garden, Dyke spent some of the time pumping the assembled TV notables about the BBC – its internal politics, the problems and prospects, how the whole structure worked and what the Governors were like. He had not yet finally made up his mind about applying for the job, but it was clear to many of those present that he was now thinking about it very seriously.

Then, in February 1999, just a few weeks before the BBC was due to officially advertise the vacancy, Dyke had lunch with the Culture Secretary, Chris Smith, to discuss the progress of the British film industry. In passing, Smith asked him if he was going to apply for the Director-Generalship. In theory, Smith had no direct say in who would get the job. The Culture Secretary's main power was in helping to appoint the Chairman and Governors, who would then make the decision. Dyke told him that he was thinking about it, but had not yet made up his mind. It was obvious at the time that Dyke's politics could pose a problem. The Director-General was also the BBC's editor-in-chief and so any hint of political partisanship could potentially rule him out of contention, especially in the eyes of the Governors. The Conservatives were at the time running a campaign against Tony Blair, alleging that he was abusing Prime Ministerial patronage to pack all manner of public bodies with loyal 'Tony's Cronies'. If Dyke decided to put himself forward they were bound to try and make something of such a well-known Labour supporter being in the running for Director-General.

In the weeks that followed, Dyke talked openly about his chances of getting the job with several of his friends in the business. He seemed to run hot and cold about the idea. One minute he would say that running the BBC would be a great challenge, that he could see how he could make a big impact quickly. It would be a chance to work closely again with Bland, perhaps recreating the triumphs of their LWT days. 'It's the problems . . . ' he would intone. 'There's lots of nice knotty problems to solve. That's what I like.' The next minute he would tell a different story, describing the Director-Generalship as a 'nightmare job' and 'not worth all the hassle'. For some, the decisive moment was when Dyke spent a fortune on some expensive dental work and shaved off his beard, as David Starkey had predicted, so that he could at least look more like the part. 'It's like *Stars In Their Eyes*, innit?' Dyke said of the make-over. 'You go in looking like Barry Gibb. Then there's a big puff of smoke . . . And you come out looking like 'Enry Cooper!'

All along, Dyke's main concern was the effect that doing the job would have on Sue and the kids. Becoming Director-General would make him a public figure – a household name maybe. That meant setting up himself and his family for intense scrutiny from the tabloids. He and Sue were not married and, despite changing times, he knew that the tabloids might try and make something of that. When he was in the mood, Dyke would make light of the tabloid threat by saying the worst thing they could do was print a picture of him apparently riding to hounds. As part of his outdoor pursuits mania, Dyke had taken up horse-riding. He had once got lost and ended up in a field surrounded by the Hampshire Hunt.

Dyke's fears about tabloid intrusion were confirmed when he discovered that the *Daily Mail* was trying to track down Christine, his ex-wife, doubtless in the hope of finding some entertaining or damaging material on his personal life. Some thought it was odd that Dyke had effectively written Christine out of his life. She was not referred to at all in his *Who's Who* entry. As a former tabloid journalist, he was only too aware of the mischief the papers could serve up if they put their mind to it. In March 1999 the BBC officially invited applications for the £337,000-a-year job as Director-General. Dyke did not declare himself to be in the running immediately. Even so, sections of the press began running 'knocking stories' on the basis of rumours that he might be a candidate.

And that was what settled it. The first salvoes in a press campaign aimed squarely at the Governors of the BBC, and designed to prevent them appointing Greg Dyke, led to a final family conference on whether he should go for it. Sue was adamant. They were not going to be dictated to by the papers. Dyke had by now been approached by the firm of head-hunters the BBC was using to draw up a shortlist for Birt's replacement. He decided to let his name go forward.

# 29.
# The Candidate

The newspaper campaign designed to prevent Greg Dyke from becoming Director-General of the BBC began in full force the moment he announced that he was a candidate for the job. Leading the way was Rupert Murdoch's *Times* which, in the first week of May, broke the exclusive story that Dyke had made donations totalling £50,0000 to the Labour Party and the private offices of various ministers who, at the time, were shadow ministers. The paper's editor, Peter Stothard – a former BBC graduate trainee who had once written a famous series of three consecutive leading articles calling for the BBC to be broken up and privatized – now ran a leader saying that Dyke should be ruled out of contention.

Dyke, and his supporters, responded by sending a letter to the paper, published the next day. 'We find it astonishing that some commentators have suggested that Greg Dyke might be susceptible to political pressure,' they said, adding: 'He has always been known as someone who has never allowed his personal beliefs to interfere with, or encroach upon, his editorial judgement.' It was signed by Clive Jones, Dyke's number two at TV-am and TVS, now installed as chief executive of Carlton TV, and a list of other luminaries including Melvyn Bragg, Barry Cox and Adam Boulton of Sky News. In the same edition, Ray Snoddy, who had worked with Dyke when they were both rookie journalists in Uxbridge, reported that headhunters Heidrich and Struggles had finished drawing up their shortlist of candidates. The most likely 'internal' candidate, Snoddy wrote, was the BBC's director of TV, Alan Yentob, with Tony Hall, the head of BBC news, also in the running. But Dyke, Snoddy said, was 'the bookies' favourite'.

The next day Dyke was once again all over the papers. Under the headline NEW GUIDELINES THREAT TO DYKE, *Times* reporter Andrew Pierce reported the fact that an unnamed BBC Governor was 'urging the government to set new guidelines which could bar political donors such as Greg Dyke from standing for public office'. The same edition carried a letter from Peter Ainsworth, Conservative Shadow Culture Secretary, that concluded by saying: 'In order to end damaging speculation and to make a clear statement of the BBC's commitment to impartiality, the governors should rule Mr Dyke out now.'

The *Independent* weighed into the anti-Dyke campaign, opening up a second front – the allegation that Dyke was responsible for the 'dumbing-down' of television. 'Mr Dyke is often criticized for bringing such low-brow products as *Roland Rat, Gladiators* and *Blind Date* to British television,' the paper said. At least Dyke escaped having his name linked to Channel Five and its profoundly dumb 'three Fs' – Football, Fucking and Films – formula. Dyke's joint creation with Lord Hollick had lately upped the raunch factor to the point where it was featuring soft porn movies on many nights and a glut of sex documentaries including *Sex and Shopping* and *The Female Orgasm*. All that would have been a far more damaging smear than associating him with good old wholesome *Blind Date*. (Possibly the anti-Dyke journalists were working on the entirely reasonable assumption that the Governors had never heard of Channel Five or, possibly, thought that it was some sort of satellite channel beamed in from Scandinavia.) The problem was that one of Dyke's main rivals for the BBC job was none other than David 'Two

Brains' Elstein and he was now running Channel Five. Instead, Andreas Whittam-Smith, the paper's founding editor, commandeered the best part of a page to – in the nicest possible way – accuse Dyke of straightforward political payola, saying that his Labour Party donations 'ruled him out' of the job because 'all large cash contributions to political parties are attempts to buy favours'.

The *Daily Mail*, having failed to track down Dyke's first wife Christine or otherwise dig up much of interest on his personal life, weighed in on the 'dumbing-down' angle with an article squarely addressed to the Governors. Some of the Governors were keen to show that Christopher Bland could not ride roughshod over them and that they might be inclined to vote against Dyke just so Bland did not get his way. 'Greg Dyke is the man who brought *Roland Rat* to the screen,' the paper said. 'His status as favourite for the job is based on his friendship with the Chairman of the BBC Governors, Sir Christopher Bland. Critics say he is not really a programme-maker.' All this was in contrast to Alan Yentob, one of Dyke's leading rivals. After years of castigating Yentob as principal bogeyman of British television as head of BBC2 and BBC1, the *Mail* experienced a sudden conversion. Yentob, the paper purred, 'has only ever worked at the BBC . . . he is regarded as a "creative leader" responsible for all output bar news. In 1997 the RTS presented him with the Judges' Award, describing him as "a passionate champion of individual choice".' The next day the *Mail* reported a 'new twist' in the Director-General story – Dyke's lunch with Chris Smith in February, implying that the Culture Secretary had fixed Dyke up with the job there and then and wondering if the Governors were going to stand for being manipulated by politicians in this way.

# The Candidate

On and on it went. For the best part of a month the *Mail* and, especially, *The Times*, ran knocking stories on Dyke practically on a daily basis. Sometimes there were two stories on a single day, with endless variations and 'new twists' on the same basic story that Dyke was a member of the Labour Party, had made donations, was Bland's man and was responsible for *Roland Rat*. At one point *The Times* even reprinted Dyke's twenty-year-old Putney GLC manifesto, implying, in defiance of the facts, that Dyke was such a 'Tony's Crony', sycophant and placeman that he had been 'New Labour' even back then. Dyke complained that if he had known the picture was going to appear in *The Times* he would have combed his hair. The same edition carried a story again quoting an unnamed Governor as saying: 'He is not the right person for the job. I think he has been damaged by the press disclosures. I do not think he can get it now.'

In the middle of all this Dyke found the time to watch Manchester United play in the European Cup Final against Bayern Munich in Barcelona. Colleagues at Pearson noticed that Dyke's worries about the BBC and the press campaign seemed to evaporate as he concentrated on United's prospects for the game. He spent part of a day organizing a Manchester United trivia quiz, offering part of his director's allocation of tickets for the match as prizes. Such was the importance of the game that Dyke allowed his son to skip revision for final exams at Manchester University so that he could attend the match, on the grounds that, in twenty years' time, nobody would care what degree he got, but he would be able to tell everyone that he saw Man United play (and, as it happened, win) in a European Cup Final. Dyke splashed out on the hire of a private jet to take the family down to the match, moaning that it 'cost an absolute fortune' but explaining that there was no point in being a multi-millionaire if you couldn't do that sort of thing from time to time. Dyke returned to London deliriously happy with United's 2–1 win over the Germans, only to have his mood ruined by the news that *The Times* had been on to Pearson asking how its board of directors and shareholders felt about Dyke making personal use of the company jet. The Pearson press officer had replied: 'We don't have a company jet.' Dyke later went on the record to wonder why *The Times* thought that his application for a job at the BBC was bigger news than Kosovo. The answer, he was convinced, was sheer snobbery, combined with vengeance being personally directed by Murdoch in the wake of the blocked Manchester United takeover.

Although, unlike some of the other candidates, Dyke was not exactly running an organized election campaign, he did have some valuable allies in the media. The *Guardian* came out strongly in his favour, running a lengthy piece by star columnist Polly Toynbee under the headline: THE BBC MUST APPOINT THE BEST MAN: HE IS GREG DYKE. Barry Cox and Melvyn Bragg, meanwhile, helped him rehearse his impending interview with the Governors during a face-to-face session at Bragg's house in Hampstead. He did something similar over the phone with Liz Forgan, the former head of BBC radio who had left the Corporation after clashing with John Birt.

The day of Dyke's interview was marked by a final flurry of black propaganda aimed at the Governors. *The Times* rehashed its original Labour donations 'story' for the umpteenth time under the headline: UNEASE AT BBC OVER DYKE CASH TO LABOUR, quoting yet more unnamed sources and, at the same time, boosting Alan Yentob, the man with the best chance of beating Dyke as a person who 'understands the ethos of the BBC because he is no ratings-chaser'. The *Mail* reported FURY OVER MINISTERS' LINK WITH TV MOGUL, also a reworking of the original donations story. In Dyke's corner, the *Guardian* countered with the angle that Dyke, if made DG, planned to make Yentob his deputy, thus creating a 'Dream Ticket'. Dyke was cast as 'a successful businessman and effective leader', whereas Yentob was 'creative with an arts background – but disorganized and not a charismatic leader'. Working together in this way, the *Guardian* thought, they would be 'perfect'.

Dyke approached his interview with the Governors in his normal happy-go-lucky way. By chance he met Tom Gutteridge, once his rival in the LWT franchise bid, for a meeting the day before. Dyke seemed to Gutteridge 'the same as ever' and perfectly relaxed as both men exchanged ideas about the BBC. The interview itself took place in front of all twelve Governors in the oak-panelled council chamber at the heart of Broadcasting House. What transpired was to remain confidential, though Dyke later claimed he had started off by cracking a joke: 'Some of you may have read that I once said that the reason why there is a crisis in the Church of England is that in the 1950s the English aristocracy stopped sending their idiot sons into the clergy and got them jobs in the BBC instead. I now wish to retract that statement.' He also claimed to have retracted a complaint that the BBC won more BAFTA awards than ITV only because the jury was 'fixed' and said that he had been 'only joking' when he made his famous Pebble Mill pronouncement that Saddam Hussein was more likely to get the DG job than himself.

The Governors completed their interviews with all the candidates over a number of days, finishing on 25 May. They then spent almost a month mulling over their decision. The press campaign was cranked up again, with Tory leader William Hague issuing a statement calling on the Governors to reject Dyke. This was to be a turning point in the saga and many believed that Hague had inadvertently done Dyke a favour by taking such a blatant political stand against him. On 23 June Bland, as BBC Chairman, called a special meeting of the Governors so they could make a final decision. Bland had wanted the decision to be unanimous, but this was proving to be impossible. Several of the Governors had reportedly accepted Bland's case that Dyke was the best man for the job, but some refused to come round. Others, as *The Times* had correctly deduced, simply wanted to assert their authority by defying the sometimes overbearing Bland on a matter of such great importance.

The special Governors' meeting lasted for five hours, taking up the whole of the afternoon. Bland failed to get his way on one point – the decision was not to be unanimous. No vote was taken and the Governors reached what was described as a 'consensus' in favour of Dyke by the narrow margin of seven to five. The decision to appoint Dyke was such a close-run thing that the Governors insisted, as part of his conditions of employment, that he would not bring his long-standing personal assistant, Fiona Hillary, to work with him at the BBC because she lived with Barry Cox, the man who had helped run Tony Blair's leadership campaign and who was still closely linked to the New Labour establishment.

Finally, the Governors decided to wait two days until Friday morning before announcing their decision at a press conference. They then had dinner, which lasted until beyond midnight. Dyke, meanwhile, had spent a nervous evening – mobile phone at the ready – at Bertorelli's restaurant in London's West End in the company of Sue and, of all people, Jeremy Beadle. At 1.45am on Thursday morning Dyke took a call from Christopher Bland on his mobile as he was travelling home in his Pearson Jaguar. He had got it.

On Thursday morning Dyke had breakfast as usual with Sue and the kids. His 14-year-old daughter Alice was distinctly underwhelmed. 'Well, I don't think you should get that job,' she grumbled. 'You'll spoil Radio One by putting adverts on it.' Dyke cheered her up by saying that the family would now be able to get into the hospitality tent at Glastonbury. Alison's mood changed immediately and for the next few weeks Dyke had the unaccustomed pleasure of her trying to get into his good books.

News of the appointment leaked immediately and – bizarrely – from William Hague's office rather than the BBC. By Thursday afternoon it was common knowledge in the BBC newsroom. As word spread, there was spontaneous cheering in parts of the organization. Dyke's appointment might not have played well in the Tory party or in the Wapping headquarters of *The Times*, but it was an immediate hit with most of the people in the BBC and with the overwhelming majority of people in the TV business. Quite apart from his various qualities, Dyke had one huge and overwhelming advantage as far as the troops were concerned – he was not John Birt. (Michael Grade later compared the end of the Birt era to the finale of Beethoven's *Fidelio*, as prisoners grope their way out of Pizarro's dungeon, 'blinded by the unaccustomed sunlight, their years of incarceration behind them'.)

By Friday morning photographers had gathered on the steps of Broadcasting House in the hope of getting the first pictures of The Great Liberator or Monstrous Fat Cat Dumbed Down Tony Crony, according to proprietorial preference. They were to be disappointed. The BBC's army of 'Birtist' spin-doctors were still quixotically clinging to the idea that the decision was secret until the press conference, so Dyke had been smuggled into the building through a sinister-sounding tunnel which connected the basement of Broadcasting House to a spur of the London Underground nuclear bunker system at Oxford Circus tube station.

Over the weekend *The Times* vented its spleen one last time, based on the news that William Hague was 'seeking an urgent meeting' with Christopher Bland to win assurances that the BBC would remain politically neutral. The paper had one last push at the Governors, saying that their 'farcical' decision to appoint Dyke showed they were ROTTING AT THE CORE and that, for good measure, they had SCRIPTED A TRAGEDY. *The Times* suggested that they could redeem themselves, slightly, even at this late stage by appointing Tony Hall, the defeated Wapping-approved 'Birtist' candidate for DG, as editor-in-chief with a specific role to ensure that Dyke did not somehow turn the Corporation into an extension of the Labour propaganda machine.

Dyke spent much of the weekend taking congratulatory phone calls and reading the mountain of letters that began to pour in. One of the letters was from Paul Bonner, the former chairman of the ITV network controllers' committee who had presided over Dyke's battling for LWT against the other companies in the ITV system and who used to play the role of referee during the slanging matches with Granada.

Dyke wrote to Bonner to thank him for his best wishes, signing off with a characteristic flourish: 'Now we can *really* fuck Granada.'

# Chronology

1947: Born 20 May.

1959: Attends Hayes Grammar School.

1965: Leaves school: spends three months at Marks & Spencer as trainee manager.

1966: Commences work as a junior reporter on the *Hillingdon Mirror*, subsequently working for the *Slough Evening Mail*.

1971: Attends York University to read politics, where he meets and marries Christine.

1974: Graduates from York and starts work at the *Newcastle Journal*.

1976: Returns to London to take a job working for Wandsworth Community Relations Council.

1977: Stands as Labour candidate for the Greater London Council in Putney.

1977: Joins London Weekend Television as a researcher on *The London Programme*.

1978: Promoted to producer, *Weekend World*.

1979: Becomes deputy editor of *The London Programme*. Dyke is active in an 11-week ITV strike.

1981
May: Appointed editor of *The Six O'Clock Show*.

# Citizen Greg

**1982**

Jan:    *The Six O'Clock Show* is launched. He and Christine are divorced the same year.

Dyke's new partner is Sue Howes, a school teacher.

Nov:  Channel Four launched.

**1983**

Jan:    BBC *Breakfast Time* begins.

Feb:   TV-am is launched.

Mar:  Appointed editor in chief, TV-am.

May:  *Roland Rat* begins to make an impact on TV-am's ratings.

June: Tory landslide in general election.

Aug:  *Roland Rat* helps TV-am to overtake BBC in ratings.

Oct:   Neil Kinnock succeeds Michael Foot as Labour leader.

**1984**

Jan:    Rupert Murdoch relaunches Sky, a pan-European cable service.

Mar:  Miners' strike begins. Thatcherism is rampant.

May:  Bruce Gygnell arrives as the new boss of TV-am.

Dyke leaves TV-am to join TVS as director of programmes.

Nov:  Michael Grade becomes controller of BBC 1.

**1985**

Jan:    Dyke embroiled in row over TVS Greek Civil War documentary made for Channel Four.

Mar:  Peacock Committee set up to investigate BBC finance.

**1986**

Mar:  Press reports that Dyke is being 'wooed by the BBC'.

Apr:   Peacock Report puts idea of auctioning ITV franchises on Thatcher agenda.

Jun:   TVS announces Dyke's appointment to group board.

Jul:    Dyke gets £100,000 share windfall from TV-am.

Oct:   Marmaduke Hussey appointed Chairman of the BBC.

Dec: British Satellite Broadcasting wins contract from IBA for satellite service.

**1987**

Jan: Dyke attacks northern domination of ITV.

Mar: LWT's director of programmes, John Birt, becomes BBC Deputy Director-General.

Apr: Dyke is appointed Birt's successor as LWT director of programmes.

Jun: Tories re-elected with big majority.

Oct: Dyke shakes up LWT programme schedule and says that ITV needs to be more like Sainsbury's and not the Co-op. Makes comparison with outdated Labour Party.

Nov: TV-am strike starts.

Negotiations begin between Football League and TV companies for screening of live Sunday matches. Dyke heads negotiations as head of ITV sport.

**1988**

Feb: Gyngell wins TV-am strike.

Dyke attacks LWT unions after a drama is scrapped because of pay demand.

June: Murdoch announces plan for launch of Sky TV as satellite service.

ITV pays £11 million for football rights as part of Dyke's plan for live, exclusive sport.

July: Dyke reveals details of 'ITV ten' football superleague initiative.

Aug: Announces plans to axe Sunday evening 'God Slot' but plan is scuppered by IBA.

Nov: Broadcasting White Paper published. Hostile to ITV with plan to auction franchises.

Dyke drops plan to axe 'downmarket' darts from ITV after viewer protests.

**1989**

Feb: Sky TV launched as direct-to-home satellite service.

Oct: Dyke appointed managing director of LWT. He attends a three-month course at Harvard.

Fifty-four LWT managers invest just over £3 million with shares valued at 83p.

By September 1993 the shares are worth 470p.

## 1990

Feb: Dyke becomes LWT managing director. *Sun* runs headline: ROLAND RAT'S DAD GETS TOP TELLY JOB.

Mar: Sky reaches one million homes.

Apr: Delayed launch of BSB.

Jul: BBC ratings are at a six year low. ITV share is 44 per cent with BBC at 37 per cent.

Dyke declares that ITV can no longer be seen 'as a downmarket, ageing channel'.

Sep: Sam Chisholm joins Sky and acts quickly to 'merge' station with BSB.

Nov: Broadcasting Act published.

Thatcher resigns.

Dyke says *World In Action* is 'a luxury ITV can no longer afford'. The network must get in shape to face the challenge of satellite TV.

## 1991

Feb: Dyke denounces franchise auction.

Apr: He advises BBC to 'hack' at staff numbers following his example at LWT.

May: Applications for LWT and Sunrise go in to IBA.

Jul: LWT's profits soar on the back of Dyke's cost cutting – despite recession. Birt made Director-General designate.

Oct: Dyke is double winner in franchise race as LWT and Sunrise triumph.

Nov: LWT winning 56 per cent of the audience on Sunday nights thanks to investment in drama. 'We are out BBC-ing the BBC,' crows Dyke, now group chief executive at LWT and chairman of ITV Council.

# Chronology

1992

Feb: Dyke resigns from ITN board in row over Oracle, ITV's teletext service.

Dec: Dyke approached to be ITV network central scheduler.

Mar: BSkyB achieves breakeven.

Apr: John Major wins the General Election on reduced majority.

May: ITV network centre announces it will have £500 million programme budget.
ITV's bid for Premier League football beaten by joint bid from Sky and BBC. Five-year deal worth £304 milllion.

Aug: Michael Grade attacks John Birt's 'pseudo-Leninist' management style at BBC.

1993

Jan: New era of ITV dawns as ITV's new licences kick in. GMTV (the renamed Sunrise franchise winner) goes on air.

Feb: Dyke appointed chairman of GMTV following disastrous launch.

July: Granada takes a 17 per cent stake in LWT. Opening salvo in bitter takeover battle.
Dyke clashes with MPs over attempt to axe *News At Ten*.

Aug: 'Golden handcuffs' share deal pays out. Dyke pockets around £5 million.

Nov: ITV ownership rules relaxed by Government.

Dec: Granada formally launches hostile takeover for LWT.
Dyke tells the *Daily Telegraph* that Saddam Hussein stands better chance of running the BBC than he has.

1994

Feb: LWT takeover by Granada. Dyke says he is quitting TV – maybe for good. He gets a 'six figure' payout.

Apr: Resigns as chairman of GMTV.

Jul: Tony Blair becomes leader of the Labour Party. Dyke has contributed to Blair's leadership campaign, which is run by his former LWT boss, Barry Cox.

Aug: Dyke gives the MacTaggart Lecture at Edinburgh TV festival.

BSkyB announces £93 million profit, fruits of 1992 football rights deal.

Dec: Reports that Dyke might join the BBC as a channel controller.

**1995**

Mar: Dyke becomes chairman and chief executive of Pearson TV.

Pearson buys Grundy, makers of *Neighbours*, for £175 million.

Aug: BSkyB profits top £155 million.

Sep: Pearson sells stake in BSkyB for £492 million. Dyke resigns from BSkyB board.

Oct: Pearson-United consortium wins Channel Five licence chaired by Dyke.

**1996**

Jan: Marjorie Scardino appointed chief executive of Pearson Group.

Apr: Christopher Bland becomes BBC Chairman.

Jun: BSkyB renews Premier League deal for £670 million.

Birt announces his most radical reform yet, splitting BBC into separate Production and Broadcast divisions. Colleagues are outraged.

Dec: Speculation that Dyke is preparing a management buy-out of Pearson TV.

**1997**

Mar: Channel Five launched.

May: Tony Blair's New Labour wins by a landslide at the General Election.

Aug: Scardino dismisses rumours of a rift between her and Dyke as 'bunkum'.

Sep: Dyke becomes a director of Manchester United.

David Starkey's attack on '1789' (mob rule) brought about by TV's coverage of Diana's death at RTS event hosted by Dyke and Pearson TV. Deep embarrassment.

Oct: Pearson buys All-American (*Baywatch*, *Blind Date*, etc) for £233 million.

Article by Dyke on National Health Service appears in *Daily Mirror* following his appointment to chair committee investigating NHS patients' charter.


1998.

Feb: Michael Wearing resigns as head of serials at the BBC claiming that Birt's reforms have stifled creativity.

Aug: Sky launches takeover bid for Manchester United. Dyke isolated on United board in opposing sell-out at the price offered.

Oct: BBC loses cricket coverage to Channel Four.

Sky Digital launches.

Nov: OnDigital launches.


1999

Mar: BBC advertises for a new Director-General to replace Birt.

Apr: Dyke buys £100,000 extra Man Utd shares, 'fuelling speculation' that he might be Club's next chief executive. Dyke's candidature for D-G opposed by Tories because of his donations to Labour

Jun: BBC axes *Vanessa* show after row over faked guests.

Dyke appointed Director-General of the BBC.

# Selected Bibliography

Bose, Mihir, *Manchester Unlimited: The Rise and Rise of the World's Premier Football Club*, Orion, 1999.

Bonner, Paul (with Lesley Aston), *Independent Television in Britain*; Volume 5, *ITV and IBA, 1981–92, The Old Relationship Changes*, Macmillan, 1998.

Davidson, Andrew, *Under the Hammer*, Heinemann, 1992.

Docherty, David, *Running The Show: The Inside Story of a Television Station*, Boxtree Books, 1990.

Grade, Michael, *It Seemed Like A Good Idea At The Time: An autobiography*, Macmillan, 1999.

Grout, Jeff and Lynne Curry, *The Adventure Capitalists*, Kogan Page, 1998.

Horrie, Chris and Steve Clarke, *Fuzzy Monsters: Fear and Loathing at the BBC*, Heinemann, 1994.

Horsman, Mathew, *Sky High*, Orion, 1997.

Kay, William, *Lord of the Dance: The Story of Gerry Robinson*, Orion, 1999.

Snoddy, Ray, *Greenfinger: The Rise of Michael Green and Carlton Communication*, Faber & Faber, 1996.

# Index

*283*

# Index

# Index

# Citizen Greg